Praise for Self-Compassion for Parents

"This book goes to the heart of what parents struggle with—feeling deficient—and offers expert guidance in healing ourselves with self-compassion. You'll nod your head reading the stories, and will transform your relationship with your children by following the guided reflections and meditations. Parenting can be a more light, fun, wise, and loving path—Dr. Pollak shows us how."
—*Tara Brach, PhD, author of* Radical Acceptance *and* True Refuge

"This should be a required self-care book for all parents! Dr. Pollak takes on the mighty job of parenting and the everyday struggles modern families face. She offers easy-to-implement exercises that are helping me to bring more kindness to myself—and my kids. The book is easy to read all at once or in smaller chunks. I appreciate Dr. Pollak's honesty and down-to-earth humor, especially at the end of a hard day."
—*Laura W., Cambridge, Massachusetts*

"How we wish we'd had this book during the years of hands-on parenting! With infinite warmth, kindness, and 30+ years of experience, Dr. Pollak offers a wide range of playful, creative tools to help parents explore the inner and outer landscapes of raising children in wondrous new ways."
—*Trudy Goodman, PhD, mindfulness teacher, and Jack Kornfield, PhD, author of* A Path with Heart

"After reading this book, I find myself reacting differently to my children's behavior. Instead of tension, there is connection and compassion. This book is a life changer!"
—*Daniel F., Boston, Massachusetts*

"Ever feel inadequate raising your kids, like you can't quite get it right? There's hope! Seamlessly weaving together insights from ancient wisdom traditions, modern psychological research, years of clinical practice, and vivid firsthand experience as a mother, Dr. Pollak has created a lucid, practical guide to parenting as sanely as is humanly possible. Filled with warmth, humor, kindness, and sage advice, this book provides time-tested practices anyone can use to have a richer, happier, more rewarding experience raising kids—and helping them to flourish."
—*Ronald D. Siegel, PsyD, author of* The Mindfulness Solution

"Reading this wonderful book is like talking with a warm and wise friend who happens to be a world-class parent educator and therapist. Applying the healing power of compassion to ourselves makes us better parents and partners, and happier along the way. Chock-full of practical tools, clear examples, and tremendous encouragement, this book offers real help for the most important job in the world: raising a family."

—*Rick Hanson, PhD, author of* Resilient

"Consider this book a gift to yourself *and* your family. There is well-earned wisdom and authenticity on each page. You will find yourself going back to this book throughout your entire life as a parent."

—*Christopher Willard, PsyD, author of* Growing Up Mindful

Self-Compassion for Parents

Also Available

Sitting Together:
Essential Skills for Mindfulness-Based Psychotherapy
Susan M. Pollak, Thomas Pedulla, and Ronald D. Siegel

Self-Compassion for Parents

Nurture Your Child by Caring for Yourself

Susan M. Pollak, EdD

Foreword by Christopher Germer

THE GUILFORD PRESS
New York   London

Copyright © 2019 The Guilford Press
A Division of Guilford Publications, Inc.
370 Seventh Avenue, Suite 1200, New York, NY 10001
www.guilford.com

The information in this volume is not intended as a substitute for consultation
with healthcare professionals. Each individual's health concerns should be
evaluated by a qualified professional.

Printed in the United States of America

This book is printed on acid-free paper.

Last digit is print number: 9   8   7   6   5   4   3   2   1

Library of Congress Cataloging-in-Publication Data is available
from the publisher.

ISBN 978-1-4625-3309-1 (paperback) — ISBN 978-1-4625-3953-6 (hardcover)

To Adam, Nathaniel, and Hillary,
for the laughter, joy, and beauty you bring

Contents

Purchasers of this book can download audio files at
www.guilford.com/pollak2-materials for personal
use or use with clients (see page 246 for details).

Foreword

As a parent, have you ever had the wish that a wise and compassionate person would show up at your doorstep just when you needed it the most—when your toddler has a meltdown, when your daughter gets bullied in high school, when you disagree with your partner about parenting, as holiday stress starts mounting, or when you're just plain overwhelmed? If so, this book is for you.

Dr. Susan Pollak has been a mother for over 30 years and has been practicing clinical psychology for even longer. She has been engaged in meditation practice for decades and is a leader in the integration of mindfulness and self-compassion into psychotherapy and daily life. Using compelling examples, Dr. Pollak makes it clear that she knows the challenges of parenthood from the inside out, and she gently leads readers into a new relationship with themselves and their families—a relationship of loving, connected presence. That's self-compassion.

When parents hear about self-compassion for the first time, they're likely to say, "Oh, I need that!" Parents often find themselves at the edge of their capacity to be kind and compassionate to their loved ones, and they instinctively understand that they need to nourish themselves to have more to give to others. However, there are many obstacles to self-compassion—to giving ourselves the same kindness and understanding that we so readily give to others. There are the misconceptions that self-compassion is a lot like self-pity, self-indulgence, selfishness, or that it will make us weak and unmotivated. Actually, burgeoning research shows precisely the opposite—that self-compassionate people behave *more* compassionately toward others, they take better care of themselves, they're more emotionally resilient, they have greater perspective on their problems, and they are more motivated to achieve their goals. Other obstacles to self-compassion are personal, such as messages from the past that we should disregard ourselves and only pay attention to others, especially one's family, or that we just don't deserve to stop and nourish ourselves because there is so much that needs to be done.

The good news is that anyone can learn to be more self-compassionate. Kristin Neff, a research psychologist at the University of Texas, Austin, and I developed an eight-week training program starting in 2010 that is currently taught around the world, Mindful Self-Compassion (MSC). Interest in this subject is enormous, perhaps because the impact of self-compassion can be felt almost immediately. It can also be an epiphany to discover that each of us has the capacity to give ourselves much of the kindness and understanding that we seek, often in vain, from others.

Susan Pollak understood the power of self-compassion early on. She was one of the very first MSC teachers and is currently an MSC teacher trainer. I am so glad that Susan is sharing in this book her deep insight into self-compassion and her intimate knowledge of MSC. Parents are especially ripe for self-compassion—they know struggle and they know compassion. They simply need to make an occasional U-turn with their compassion and discover the positive influence it can have on themselves as well as their families.

This book is one of the most effortless introductions to self-compassion that I know. It does not teach *about* self-compassion, but connects with the direct experience of parenting through detailed examples, personal anecdotes, and elegant exercises how to transform parenting struggles through mindfulness and self-compassion. It is indeed like having a wise and compassionate friend at your side, but better than that, it shows readers how to be their *own* wise and compassionate friend. You don't need to wait even a minute for your friend to show up.

The invitation of this book is to let go of all those behaviors that make parenting more difficult than it already is—comparing yourself to other parents, comparing your kids to other kids, blaming yourself for inevitable mistakes, or needlessly quarreling with your kids or a partner. Instead, the invitation is to turn toward yourself in a genuine way in the midst of struggle, become curious about what you're feeling, and then begin to tend to yourself—tend to your heart—allowing yourself to be, in that moment, just as you are.

CHRISTOPHER GERMER, PHD
Harvard Medical School/Cambridge Health Alliance

Acknowledgments

The meditation practices in this book are the fruit of decades of practice and study with many teachers and in many traditions. For this wisdom, compassion, and inspiration, I offer profound thanks to all from whom I've had the privilege of learning, in particular, His Holiness the Dalai Lama, Jack Kornfield, Sharon Salzberg, Joseph Goldstein, Trudy Goodman, Pema Chodron, Ram Das, Thich Nhat Hanh, Pir Vilayat Khan, Pir Zia Inayat Khan, Kalu Rinpoche, Sylvia Boorstein, Tara Brach, Narayan Helen Liebenson, Larry Rosenberg, and Lama Willa Miller.

I'd also like to thank some of the pioneers who have advanced our understanding of mindfulness and compassion practices and how they can help with the problems of daily life as well as more serious disorders, including Sylvia Boorstein, Richard Davidson, Jack Engler, Mark Epstein, Paul Gilbert, Daniel Goleman, Rick Hanson, Steven Hayes, Jon Kabat-Zinn, Marsha Linehan, Alan Marlatt, Richard Schwartz, Zindel Segal, Daniel Siegel, Tania Singer, John Teasdale, and Mark Williams. I'd also like to express deep gratitude to Chris Germer and Kristin Neff for their work in creating and implementing the Mindful Self-Compassion Program. I want to acknowledge my colleagues Michelle Becker, Christine Braehler, and Steve Hickman at the Center for Mindful Self-Compassion.

I am also grateful for the guidance of many clinical supervisors and professors who have helped me understand the art and science of psychotherapy, the complexities of human development, and of parenting. In particular, I'd like to thank Robert Bosnak, Diana Eck, Janina Fisher, Howard Gardner, Carol Gilligan, Judith Lewis Herman, Alfred Margulies, Richard Niebuhr, Bennett Simon, and Merry White.

I am indebted to a "dream team" at The Guilford Press. Executive Editor Kitty Moore and Christine Benton, developmental editor, are two of the smartest, funniest, and most literate women I know. We laughed nearly as much as we worked. I thank them for their unflagging support of this book and so many other books on mindfulness and compassion. I am particularly grateful to Art Director Paul Gordon for his intuitive brilliance in the whimsical cover design.

My longtime friends and colleagues at the Institute for Meditation and Psychotherapy have contributed to my understanding of the relationship between these fields. I thank Doug Baker, Paul Fulton, Trudy Goodman, Inna Khazan, Sara Lazar, Bill Morgan, Susan Morgan, Andrew Olendzki, Meghan Searles, Dave Shannon, Ron Siegel, Charles Styron, Janet Surrey, Laura Warren, and Christopher Willard. In fact, this book grew out of a series of conversations with Chris.

Harvard Medical School/Cambridge Health Alliance (CHA) has provided a home where I've taught mindfulness since 1996. At our Center for Mindfulness and Compassion, I thank Liz Gaufberg, Richa Gawande, Todd Griswold, Bridget Kiley, and Zev Schuman-Olivier, as well as Deb Hulihan at CHA for supporting mindfulness and compassion in health care.

My most powerful teachers, however, have been my patients, who have opened their hearts and trusted me with their deepest doubts, frustrations, and worries. They are the guiding force behind this book. Although their stories are front and center, their identities have been disguised to protect confidentiality.

Finally, I'm indebted to my friends who have sustained me. A remarkable group of women have been meeting for breakfast since our children were young. We have been there for each other through the joys and sorrows of mothering. These stalwart women include Maggie Booz, Lisa Dobberteen, Heather Faris, Christine Herbes-Sommers, Pattie Heyman, and Carrie Jones.

I'd also like to thank the members of the Wednesday meditation group: Jerry Bass, Matt Czaplinski, Dan Foley, Suzanne Hoffman, Joshua Lowenstein, Tom Pedulla, Tom Putnam, Janet Yassen, and Ed Yeats. While some members have passed or moved on, our meditation, study, conversation, and friendship for over 25 years has been a true refuge.

I am grateful to my dear friends Elissa Ely, Stephanie Morgan, Carin Roberge, Sally Anne Schreiber, Niti Seth, Janna Malamud Smith, Lori Stern, and Sherry Turkle, all of whom have provided wise counsel.

And of course, none of this would be possible without my parents,

Rita and Robert Pollak; my aunt, Faye Levey, who introduced me to meditation and yoga when I was in elementary school; and my brother, Rick Pollak, and his wife, Anita.

I owe the greatest debt to my husband, Adam, who read and commented on drafts, provided comfort and tech support, and graciously tolerated my distracted mind and more than occasional lack of presence over two years of writing. I also want to thank our children, Nathaniel and Hillary, and daughter-in-law, Katharine, for their unfailing encouragement and good humor.

May many parents and children benefit from this book.

Self-Compassion for Parents

Introduction

Recently I was helping some cousins with preparations at a family wedding in the countryside. One of them was a mom who had three young kids, including a newborn. We began to talk about parenting. "So how am I doing?" Emma asked me point blank, looking anxious. "I'm the last person to judge," I reassured her. As one child pulled on her leg, demanding attention, I paraphrased a line from one of my favorite essays by the writer Tillie Olsen and shared it: "To be a mother is to be constantly interruptible." She laughed and said, "And, to be constantly correctable. And constantly criticized. I never feel like I'm doing it right. Sometimes when my kids are rambunctious, people stare at me like I'm raising juvenile delinquents. I refuse to put them in straitjackets with muzzles or keep them on a tight leash like a trained dog. When I was a kid I felt free to run and climb and yell and be wild. Now it seems that it's not OK for kids to make noise and have fun. It's like they should be constantly quiet and contained," she confided. "It's impossible."

Emma's words stayed with me and troubled me. She articulated something I hear from almost all the parents I know. Parenting is hard for everyone. We never feel good enough. Things rarely go the way we imagine they will. And when they don't, we blame ourselves, criticize our kids, push harder, and try to exert more control. We become anxious and depressed. Our kids become anxious and depressed. We look over our shoulder, comparing ourselves with our friends, families, neighbors. We lose sleep. What are we doing wrong? Is there some way off this interminable and joyless merry-go-round?

Stop. Breathe. Listen. Stop beating yourself up. Cut yourself some slack. Stop fighting with your kid, yourself, your partner. Freud was on to something, as was Emma—parenting is an impossible profession. And trying to dominate or muzzle our kids is a losing battle. The experts tell us that ultimately very little can be predicted or controlled.

We are all exhausted, anxious, and worried. And we are not alone. One historian of American culture noted that "in no other country has there been so pervasive a cultural anxiety about the rearing of children." We wonder if someone, someplace does it better. Do French parents have the magic recipe? Do "tiger mothers" get a better return on their investment? Anthropologists tell us that Japanese babies sleep and Mexican siblings don't fight—should we relocate?

Make a "U-Turn"

No. Start where you are. This book offers a radical shift in perspective, based on decades of research on mindfulness and compassion. The seeds for happier and less combative parenting are within us, not on another continent. We don't have to feel angry or helpless and drive our children and ourselves to exhaustion. There is another way. Instead of the constant struggle to fix or change your kids, try a U-turn. Extend some kindness and compassion to yourself. Begin to nurture yourself so your kids can thrive. Huh? You shake your head. You roll your eyes. You are busy, you don't have time for this. It sounds too selfish, and silly. Most parents tell me this.

As a Harvard-trained psychologist with two grown children and over 30 years of clinical experience, I've worked with a lot of parents and children. And I've read a lot of books on how to parent. The predominant focus is often on how to fix our kids, how to make them behave, how to get them to sleep, how to get them into a good college and guarantee success. In short, how to make them into what we want them to be. But rarely do we achieve the results we want.

What happened to joy? Happiness? Exuberance? We don't need to be so hard on them or ourselves. The current research says that we can motivate more with compassion than criticism. Really. We can shift the focus from constant doing to simply being. We can stop running, turning ourselves into frantic, raging parents racing to get the kids to soccer, Little League, and ballet in rush-hour traffic while they are biting and punching each other in the car. No judgment here; I've been there. I was the frantic mother in the car, spread too thin, running on empty, trying to do way too much—and losing it. It was not sustainable for anyone. I tried to find a way back to balance and sanity.

This book draws from over three decades of parenting, clinical work, and meditation. The theoretical and scientific foundation of this book is the pioneering work of my colleagues Drs. Chris Germer and Kristin Neff, who developed the transformative Mindful Self-Compassion (MSC) course, which I have been teaching since its inception in 2010. In addition to MSC, which has been taught to tens of thousands of people, this parenting guide is full of stories and examples from my years of clinical practice with parents and children and my own experience as a parent. (The illustrations are composites to protect privacy.) I have paired these stories with practices and reflections drawn from my understanding of what is effective and from the experiences of many people who have been helped by these exercises.

My hope is that this book will speak to you where you are and will help you with your parenting dilemmas. Things don't have to be so hard, and we don't have to suffer so much. Nor do our children. May this book help bring you and your family some joy, happiness, laughter, and compassion.

How to Use This Book

There is no "right" way to use this book. You don't have to read sequentially. Just jump right in and find a chapter or story that speaks to you and start there. If you're new to mindfulness, the first few chapters have practices for beginners. I've tried to mix mindfulness and compassion exercises with reflections to make the material accessible to everyone. The reflections are designed to help you focus on what you need, so grab a notebook and pen, or record your responses on your phone or tablet if that is easier. Don't have time to read? I get it—I didn't either when my kids were little. Just go to Guilford's website (see the box at the end of the Contents for information) and download the selected audio practices (audio track numbers are provided with the practice instructions in the following chapters) to use while you are doing the dishes, drinking your morning coffee, making school lunches, or driving (please keep your eyes open). In a crisis? Turn to the "Toolbox" in the back of the book for immediate support—from colic to tantrums, sibling rivalry, an ill child, a power struggle with a teen, and other common challenges.

But the most important thing to remember, as one of my mindfulness teachers told me years ago, is that there is no way to do this wrong. "Come on, really?" you say. Yup, really. I'd spent a lifetime castigating myself for the most minor mistakes. "No way to fail," she would tell us. Was this teacher an alien from another universe? What substance was she on? (And would she share it?) Basking in the presence of her compassion, humor, and wisdom, I thought of that unforgettable line from *When Harry Met Sally*—I decided that I wanted to "have what she was having."

The good news is that mindfulness and compassion are available to all of us—and we can share them with those around us. These are skills you can develop. The practices aren't for already serene people who have everything together. You don't have to be good at sitting still. You don't have to be vegan, sugar-free, and decaffeinated. You can be as you are—overworked, anxious, neurotic, sleep deprived, and barely keeping it together. It's fine to be a mess. I certainly was. If you can breathe (and don't look now—you're already doing it), you can do this. Welcome.

1 "Make It Stop— I Can't Keep Up!"

PARENTING IS OVERWHELMING

Out of Gas

It was one of those mornings. The baby hadn't slept, Amy's husband was out of town, and three-year-old Sophie insisted on wearing her new tutu to nursery school as snowflakes began to pile up on the New England January morning. Plus, they were late. Of course, they were late. Amy had time to feed the kids, but no time to feed herself.

"You can't wear your tutu and ballet slippers to school today," Amy insisted. "It's snowing."

"I don't care," Sophie retorted and resumed pirouettes.

Amy was in no mood for a fight. "Honey, we're late," she pleaded, her voice rising.

"We're late, we're late," Sophie mocked, imitating her high-pitched voice.

"Enough, no backtalk, we are going. NOW. Put on that jacket," Amy said, trying to sound firm but calm, as all the good parenting books recommend.

"You can't make me, you can't make me," Sophie chanted in a singsong. She gave up the dance and plopped down defiantly and stuck out her tongue.

Amy was furious. "Enough! I've had it," she yelled, picking up both kids and dragging them to the car, jackets spilling out of her hands. Opening the door one-handed to get the baby in, she tossed Sophie her jacket. Sophie immediately sensed a new stand she could take with her mother's conviction and compassion waning and rage seething: she promptly refused.

"You're not the boss of me," Sophie taunted.

"You can just freeze, see if I care," Amy retorted as she buckled both kids into their car seats and sped off.

Sophie started to wail, and then the baby joined in.

"Stop it *now*," Amy hissed, feeling overwhelmed and helpless. Clearly this was not one of her finer moments in parenting.

"I want my daddy," Sophie cried. "He isn't a meanie like you."

It was a relief, for everyone, to get to school. The teacher was understanding as she greeted them, wiped Sophie's tears, and led her inside with a sympathetic smile to Amy. Within minutes Sophie was coloring and laughing with her classmates.

Amy left, shamefacedly waving good-bye and feeling like a terrible mother. While Sophie had moved on, Amy's anger boomeranged as hot shame, guilt, and regret. She began to berate herself, saying, "I really suck at this. I'm an awful mother."

As she was driving home, the car began to sputter and spurt, then finally stopped. "Oh shit," she thought. Tom, her husband, usually filled up the car, but with him out of town she hadn't even remembered to check the tank, which was, of course, empty.

Amy sighed, packed the baby in his carrier, and started to walk to a gas station. The snow was coming down harder now. "Great, just what I goddamned need," she thought as she began to cry. She surprised herself with the intensity of her sobs. "How am I going to do this? How can I get through the next 15 years without driving myself and the kids crazy?"

It's Hard for Everyone

Maybe your terrible, horrible, no good, very bad day wasn't as dramatic as Amy's, or maybe it was worse, but we all have at least one story to tell about "that day." Hungry, angry, lonely, and tired, we've all run out of gas, or worse. Parenting is hard for everyone, but especially hard when family is far, and the village that it's supposed to take seems full of idiots or other parents who don't have the time for us. And this is how most of us parent these days, without a network and without a net to catch us or a hand when something inevitably goes south. The promise of parenting was connection and love, yet we find ourselves lonely and overwhelmed much of the time. And even if we do have some help, there is always a price to pay. It is so easy to run out of gas.

How can we gas up and not lock up the brakes? If we restore our own well-being, might the quality of our parenting expand? Our aim in this book is to offer you a toolbox of techniques, anecdotes, humor, support, and guidance to help keep you sane during the parenting years and to help you find joy as well. And we'll help you learn to see the problems that arise not as intrusions or interruptions of your former child-free life, but as opportunities for wisdom and growth.

"Replenishment," you scoff. "What about anger management? Or Xanax? How about a double martini?"

I get it. We've all been there. But what I hope to teach you in this book is that it is easier to manage your anger, take responsibility, keep your mood steady, and enjoy your child (or children) while you are taking care of yourself. The writer Audre Lorde put it succinctly, stating that caring for oneself is not self-indulgence but self-preservation.

Offering yourself mindfulness and compassion isn't about giving yourself free rein to be lazy, to shirk responsibility, or to sit on a cushion and contemplate your navel while your kids are fighting and destroying the house. It's not about being soft on ourselves. On the contrary, mindfulness helps us see clearly and act from a place of kindness and wisdom. In fact, one definition of mindfulness is "clear seeing."

So what is mindfulness? There are many definitions, but the one that has guided me as a parent and psychologist is a very simple no-fuss, no-frills definition: "awareness of the present moment with kindness and acceptance." With the constant stresses and strains of being a parent, whether it's a night without sleep, a child's tantrum, sibling rivalry, difficult in-laws, or a critical partner, we need a warm and compassionate response to our experience.

"Sounds nice," you might argue, "but that isn't realistic. The world is tough; we're all constantly judged. It's out of touch to think you should always be kind and accepting. And sometimes I just get angry. And how do you teach kids right from wrong? How can you motivate them to do their best if you don't push? And we need to think about the future. It simply isn't practical."

These are all excellent questions, and I'll address them. What I'm proposing is a radical way to parent, to be a parent, a different way to be with our kids and to be with ourselves. Most of us are used to motivating ourselves with criticism, thinking that if we yell at and berate ourselves we will be better and more effective, happier and more successful.

In fact, self-criticism rarely works. Kristin Neff, widely known for her comprehensive research on self-compassion (see Chapter 2), has written extensively about this. Motivating ourselves with kindness and compassion is actually more effective than using criticism. "Yeah, sure, more stupid psychobabble," you protest, ready to put down this book. Hold on. These ideas are impacting the business sector as well. Charles Schwab, financial leader and philanthropist, wrote, "I have yet to find the man, however exalted his station, who did not do better work and put forth greater efforts under a spirit of approval than under a spirit of criticism." Let's illustrate this by returning to Amy, who consulted with me not for therapy but for "sanity" as she put it.

"I don't need therapy," she protested, "but I do need a parenting coach. I don't know what I'm doing, my parents and my sisters, who also have young kids, are two flights away, I have no help, and I don't want to push away the new parent friends I am just barely making."

As we talked more, Amy's story unfolded. She had moved to the East Coast for her husband's job, leaving behind friends and family. "People are cold here, just like the weather," she said sadly. "And everyone looks so together. I feel like such a mess." She began to cry. "We moved here for Tom's job—not that he's ever here; they have him traveling twice a month. And when he gets home, he's exhausted and hungry and wants the kids to be all fun and the house to be all clean, and he forgets the house isn't a hotel room and doesn't have daily maid service . . ." She paused and drew a breath. "It just isn't happening." She was silent for a moment. "I'm taking care of everyone, I'm not sleeping, I'm lonely, eating the kids' leftovers because I gained so much weight, but now I'm hungry most of the time. Sometimes I feel I'm going so fast that I'm barely breathing. But what is scariest is that I feel that I'm losing myself and my brain is just *mush*. I've lost my old competent self. No one is taking care of me. I need some help and I need it now. That horrible morning when I ran out of gas and had to walk to a station in the snow, I saw the sign that said 'Full Service,' and I wondered, 'Will I ever feel full again? Am I always going to feel depleted?'"

I tried the following reflection with Amy, which helped her reconnect with feeling competent.

Reflection: Finding Yourself

Do you feel like you lost yourself when you became a parent? Take a moment and ask yourself the question "Who am I?" Ask it again. And again. Did "parent" come up in one of the first answers? That's wonderful, but who ELSE are you besides a parent? We can't lose this essence of who we are as we become overwhelmed with parenting.

As our work progressed, I added the following practice, inspired by Christopher Germer's *The Mindful Path to Self-Compassion* (2009), which Amy did when she woke up in the morning. This is a great place to start. We know that you're busy and don't have free time. Don't worry. Set a timer; it takes only three minutes. (Don't tell me you don't have three minutes.)

 Tending to Yourself

🎧 *Audio Track 1*

- Take a moment and find a comfortable seat.
- Let yourself settle for a few moments.
- Find your breath. Sometimes we are so busy we don't realize that we're breathing. Where is it? Where do you most notice the sensation of breathing? Focus there and feel the breath move in and out.
- Let yourself feel one breath fully.
- Ask yourself, *How do I know that I'm breathing?*
- Notice any sensations in your body.
- What are you noticing? Are you hungry? Tired? What emotions are you aware of? What are you feeling?
- Just as you rock or hold your child, let yourself be gently rocked and held by each inbreath and each outbreath.
- Let the inhalation and exhalation soothe and comfort you, anchor you.
- If you like, put a hand on your chest or a hand on your chest and belly.
- Feel the comfort of your warm touch.
- Let yourself take five breaths. Yes, you have time for five breaths. You are breathing anyway.
- Give yourself permission to tend to yourself, to be kind to yourself. You spend so much time taking care of others, attending to their needs. Take a moment. What do you need?
- Give yourself permission to eat, to shower, to rest, to stop and breathe.

Amy tried this for a few weeks. Some days all she could manage was three breaths, but even that seemed to help. Even though this seemed so simple, she felt that it grounded her.

"Sometimes I'm so frantic that I forget to eat or don't have time to shower. I was running on empty. And now I'm realizing the truth of the saying that I grew up with in the South," she said with a laugh. " 'If Mama ain't happy, ain't nobody happy.' I can't not sleep or eat and expect the family to run smoothly. If I have nothing to give, everyone suffers. What I realized, which was a big breakthrough for me, is that I don't have to depend on someone else to fill me up. I can do it myself. I don't need my husband, my sisters, or my parents to nourish me. That was very freeing."

There are many ways to practice mindfulness and compassion. Not everyone likes to sit quietly and look inside. No problem. One size doesn't fit all. I'll help you find what works for you. I like to teach people short reflections, where they set aside a few moments (maybe when the kids have gone to bed) to take time for themselves and to consider their needs and desires. After this exercise, feel free to jot down what comes up for you.

Reflection: What Do I Need?

Find a quiet moment, either early in the morning or after the kids have gone to bed. If you like, in your mind's eye, imagine a powerful tree with deep roots and a strong trunk. Notice that the branches of the tree reach as high as the roots are deep. You might even imagine you are breathing in through the top of your head and out through your "roots" or feet.

Ask yourself, "What do I need?"

Pause and listen for words or images to arise.

Ask again, "What do I really need?"

Take a few minutes to be open to whatever comes up, without judging or censoring your response.

Write down what comes up for you.

When Amy tried this reflection, she found herself connecting with the image of the deeply rooted tree. "I left my family and sibs and community to come here, and I really miss that feeling of connection. I had this fantasy that once I had a partner, a home, and kids, all would be wonderful and I would have everything I needed. That I would feel full. I was so wrong. I feel so isolated here, so alone. And I thought I could do it all, but I can't. I need some downtime. I can't be there for everyone 24/7. That tree needs sunshine, water, and some fertilizer!"

Amy is not alone. So many of us feel isolated. Over the past 30 years, as I've talked to hundreds of parents, I've seen so many paths that lead to isolation. Sometimes we wait until we think we have all the pieces of the puzzle in place—the career, the house or condo, a decent income—and we think, "Yes, the time is right." But then we may have trouble conceiving, and when we finally do have children, most of our friends have already had their kids or have returned to work. Instead of being with our friends pushing our kids on the swings, bathed in golden sunlight, we find nannies and babysitters. Suddenly, we feel out of sync. Or the company we work for transferred us to another state or even another country. So much for that dream. Or it may be that our partner feels that it is her turn to focus on her career, and most days we are the only guy at the playground, and the moms and babysitters aren't very friendly and there is no one to talk to—no matter how hard we try, how much we plan, it is never perfect and we realize how little control we have. (If this is the situation you find yourself in, you might also enjoy a practice in Chapter 5 called You Don't Have to Control Everything.)

Learning to Pause

People often complain that they don't have time to practice mindfulness, especially with small children. No worries; I understand. I didn't either. This is why the practices that I offer, especially in the beginning chapters, are designed for parents who are spread too thin and don't have time for themselves. Most can be done in three minutes or less. Researchers tell us that consistency is what matters, not large chunks of time. Think about it: What would your dentist recommend, one 40-minute tooth brushing a week or three minutes twice a day? And you don't have to sit still to practice mindfulness. It can be done walking, standing, driving (keep your eyes open), lying in bed, and even changing a diaper (see the Mindfulness in Daily Life exercises below).

Mindfulness doesn't have to be something you do alone in silence in a meditation hall on a remote mountaintop, but something that can become part of your crazy, busy life as a frantic parent trying to juggle way too much. Which is, in fact, when you need it the most.

One of the most accessible practices is the Parenting Pause, adapted from psychologist and meditation teacher Tara Brach. Brach teaches that a simple pause of just a moment or two has the power to shift the tone and direction of an interaction, an invaluable skill to have as a parent and in all relationships (especially intimate ones).

Why Can't You Get the F#k to Sleep!*

Lionel had a busy and stressful job in sales. Before they were married, he and Kyra, his wife, had agreed to split the childcare 50/50. This had sounded good in theory, but Tyrone was premature and had trouble breathing. Things were getting better, but both parents still worried about him. Now that Tyrone was seven months old and still not sleeping through the night, no one in the house was sleeping through the night. Kyra worked in retail, which meant long hours and often weekends. For the first few months, when she was on maternity leave, they were feeding the baby on demand, and they worried about every cry. Now that she was back at work, her boss didn't take kindly to her pumping during the day. Feeding the baby every two hours at night was an added stress.

Lionel was sure he could do a better job and generously offered to handle the night feedings. "No problem, I've got this," he reassured Kyra. However, it wasn't as simple as he thought. Wanting to do it "right" and show Kyra how competent he was, he got up whenever Tyrone whimpered, fed him, and then tried to put him to sleep. However, Tyrone, delighted to see his dad in the middle of the night, decided it was party time and refused to go back to sleep. The night feedings went from five minutes to 50, and Lionel's exhaustion was showing up at work, with careless errors on the job.

Nights were getting worse, not better. "We need to do sleep training," Lionel said. "My job is on the line. I'm making mistakes and falling asleep on the job."

"No way," Kyra insisted. "It's abusive and sadistic. We are not doing that to our baby."

When Lionel and Kyra came in for counseling, they were barely speaking (or sleeping). Their disagreement over Tyrone's sleeping habits was causing a rift in the marriage. Not only were they severely sleep deprived, but the problem had stirred up issues from Kyra's own family. She was certain that "crying it out" would harm Tyrone. Lionel insisted that Tyrone was fine and thought she was being "overly emotional" and told her so. This kind of disrespect triggered Kyra's memories of how her father had treated her mother, and she fought back, telling him he was insensitive. They were caught in a vicious cycle, and neither one could stand down. By this point, Tyrone was almost a year old.

After watching this pattern of escalating conflict, I asked, "Can we try something different here? We just keep going around and around in circles. Can I teach you a mindfulness practice that might help interrupt the cycle?"

"No way," Kyra responded defensively. "That is too woo-woo for us. We already have a church. I don't want any trendy bullshit. Not going there."

"OK, what I want to teach isn't out there at all. It is about reducing your stress, reducing the constant fighting, and getting some sleep."

"Well, that would be a miracle," Kyra said sarcastically.

"No harm in trying. If it doesn't work, you don't have to do it."

Desperate, Kyra and Lionel agreed to try.

While this practice is effective with couples, it is also helpful for tensions between a parent and child. Set a timer for three to five minutes.

 The Parenting Pause

- Start by sitting comfortably and taking a few calming breaths.
- If you and your partner have been fighting, it is fine to go to separate rooms.
- Let yourself stop. Just sit and give yourself a break. Don't try to fix anything right now.
- If you find yourself ruminating and your thoughts are spinning, or you are fuming, just acknowledge that.
- Just be with it, whatever you are feeling, even if it is difficult.
- You might say to yourself, *This is hard; this hurts.*
- Pause. No need to act right now. No need to fight right now.
- Feel your feet on the ground and notice any sensations in the body.
- Know that whatever you are feeling, it will pass.
- Try to bring a little kindness to yourself.
- Take a few more grounding and centering breaths.
- Before you return to your day, see if you can tune in to what you need right now.
- As you go through your day, take a pause whenever you need to anchor and get perspective.

"So, what did you notice?" I asked.

Kyra laughed. "I fell asleep. Sitting up. Can you believe that?"

"I dozed off too," Lionel joked. "Hey, this might help with the sleep deprivation."

The two were able to acknowledge just how exhausted they were, where before they had denied it and argued about it. Their homework was to practice pausing for three minutes a day. They reminded each other to pause when they started to get into a fight, and it seemed to bring some humor and perspective. Tara Brach writes, "When we pause, we don't know what will happen next. By disrupting our habitual behaviors, we open to the possibility of new and creative ways of responding to our wants and fears."

I think of the Parenting Pause as a kind of flotation device that has kept me, and my clients, from going under. I have used it during those times when the kids are fighting and don't seem able to stop and I've had more than enough. It was a lifesaver when my aging father kept asking the same stupid questions over and over again and I could barely hold it together any longer and just wanted to scream, "Why are you asking me that again? I just told you!" It is one of my favorite practices when you have reached the end of your rope.

Tatiana used this practice when her mother humiliated her in front of her children by talking about all the mistakes she had made when she was young and what a difficult child she was. "I felt like I was an inch away from disowning her and denying her access to her grandchildren forever. Luckily, I was able to pause and collect myself before I did major damage." Jonathan used it when the kids badgered him to buy them toys or a sugary breakfast cereal they had seen advertised on TV. Al, whose in-laws treated him like he was an incompetent father, found it was his go-to practice when his mother-in-law criticized his parenting and told him how it should be done. "It really helped me keep my shit together. It would have been so easy for me to erupt in anger and say, 'Given what kind of mother you were to Diane, how dare you give me any advice!' That of course would've had disastrous consequences. I'm so glad I held my temper. I think of pausing as my 'superpower' that I turn to when I've run dry."

After a few weeks of practice, I made a suggestion to Kyra and Lionel: "I don't know if you're open to this, but you could try the pause with Tyrone."

"That's absurd," Kyra countered. "He can barely talk."

"But babies understand a lot, more than we realize."

"So what are we going to say?" Kyra mocked. " 'Tyrone, now just take a deep breath and pause'? Are you kidding me?"

Everyone laughed. "Let's talk this through. I hear you, Kyra," I said.

"For next week, Lionel, how about if you try pausing before you go into his room? Even if he is fussing and whimpering. It's OK. Babies fuss, it just goes with the territory. It doesn't mean something is wrong. You want him to learn to soothe himself."

"Trust me, that won't happen." Lionel challenged. "Not with this kid."

"I hear you. And I've been there," I said. "Let me tell you a story. One of my kids was waking up so frequently, nearly every two hours, that I started to fall asleep with my patients! I was so exhausted I couldn't keep my eyes open. Not good form. A snoring therapist is not very helpful, and my patients were not amused. I had to figure it out before I lost my job!" The couple nodded.

"Think of it as something that you're going to teach him, just as pretty soon you'll teach him to play catch."

"I will not allow him to scream bloody murder," Kyra insisted. "Or I'll put a stop to this," she warned.

No Trendy Bullshit

Over the next few weeks, everyone worked together to help Tyrone sleep through the night. They started gently and slowly. Rather than picking him up to feed him, Lionel came in and put a warm hand on the baby's back.

"It's OK, big guy, you don't need another dinner. You're good. I'm here, I love you."

Sometimes he would sing, often the songs his mother and grandmother sang to him or ones he learned from church. When he sang, Tyrone smiled, snuggled with his blanket and teddy bear. As he got used to this, sometimes all Tyrone needed was a pat on the back and gentle words. "I'm here, you go back to sleep. Everything is OK. Mommy and Daddy love you."

While Tyrone would still fuss at times, and it didn't work every night, it was getting better. Things were going in the right direction. Tyrone was learning that he could fall back asleep without being held and fed.

"It's like he's finding his own rhythm. You know, it's like he's taking in the rhythm of the songs, the words and the beat, and feeling them in his body. Really, I swear," Lionel smiled proudly. "I'm from a family of musicians; he has it in his blood and bones."

Over weeks of work, as Tyrone's parents learned to understand and respect his natural cycles of sleep, and that he no longer needed to be fed on demand, it was easier for them to let go. As Lionel and Kyra themselves began to pause and settle, and to work together on the sleep problem, their constant bickering diminished, and they started to enjoy each other again. And everyone was finally sleeping through the night, or close enough, anyway. "You know, I thought no way at first," said Lionel, "but this stuff has really helped."

"Mommy Doesn't Love Me Anymore"

It had been a rough year. Meghan had spent the last few months of her high-risk pregnancy on bed rest, and the labor and birth were complicated. She needed an emergency C-section so she and the baby would survive. Both she and Lila were still struggling with health issues, and Meghan barely had enough energy to take care of herself, let alone a fragile baby and her rambunctious five-year-old, Johnny.

And, to make matters worse, Meghan was struggling with the death of her mother, who had passed away when she was pregnant. She had been on bed rest, so she wasn't able to see her or say good-bye. Theirs was a deeply ambivalent relationship, but the force of Meghan's grief took her by surprise. She had no idea she would ever miss her mother this much and often wished that her mother would magically appear to help, especially now.

In fact, she was thinking about her mother as she was trying to cook dinner one night. Her husband was at work, having taken on an additional job to help cover the medical expenses. The insurance had covered only a small portion of the costs. He was doing as much as he could, but he was exhausted and irritable as well. They thought that giving Johnny a playmate would be fun and make their lives easier—no one had bargained for this nightmare.

"Johnny, could you please play with Lila while I make dinner?" Meghan asked.

"What should I do?" he asked.

"Oh, just tell her a story or sing to her; anything is fine," Meghan said.

Johnny started by singing his favorite songs, but then quickly ran out of material. The baby started to cry. On top of everything else, she had colic and cried constantly. It put everyone on edge.

"Try something else," Meghan suggested. "Dinner's almost done. Just a few more minutes."

"Can't we send her back to the hospital?" Johnny suggested. "I don't like her. Too much noise."

"Stop that. She's your sister, and she's been sick. She's here to stay."

Giving his mother a mischievous grin, Johnny made up his own song and sang it in a singsong rhythm.

Mommy loves you
She doesn't love me
But I don't care
I don't need Mommy anymore
You can have grumpy Mommy
I don't care
She's all yours
I don't need a mommy anymore.

Meghan was speechless. She didn't know what to say or do. She wanted to yell and scream and give Johnny a time-out. She even wanted to spank him, which she swore she would never do, but she didn't have the energy to do anything but go to bed. And he was doing what he had been asked. She just hadn't asked for the aggression. "Wow," Meghan thought, "now I get why my mother hit us so much. I had no idea I would get so angry with my own child."

"But I do love you," she protested. Johnny didn't look convinced. And truth be told, she was furious with him.

They ate in stony silence, the only soundtrack the cries of the new baby.

Meghan put the children to bed and then went to her room. She felt ice cold and numb. When her husband returned home from work, she could barely speak. She'd been crying for hours, wrapped in blankets, shivering, hugging the baby's stuffed animal.

"Another hard day? What's up?" Her husband did little to hide his annoyance.

"I'm damaged. I'm deeply flawed. And I've damaged Johnny; he hates me. I can't do this—it is too much," Meghan sobbed. "I'm a horrible mother."

At the hospital clinic, Meghan was diagnosed with postpartum depression and started on medication. As she began to stabilize, we worked on helping her get her health back, mourn her mother, and get more support.

Meghan had no time or interest in any formal mindfulness practice. Just getting through the day was a victory, but she was interested in anything informal to help her "get a grip," especially on those days when Johnny was challenging and the baby was colicky.

We created the following practice together. As mentioned earlier in this chapter, you don't have to sit to practice mindfulness; it is fine to practice walking, standing, or lying down.

♥ Bouncing the Baby Meditation

- Start by standing, feeling your feet on the ground.
- Find a comfortable position to hold the baby.
- Rock from side to side, back and forth.
- Feel the warmth of the baby against your body.
- Hold the baby against your heart, letting him or her listen to the heartbeat.
- Bend your knees, gently bouncing the baby up and down.
- Let yourself feel held by the earth, feeling your bodies in space.
- Feel free to turn, to dance a little, even to sing.
- Tune in to your breath, perhaps synchronizing your breath with gentle movement.
- Let the baby be rocked by your breath.

You might want to add some phrases that you recite to the baby. Feel free to create your own, but Meghan created the following rhythm that soothed her and the baby: *You're my baby and I love you like crazy.* The other phrase that helped was *I'm here for you. Things have been tough, but we'll get through. Yes, we'll get through this together. We'll find a way.*

It is fine to walk, to dance. Feel free to make this practice your own.

The doctor was right—the colic subsided in a few months. As Meghan recovered, she turned some of her attention back to her relationship with Johnny, but she was still angry.

"I know that this is an awful thing to say, and please don't lock me up, but I don't like him anymore. I don't want to be with him. He's . . . kind of a jerk! Sometimes he pinches the baby just to piss me off. She cries, and I go into a rage." She paused. "I'm a pretty pathetic excuse for a mother," she said, shaking her head.

This is something that parents rarely talk about outside of the consulting room, but there are often periods in the parent–child relationship where there is tension and anger—long ones. Yet tough times in any relationship are an inevitable part of being human. While we are used to discord in adolescence, and even expect it, negative feelings can arise at any time. It's perfectly normal to feel irritated with your child (and with your partner as well). However, we tend to feel guilty about having such feelings and deny or suppress them, believing that something is wrong with us.

Reflection: What Pushes Your Buttons?

Let's take a moment to look at what sorts of things typically come up that cause negative feelings for parents.

- Let yourself pause. Ahhh, you need and deserve this moment of reflection.
- Take a few breaths or listen to the sounds around you. Take this in. Let yourself fill up.
- Sometimes it is easiest to start by remembering what caused your parents to lose it. Was it when you . . .
    Didn't do chores?
    Didn't clean up after dinner?
    Talked back?
    Spilled milk or food?
    Didn't clean your room?
    Fought with your siblings?
    Got into fights with kids at school?
    Didn't do your homework?
    Didn't get good grades?
- How about you? What makes you angry? What brings up negative feelings for you? Jot it down, paying attention to any patterns you might notice.
- Finally, bring some compassion to yourself (and even your parents if you can). We're all human, and we all lose it at times.

Researchers tell us that "what we resist persists." So, if you are noticing irritation, don't fight it. Notice it, acknowledge it, and then let it go. Thoughts and feelings rarely last more than 30 seconds. Try not to create a story about it or turn it into more than a passing, and human, moment of irritation. If it's still nagging at you, make a practice of what we call the compassionate **NAG**.

Notice the feeling or sensation.

Allow it to linger, without fighting it off, watching it wax and wane, and eventually

Let it **G**o.

Often seeing your child with what the meditation teachers call "Beginner's Mind" can help reset the relationship. It is very easy to get stuck in negative patterns of behavior. Fortunately, we can shift this way of seeing and relating. Try this reflection practice when you need to clean the slate and shift the dynamic of a relationship.

Reflection: Seeing with Kind Eyes

Try doing this practice when your child is sleeping.

- Without disturbing his or her sleep, quietly sit by your child.
- Watch your child breathe. If you like, try to coordinate your inhalation and exhalation with that of your child.
- Without being hard on yourself, reflect honestly on how you see your child. What thoughts or feelings are arising right now?
- Often our thoughts are neutral or critical. Do you often say, "Why are you wearing that to school today?" "Why are you so messy?" "Do you have to complain about everything I say and do?" "Why won't you eat your vegetables?"
- How are you reacting and interacting with your child? Don't judge and berate yourself, but get curious. Do you notice the stain on a T-shirt, the fire engine that is left in the living room?
- Try looking at your child as if it is the first time, as if you have never seen him or her before. Rest there.
- What do you notice? See if you can see something new in your child's face.
- Spend a moment with your child's vulnerability. See the strengths as well as the weaknesses.
- What might be causing his or her suffering?
- Reflect on how your child, like all beings, wants to be happy.
- Can you allow your heart to soften as you see your child from this new perspective?

Meghan practiced this a number of times, and it helped her reconnect with the things she loved in Johnny. She began to see things from his perspective—how hard it must have been when she was on bed rest, the disruption to the equilibrium of his old family structure, the ways he had felt displaced. Of course he was angry and acting out. She could see that now and began to soften. For the first time she saw the possibility that her anger wouldn't last for his entire life.

I suggested that they try to do something together, just the two of them. Could Dad watch the baby on the weekend for an hour or two while they had some special time together?

It took some negotiation, but Johnny liked the idea and helped make it happen. At first it was pizza lunch, his favorite food, at the neighborhood pizza place. This evolved into lunch and then kicking a soccer ball together in the playground. Meghan had played soccer in school, and she was able to show Johnny some fancy footwork, which he tried to imitate. It felt good for her to be physically active again, and Johnny was impressed.

"Cool, Mom," he said with admiration. "That is awesome!" Things were on the upswing.

Just a Bad Cold

It seemed like just a bad cold. "Don't worry so much, Valerie," her husband chided. "Kids get colds all the time. You always overreact." Four-year-old Matt, however, was miserable. He was so stuffed up it was hard to breathe, he couldn't sleep, and he was achy and irritable. "Just send him to school. It's not a big deal—don't make a sissy out of him." Matt was their first child, and Valerie had heard all her life that she was too emotional. So she packed him up with a warm sweater, scarf, gloves, and hat and took him to daycare. He barely had a fever, and she needed to get to work herself.

A few hours later the teacher called. "Matt just threw up. You need to come and get him," she insisted.

"Great," Valerie thought, "so much for getting any work done."

By the time she arrived at daycare Matt's temperature was over 100 degrees and he seemed unusually pale and listless, but glad to see her.

She gave him something for the temperature, but the fever didn't go down. In fact, it went up.

"This isn't right," Valerie told her husband, "I'm taking him to the doctor; something is wrong."

"Jesus, Valerie, let him sleep it off. You can't call the doctor at night, and we both need to rest. Don't bother her; it's just the flu."

When the fever persisted the next morning, Valerie had to call in to her workplace to take off another day. "How on earth do people keep a job when they have kids?" she wondered, feeling angry, trapped, and worried.

The fever continued to climb, and Valerie took Matt to see the pediatrician. He was listless, struggling to breathe, and his heart was racing.

The pediatrician examined him and in a calm but no-nonsense voice said, "Take him to the hospital, let's get him on medication immediately.

And Valerie—" The doctor paused and put a hand on her shoulder. "I don't want you to worry, but go directly to the hospital; don't stop at home."

Of course Valerie began to worry. She bundled Matt into the car and drove as quickly as she could to the children's hospital in the city. She hated driving in city traffic, especially during rush hour, but she had no choice.

By the time they arrived at the hospital, his fever had spiked to over 103. He was still having trouble breathing. The wait was interminable. Valerie felt so alone. "Please, he is struggling to breathe, can someone look at him already?" Valerie grabbed a triage nurse, trying to get some help.

Within moments they were in the emergency room, with Matt on a metal table with bright lights on him, surrounded by a circle of doctors, nurses, and young residents. Suddenly there were machines, tubes, and monitors attached to his little body. Things moved so quickly. It seemed surreal.

"It's good you brought him in when you did," the attending doctor said. "Your little guy has a serious respiratory infection. I want him to spend the night here so we can keep an eye on him."

Valerie was frantic but relieved that Matt was in good hands and that her concerns were being heard. She had tried mindfulness, but there was no way she could focus on her breath while Matt was struggling with his. When she tried to find her breath, all she could think of was his pain and suffering and how he was struggling to breathe. But she needed something to get through this ordeal. She was exhausted, her body was shaking, and she would spend the night trying to sleep in a chair by his hospital bed.

Valerie liked listening to sounds, another popular and practical way to meditate, and found this to work better for her than trying to follow her breath. She adapted that basic practice for the hospital.

♥ The Sounds of Life

- Start by sitting, standing, or lying down. The posture doesn't matter. Let yourself get as comfortable as possible.
- Begin to listen to the sounds around you. This may include the heat, the air conditioning, wind, rain, or traffic.
- No need to name the sounds, to hold on to them or push them away. Allow yourself to listen to the sounds as they are.
- Imagine that you are listening with your entire body, picking up 360 degrees of sound. Above you, below you, behind you, in front of you.
- Notice that each sound, like every story, has a beginning, a middle, and an end.

- It may be that some sounds are annoying or irritating, while others don't evoke a response. Don't judge the sounds; just listen.
- When your mind wanders, no problem, just bring it back to the sounds in the room and to the present moment.
- See if you can allow yourself to rest in the sounds of the moment just as they are.
- Even if this is a difficult moment, know that this constellation of sounds will never appear again in exactly this way.
- When you're ready, take a deep breath, find some movement in your hands and legs, and open your eyes if they have been closed.

When Valerie reflected about the experience, she realized that listening to the sounds in Matt's room helped her stay present and not spin out into worry or catastrophic thinking, which was so easy for her to do. "Usually I would have been annoyed by the noise and beeps of the monitors, the presence of the IV, the respirator, but these sounds felt protective. I knew that the machines, even with their lights and activity, were keeping him alive. And knowing that helped keep me from being a total hysterical mess."

While the practice helped Valerie get through a dramatic situation, this practice is also useful in daily life. Although meditation and yoga teachers may focus on the breath, this is not the best route for many. Bringing attention to and anchoring in the inner, rather than outer, world may stir up uncomfortable emotions and memories. For folks with a history of anxiety and trauma, a gentle way to bring mindfulness into daily life is to bring attention to the sounds around us. For many people who are skeptical of meditation, the practice of listening to sounds is generally more accessible. And it's easy. We don't have to make the sounds come or go. We don't have to manipulate them. We can listen to sounds without making any effort. The sound appears, we hear it, and we're present.

Rosa came to see me to help manage the stress of three small children and an aging mother who required care after her knee replacement. She didn't think mindfulness would work for someone with such a busy life. I told her that the practice is like puppy training, requiring patience, humor, and self-acceptance. She set aside just three minutes a day and found that she could return to the present moment "one sound at a time." Tuning in to the sounds around her as she ran between soccer games and her mother's rehab helped her feel less agitated.

Alessandra had a history of trauma and sexual abuse. She wanted to try mindfulness but became agitated when she tried to feel her breath.

Listening to sounds became a way for her to stabilize and come into the present moment. When she began to feel overwhelmed by memories of the past, or fears that something bad would happen to her daughter, listening to the hum of her air conditioner or the sounds of street traffic helped her anchor her awareness in the moment and in her present life, so different from the rural home where her abuse had occurred. With practice, as she focused on the sounds of her hard-won new life and child, her ruminations about the trauma began to subside. We can also listen to sounds and tune in to our other senses as we walk, sit on a bus, or wash dishes. While our minds race to the future or get stuck in the past, our senses are always in the present.

Mindfulness and compassion are not just practices for exhausted, stressed-out parents who are trying to juggle too many balls without dropping them all. They are tools for life. These are skills that can help you manage the consequences of the truly challenging situations that we all face—families that didn't meet our needs or who were abusive, the emotional strains of illness, financial burdens, being a single parent, trauma, and the aftermath of addictions. Mindfulness and compassion offer the promise of a different relationship with our burdens and the freedom not to be defined by our histories and the events of our lives.

"I'm Drowning"

Rob was raised not to talk about problems. In his self-reliant family, needing help was a sign of weakness. His wife could see he was down and needed help managing his stress. He was a hard worker, the oldest of five. "I'm loyal. I try to be the person who is always there, someone you can trust. I won't let anyone down," he told me.

"I don't complain, feel it is disrespectful. My mom was a nurse. She's tough, no nonsense. If you were sick you went to school anyway unless you were bleeding from the head. She's a good honest woman. My dad worked construction. Proud. Street smart. When I was a teen he was hurt on a job. Had to go on disability. Got down, started drinking. My mom stepped up to the plate, started to work extra shifts. I stepped up as well. Had a paper route, started to bag at the local grocery store. You can't make much when you're 15. I had to help with the younger kids as well while my mom was working. We were eating cereal for dinner, and then I decided to learn how to cook dinner. Nothing fancy, but I can boil water." He smiled. "Dad is pretty much bed-ridden now, with some dementia. Sad, really sad." He shook his head, looking down at the floor. "I still try to help out and support them; he has lots of medical expenses. My sibs try to help out too. But we all have our own families and expenses. The disability payments don't cover shit."

"After school I went into the family furniture business. Hoped they would pass it on to me. I learned accounting. And it was a steady job. And they treated me well; things were good for a while. I started a family, felt like I was going someplace. But then my uncle got sick, cancer, and he couldn't keep the store running. And I didn't have money to buy the business. That was it. 'Sorry, kid,' he said. 'Wish I could do more for you.'"

"So, a dozen years of hard work and nothing to show for it. Not even much of a severance. I'm out on the street. I have a wife, three young kids. I pride myself on being a good provider. I've been looking for a new job, sending out résumés, doing searches, calling friends, but nothing. And it's been months. I'm worried. Money is tight, so I'm driving an Uber. People treat me like a servant. My parents and family depend on me to help. My wife teaches nursery school, but that's not enough to support us. I feel like I'm useless. Sometimes I wake up in a panic in the middle of the night, in a cold sweat; it's hard to breathe. And some days, when it's bad, I feel like I'm drowning."

"And some days I hate myself," Rob said. "I'm distracted, angry, I feel like I can't do anything right. I beat myself up if I forget to pick up some milk at the store."

It was clear how devoted Rob was to his family and how hard he tried. And also how hard he was on himself when things didn't work out as planned. It turns out that 75% of us are harder on ourselves than we would be on a friend. To help him get perspective, I asked what his best friend would say.

"Oh, probably that I'm going through a tough time, but it'll get better."

"OK, how about if we try an exercise that might help keep that perspective?" I suggested.

"You think an exercise can help? How would it do that? Will it help me get a job and feed my family? I'm not into simplistic solutions," he said skeptically.

"There's good research behind this. Let's give it a try; I'll do it with you," I said.

The following reflection is adapted from Germer and Neff's Mindful Self-Compassion (MSC) course. It can soothe and help us through life's more challenging trials.

Reflection: What Would Your Best Friend Say?

- Take a moment and sit quietly. Think of a kind and loving friend. It could also be a teacher, mentor, relative, or even an animal or spiritual being.
- Notice how you feel in the friend's presence, in your body and mind.
- Tell this friend what you are going through and how hard it has been for you.
- What would this friend say to you? Imagine the words, the tone, even the facial expression. Feel free to write it down in the form of a letter or a note.
- Be open to any words, images, and feelings that arise.
- What would he or she do? Consider offering yourself a pat on the back, hug, or gentle squeeze if it feels right.
- If it is helpful, write this response down and carry it with you, in your wallet or purse, and then turn to it whenever you need some support or comfort.

Rob imagined his best friend from high school, Jack, who was his rock-climbing partner and still a good friend but had moved away.

"When I was doing the exercise," he told me, "I felt him say, 'Buddy, it's not your fault. It isn't. Ease up on yourself, man. Just hang in. You can't control life. You're a good man. I used to trust you with my life, and you never let me down. You'll turn this around. If ever there was someone you could count on, it's you.' It felt like the kindest thing anyone has said to me in years." A tear leaked out of the corner of his eye. "Maybe I'm not so bad after all." He paused. "And it feels good not to keep it all in. These worries have been eating me alive."

"Rob," I said, "What Jack said to you is almost the same as what the meditation teacher Wes Nisker teaches, and I find it so true. He tells people, "You are not your fault."

"I feel like I'm at fault. I shouldn't have worked in the family business. But I didn't know; it seemed like a safe decision. I can't blame my uncle. I feel like I have to take responsibility for things not working out." He paused. "Sometimes I feel like an idiot."

"Rob, we make the best decisions we can. We don't know what the future will bring. You couldn't see this coming. If we think about it, who we are and what happens in our lives involve a whole constellation of factors—our parents, our genetic inheritance, our culture, where we grew up, our economic situation, world events. It doesn't mean abdicating responsibility for our behavior and our actions, but it also doesn't mean blaming ourselves for every little thing, every deficiency, every flaw, every time we forget the milk. We can't predict which job will last, we can't predict who will get ill, we can't predict the swings of the stock market, the weather, or the impact of natural disasters."

The following practice, inspired by Mark Coleman, which Rob did daily, helped him begin to ease up on himself.

You Are Not Your Fault

- Start by sitting comfortably, letting yourself settle. You can do this practice sitting, standing, or lying down.
- Reflect on how you are not your fault. Did you order this body? Did you ask for this critical mind? Your ethnicity? Your personality style?
- Did you order your dysfunctional family online?
- There are so many factors and variables that shape our lives that are totally outside our control.
- Take the largest perspective you can. The big picture can help us develop compassion for our quirks and challenges.
- The psychologist Carl Jung suggested that we are not what has happened to us but what we choose to become.
- Instead of judging, blaming, and berating ourselves, what if we offer some kindness and compassion for our challenges?
- Reflect on what it is like to see your life from a larger perspective.

Mindfulness in Daily Life

Of course most of parenting isn't about adorable smiling babies, no matter what we all imagined years ago before we embarked on this path. There was a reason that Dr. Freud called parenting an "impossible profession." Fortunately, the practices you'll find in this book have the power to reverse much of the physical and emotional toll that comes with parenthood. The act of training our minds, like training our bodies at the gym, helps us with everyday tasks that are so important to parenting—decision making, emotional flexibility, responsiveness, and understanding. Training our attention so we can be more aware of the present moment, rather than caught up in concerns about the past or worries about the future, also nurtures qualities that are crucial to the happiness and well-being of a family—resilience, calm, equanimity, compassion, and connection with each other. Dr. Richard Davidson, a neuroscientist and pioneering researcher, stresses that our emotions can be *trained*. So can our responses to the drudgery of parenting. I'm not advocating being a Pollyanna who loves every aspect of parenting (hard to love diapers and toilet training), but I am suggesting that we do have choices about how we respond to the least pleasant aspects.

Most parents with young children change at least six to eight diapers a day. One estimate suggests each child will go through 8,000 diapers. And if you have more than one child . . . you can do the math.

No amount of mindfulness and compassion will remove unpleasant things from our daily lives. Poopy diapers will not magically disappear or suddenly turn to gold. But what happens if we bring awareness to the task of changing diapers? How we respond to the daily drudgery of parenting can have an impact on our day. While we can't make the unwanted tasks of parenting go away, we do have a choice about how we are in relationship to them. Mindfulness teacher Sharon Salzberg stresses that mindfulness doesn't depend on what is happening, but it is about "how we are relating to what is happening." It is the difference between thinking "My life is mired in shit and it always has been and always will be—this is just the current iteration" and thinking "This is an unpleasant task, but it is necessary and beneficial for my child. Let me just be with it."

When the daily demands of caring for your child feel overwhelming and are getting you down, try these practices of mindfulness in daily life. Like training a muscle, we can train ourselves through simple acts like diaper changing to be with the rest of the not-literal shit that will arise in the course of parenting, which will be even more than 8,000 changes.

Dirty Diapers

- Before changing the diaper, just stop.
- Take a breath. Feel your feet on the ground.
- Look at your baby. Look into his or her eyes. Smile.
- See if you can be with what arises during this task—the sensations, thoughts, feelings, smells—in an accepting, nonreactive way.
- When we like things, we want to hold on to them. When we dislike things, we want to push them away out of irritation or annoyance.
- One way to relate skillfully is to acknowledge, like it or not, this task is not going away.

- Be aware of the steps of changing the diaper—taking clothes on and off, using wipes, ointment, powder.
- The baby may scream, fuss, fight. This is what babies do. Take a deep breath, stay grounded. This moment will pass.
- See what it is like to allow things to be as they are, not to be repelled by the act.
- This is part of life. The Zen master Thich Nhat Hanh used to say, "No mud, no lotus."
- As you finish, know that you are keeping your baby clean and comfortable.
- If you like, end with a smile and a hug.
- Repeat 8,000 times.

Many meditation teachers emphasize that you don't need to take major chunks of time out of the day to sit quietly—what parent has that luxury? One helpful maxim is the idea that mindful moments, many times during the day, can make a huge difference in your well-being and your ability to cope with stress. One of my teachers put it simply: "Short moments, many times." Practicing mindfulness doesn't have to be a big deal. You can do it anywhere, anytime, and doing what you usually do. The aim of these practices is to learn to be present even during a mundane or unpleasant activity. The point of informal practice is to do what we always do, but know that we are doing it, perhaps by checking in more deeply with our senses.

Try the following practice on a busy morning when you barely have time for breakfast (don't worry, I won't lecture about the benefits of herbal tea). It reminds me of a meme I recently saw online that simply reads "There's a guy at this coffee shop, not on his phone, not on a laptop, just drinking coffee. Like a psychopath." How often are you just drinking your coffee when it's time to drink your coffee? Mindfulness doesn't have to be on a cushion for ten minutes, it can be with your coffee for ten minutes. OK, maybe five minutes. Because you really need two things to stay sane as a parent, your coffee and your five minutes.

💜 Drinking Coffee Meditation

- If you make your own coffee, stop and take a breath while the water boils.
- Listen to the sounds of the water or the sounds of your coffeemaker.
- Smell the coffee; let yourself inhale the fragrance.

- As you pour the coffee, use all your senses, bringing attention to the color, the smell, and the steam rising from the cup.
- If you add milk, cream, or sugar (or substitutes), notice that. Pay attention to the act of stirring.
- Stop before taking the first sip. Let yourself inhale the aroma.
- Feel the warmth of the cup.
- Let yourself enjoy the first sip. Ahhh.
- Let yourself actually taste the coffee.
- What do you notice? What does it feel like on your tongue? Feel the sensation of swallowing.
- Take a minute to sit there (or stand if it is one of those mornings) and pause as you drink the coffee, noticing as many moments as you can.
- See if you can bring this focus and awareness into the activities of your day, adding a new activity to bring complete attention to every few weeks.

Tedious Tasks

Just as mindfulness can help us see our children with a fresh perspective, it can help us bring a different attitude to things we do on autopilot or things that we resent or find to be drudgery. We haven't counted how many loads of laundry we've folded or how many dishes and pots and pans we have washed and dried, but trust me, it's even more than the numbers of diapers. For many years, cleaning up has been a dreaded chore, unpleasant but necessary. And, as with everything, we have no choice about doing the dishes, or laundry or diapers, but we do have a choice as to how we relate to these tasks. We can grumble and complain, or we can try to find something new or maybe even pleasurable in the task. Another way to bring more mindfulness to the mundane is to deliberately make it a process of discovery and get curious—as you do something for the umpteenth time, can you find something new in it? See if you can notice something you've never noticed before in the pile of laundry, the color of the dishes, and OK, well, maybe or maybe not something new in that diaper. Our children are already naturally curious; especially when they are young, they are expressive about this. Ask them to join you and notice the sensations and experiences of the chore. They'll often narrate their sensory experience without prompting: "Oooh, the water is warm, the soap is tickly, the bubbles are funny." Try to find that miracle in the mundane. If they can, you can.

Many teachers teach a deceptively simple practice of bringing awareness to the hands. I first learned the practice from Tara Brach. This is one variation I created for parents:

 ## Mindfulness of Hands

- Before washing the sink full of dishes, or folding the mountain of laundry you've been avoiding all day, allow yourself to stop for just a moment.
- Look at your hands. Begin wiggling your fingers and gently rotating your wrists. Become aware of the movement.
- Clench and unclench your hands. Feel your hands from the inside out.
- Notice sensations, pulsations, and vibrations within them. You don't have to name them; just feel them.
- Become aware of each finger, the palms, the backs of your hands.
- See what it is like to inhabit your hands. You may find that other parts of your body begin to relax and let go.
- Notice your neck, your shoulders, your jaw. Has anything shifted?
- Let your attention rest in your body before starting the next activity.

These practices can build on each other. Try the following brief reflection.

Reflection: Soap Bubbles
- *Try to remember the first time you played in soapy water.*
- *For some young children, soap bubbles can feel magical. Children often see rainbows in them, which adults, lost in the drudgery of it all, stop seeing.*
- *As you begin to wash the pots and pans from dinner, look at the soapsuds with fresh eyes.*
- *Imagine that you are seeing these bubbles for the first time, which, in fact, you are.*
- *Become aware of your hands, feel the warmth of the water, smell the soap, bring your full attention to the activity.*
- *Become aware of what you are bringing to this task. What are you feeling? Are you resenting the burden of washing and drying a pile of dishes? What happens if you approach this task as if you are doing it for the first time?*
- *See if you can carry this awareness of what you are bringing to the activity to other tasks during the day.*

Someone once asked the Zen master Thich Nhat Hanh how to practice mindfulness. "Do you want to know my secret? I try to find a way to do things that is the most pleasurable. There are many ways to perform a given task—but the one that holds my attention best is the one that is most pleasant." It's simple brain science if you think about it. And Thich Nhat Hanh always recommends smiling as you breathe. Why not enjoy the breath? And I'd take that further: why not at least try to smile at the dishes? The same applies to parenting and the tasks that go with it. When we resent the diapers, the dishes, and the laundry, we can become angry and irritable, feeling burdened by the details of running a home and caring for a family. But if we can find moments of freshness, even in mundane tasks, it can transform our experience of the daily tasks of living.

2 "Why Is This So Hard?"

USING SELF-COMPASSION
AS A LIFE RAFT

Have you ever hated yourself for something you did or said to your child? Have you ever lost your temper? Behaved in ways you don't even want to think about, and you wouldn't want anyone to know, ever? Despaired that the "parenting police" (thank God they don't exist) would come to arrest you for some infraction?

We Are All Imperfect Parents

Don't worry, you are not alone. No one is a perfect parent, and everyone screws up. (Me too—just ask my kids.) This is a judgment-free zone. Your secrets are safe. This chapter is designed to help you develop some perspective on your imperfections and to illustrate how to respond with kindness (instead of self-loathing, a bottle of booze, a quart of ice cream, recreational drugs, you know . . .).

I'm not talking about going soft or letting yourself off the hook. Learning self-compassion isn't a "get out of jail free" card. It is about accepting that we are *all* imperfect parents. There is no need to dwell on the mistakes, to replay them endlessly in your mind, or to spiral down into a black hole of shame and regret. Beating yourself up doesn't help anyone.

Chrissie's struggle with her new stepdaughter is an illustration of what self-compassion looks like in action.

Meltdown

When Chrissie, divorced with a four-year-old son, married widowed James, who had a seven-year-old, things seemed to be going well. But apparently not for his daughter, Jenny, who wasn't on board with her dad's moving beyond dating and into a new marriage. Being left with grandparents while they went on a honeymoon enraged her, and she took it as a personal insult. "You're going away with *her*?" she protested.

When they returned, Jenny missed no chance to let Chrissie know just how miserable she was with a new mother. She became increasingly rude and defiant. Every day presented a new struggle. When Chrissie asked her to put her toys away, she ignored her or challenged her authority. She couldn't do anything right; Chrissie was rapidly losing patience and confidence.

"My friends tell me to chill, that this is just a difficult stage," Chrissie explained, "and that she'll come around. I just don't know how long I can wait. This weekend was the pits. James was traveling for work, and it was just us. I tried so hard to make it fun. We saw a movie that the kids wanted to see, Jenny had a friend sleep over, and we had spaghetti, her favorite, for dinner.

"But once the friend left the next morning, Jenny had a meltdown. The girls didn't sleep much, and she was overtired. She started picking on Steven, first teasing him and calling him names and then hiding his favorite action figures. The final straw was when she destroyed a Lego tower that we had been working on all day, hours of work. Then *he* totally lost it. And I wasn't far behind.

"But I tried to remember what the stepparenting books said to do, and so I said, 'Jenny, this is unacceptable. Time out. Seven minutes' "—a minute for each year as the experts suggest.

"At first she just stood there defiantly. When I set the kitchen timer, she knew I meant business and went to her room, but first she stabbed me in the heart, screaming 'I hate you! You're not my mother. You'll never be my mother. I wish *you* were dead.' "

We All Have Negative Emotions

Chrissie told this story in my office, clutching a box of tissues as she wept and described how much she had wanted a daughter and how happily she'd looked forward to life with their new merged family.

I responded with a story of my own, about how my mentor had taken me aside after the birth of my first child and said, "No one else will ever tell you this. I want you to listen and not forget. Right now it is blissful, you barely notice the extreme sleep deprivation. It's all roses and rainbows and baby gurgles. But at some point, mark my words, you will hate your child. I guarantee it." I was stunned. This would never happen to me, never. And how dare he say this! He went on, "And when you do—it may be many years from now—remember: You are human. It happens to all of us."

Chrissie stopped crying as I explained, "At the time it almost seemed like a curse to me, like a scene from one of those fairy tales where everyone gives the child a wonderful present and someone else gives a piece of coal. But it turned out to be one of the most useful things anyone has ever told me. It helped me make room for my angry feelings and not feel so ashamed of them."

"And speaking of fairy tales," I went on, "I was reading something recently, that in the early versions of the fairy tales it wasn't the stepmother who tried to kill off her children. *It was the biological mother who wanted the child dead.* The evil stepmother became a literary device for those aspects of motherhood that we don't like to acknowledge—anger, aggression, cruelty, hatred. It's easier to split it off than to acknowledge the complexity of the mother's feelings toward the child and the child's feelings toward her.

"My mentor gave me permission to have my negative feelings, not to act on them of course, but not to add layers of guilt and shame, and not to feel that I was a bad or defective mother."

Reflection: When Have You Needed a Life Raft?

Parenting is a messy business, and we all have negative emotions toward our kids, times when we've felt overwhelmed and inadequate, lost our temper or didn't behave like Mother Teresa. You are not alone. How often have you exploded at all the little accidents?

Have you ever:

- *Freaked out when your child threw up on you? Peed or pooped on you? Spilled milk on a new rug?*
- *Lost it when your kids spilled grape juice on a nice new outfit on the way to a wedding?*
- *Flipped your lid when your kid had a tantrum and threw food in a restaurant? Or at Grandma's house? Or in your friend's living*

room (the one whose house is all neat and tidy) and everyone turned to stare at you?
- Blown up when your child refused to get dressed?
- Become furious when your child bit or scratched a sibling? Or a friend's child?
- Thought you would lose your mind with a colicky baby who cried nonstop for 12 weeks?
- Felt trapped when the kids got sick with chicken pox during Christmas and you had to cancel your plans? And you really needed a holiday?
- Felt ashamed when your child struck out in a tied baseball game? Or failed to make the winning shot in basketball?
- Decided that you had the wrong kid and are living the wrong life?
- Thought about putting the kids up for adoption and running away to an idyllic Greek island?

Add the moments when YOU really needed a flotation device . . .

Yes, *of course* we get upset. And we all lose it! The list is endless and we all melt down. Self-compassion is about giving yourself a break and making a fresh start. Remember, parenting is an impossible profession.

Chrissie nodded in recognition and said, "I think what is hardest for me is that I start to beat myself up, and I start criticizing myself. If only I were Jenny's biological mom I wouldn't yell, I would be a better mother. I would be able to love her. On a bad day I feel like I'm a grinch and my heart is a few sizes too small."

I asked Chrissie what she liked about Jenny.

"Let me think," Chrissie replied. "She's her own person. No one is going to push her around. She's determined and she's a fighter. I feel for her, I really do. Losing your mother at four years is horrible. And her mother had been sick for years before she died. And it was so hard for James as well."

How easily we extend the compassion to others that we deny ourselves.

Reflection: When Have You Shown Kindness to Others?
- Take a moment to reflect on the times you've shown compassion for other kids or to other parents who are struggling.
- Pause; choose one and write it down.

- *What was the situation?*
- *How did you respond?*
- *What did you say?*
- *What did you do?*
- *How did the other person respond?*
- *How did you feel about yourself?*
- *Allow yourself to let the experience land. Give yourself a moment or two to take it in, to remember it. Stay with it for a few moments.*

We are often so harsh with ourselves, forgetting those times when we were kind, helpful, and loving. Or when we made a difference in someone's life.

One easy way to enter a mindful state is to remember the good. In fact, one definition of mindfulness is *remembering*. Let yourself remember and savor the good that you have done. Take a second and try that right now. Yes. And then the next second, and the next.

The ABCs of Self-Compassion

Chrissie is not alone. Almost all of us feel like inadequate parents. Which is why self-compassion is so important for parents. It can help shift our inner dialogue from constant self-blame and self-criticism to acceptance, kindness, and appreciation. It can help us see that we are just as deserving of kindness and understanding as our children, friends, and other loved ones.

Self-compassion is a healthy way of relating to ourselves when things get tough. And when you're a parent, that may feel like most of the time. While it can take courage to look at ourselves and to acknowledge our imperfections, accepting ourselves as we are, it can also transform our lives and those of our families.

Dr. Kristin Neff, one of the world's experts and a pioneering researcher in self-compassion, was the first to define it and to create a scale to measure it. The MSC course rests on a solid empirical foundation. However, soon after her young son was diagnosed with autism, she had to put all her research to the test. In the shock after the initial diagnosis, she allowed herself to feel what she was feeling—grief, disappointment, and other emotions that she felt she wasn't "supposed" to feel. She didn't fight her emotions and learned to comfort herself when she was having a hard time.

After the shock, she made the decision to accept her son unconditionally and to love him no matter what. What she found has profound implications for all parents: when she could give love to herself, she could give love to her child. And this helped her find the strength and the resources to be the best mother she could be, even in the most challenging times.

Have you experienced something similar? Or has a close friend? A family member? Most of us know many people who are struggling. Perhaps a neighbor whose teen is dealing with addiction? Or struggling with mental health issues? Do you know someone dealing with loss? With disability? With major health issues?

And it isn't just the major life challenges that are hard; the daily mundane grind is enough to drive us bonkers (not a clinical term): the hormonal mood swings of a preteen, the emotionally sensitive toddler who melts down if things don't go his way, the middle school tragedy of not getting the lead in the school play, the high school slump after not making the varsity team, and so on. With kids, there is always something that can drive you crazy.

Fortunately, anyone can learn self-compassion—in part because we know what to say to others and how to treat those that we love and care about. We just need to give ourselves the permission to feel it for ourselves.

Self-compassion has three basic components:

1. Kindness to ourselves, without harsh judgment, along with the motivation to help ourselves and to inquire about what *we* need.
2. The recognition that we are all imperfect and we all lead imperfect lives. This acknowledgment of our common humanity can help us feel less isolated and alone and connect more deeply to others; other parents are going through similar struggles.
3. Self-compassion rests on a foundation of mindfulness. We learn to be present with whatever is happening, rather than to go into denial or put our heads in the sand. We often need courage and strength to do this. However, mindfulness gives us the space to step outside our immediate reactions and gain some perspective.

Let's see how Chrissie learned to use self-compassion with her stepdaughter.

"We all yell," I reminded Chrissie. "We all melt down, both kids and adults. What is important is returning to a place of kindness and working to repair any damage in the relationship. This is a tough situation, and it isn't going away any time soon. Can I teach you something that might help when it gets hard? I call it the Self-Compassion Life Saver for Parents. It's about learning how to respond with kindness when things get tough."

"Nope, sorry. Sounds silly and indulgent to me, and selfish. I just need to toughen up. Get a backbone, become a no-nonsense, no-bullshit step-mom. Zero tolerance for bad behavior."

"Hold on. People often misunderstand. Self-compassion isn't about becoming a wimp, making excuses, or letting yourself off the hook. It's about learning to respond kindly to yourself when things are difficult."

Chrissie rolled her eyes. "Yeah, as if I have time for that? I'm responsible for three people now."

"Let me try again, from another perspective. When you burn yourself cooking spaghetti for Jenny, what do you do?"

"Well, first I swear a blue streak, call myself a stupid idiot, then I apply some ice, a bit of cream, and a bandage."

"Exactly. We know how to respond kindly to our bodies, but it is harder to respond kindly when we get burnt by life."

"OK, you have a point. I'll try it, but I'm not about to get a personality transplant. Are you suggesting I say, 'You poor, poor baby. Life has been so cruel to you. Here, have chocolate cake and ice cream for breakfast! Let me buy you another toy! Do you want to stay home from school and watch TV instead?'"

"Being compassionate doesn't mean being a doormat. Of course you can still set boundaries, have rules, set limits around inappropriate behavior. Kids need structure.

"Let's do this together," I said. "It takes virtually no time. And you can put a hand on your heart. The touch is soothing and comforting."

Self-Compassion Life Saver for Parents

🎧 *Audio Track 2*

- *This is a moment of suffering.* Or, *ouch, this is hard, really, really hard.*
- Validate your feelings. Let the words feel natural.
- *Parenting is full of tough moments. Many parents feel this way. I'm not alone. This is part of life.*
- Add words of kindness. *Let me be kind to myself. Chrissie, I'm here for you.*
- Feel free to put a hand on your heart.

"It's that simple. Try it in the heat of the moment, Chrissie. When it all feels like too much. I'm not promising miracles, but it helps. I want to help you learn to respond to her rather than react."

> ### Reflection: Putting Self-Compassion to Work in Your Life
>
> *Building on the list you created in When Have You Needed a Life Raft?, see if you can brainstorm about moments when it all feels like too much and you could use this practice. For most people, there is something that happened today (or is happening right now?)—a fight before breakfast, an incident on the way to school, sibling rivalry, harsh words that we exchanged over dinner.*
>
> - *Ask yourself what has been hard for you today.*
> - *What is it that you need now?*
> - *Were there moments when you felt alone? Unappreciated? Unseen? Like staff or a servant?*
> - *Take a few moments and try the Self-Compassion Life Saver for Parents.*
> - *Jot down a few notes. What was it like? How was it to extend kindness to yourself? What did you notice?*

Chrissie came back the next week with a report.

"The self-compassion stuff helped. But the language didn't work for me. So I rewrote it a little."

"Great, I want it to be your own."

"Jenny tried to bait me this week, but I kept my sanity. I didn't totally lose it. I think you're right. She's trying to get attention, create a reaction, stir up trouble. So she takes Boo-Boo, Steven's favorite stuffed bear, the one that he sleeps with, and hides it. He's frantic. And, of course, James is working late. They start to fight, pushing each other, hitting, biting, pulling hair, the full catastrophe. I pull them apart. Another calm, peaceful bedtime," Chrissie says sarcastically.

"So I say, STOP this, everyone separate. Now. Chill-out time. In your rooms.

"We all go in our rooms, and I notice I'm losing it again, and I really feel it in my body. And I start paying attention to my thoughts. I start hating her, then hating myself, feeling I'm inadequate, blaming myself, and thinking divorce is the only way out. I was desperate, so I tried the Life Saver thing. But I changed the language so it's more realistic.

"I took out the nicey-nice sugar coating."

- *This is a moment of pure shit.*
- *Being a parent can suck. Being a stepparent really sucks. Exponentially. This is fuckin' impossible.*
- *Let me be kind to myself. This will pass. Maybe in this century.*

"And I put a hand on my heart. It almost felt like I was giving myself a hug. It felt good. I was a little calmer.

"When it was over, I said, 'OK, guys, we need to find Boo-Boo. Let's work together. We're going to be detectives.' I pulled out flashlights for everyone. 'Scavenger hunt. I hear Boo-Boo calling. He's saying, "Help! Help!" Let's go! He needs us.'"

"I got her engaged, rather than our usual futile fighting. And guess what? Boo-Boo was hidden behind the toilet. Gross. We never would have looked there. She found him, of course."

"We washed him off, cleaned him up, and Steven fell asleep, even though the bear was wet."

"When I was putting Jenny to bed, I gave her a kiss, and rather than wanting to strangle her I thought about what I liked about her. And I admired her humor, her gumption. I said to her, 'Sometimes this is hard, honey, but we'll get through this. I love you.'"

"She smiled, hugged her stuffed animal, and fell asleep."

"The practice helped me get a grip, and it might keep me from going absolute bonkers and leaving James in a fury. I don't want another marriage on the rocks. One was enough." She shook her head. "He's not objective about Jenny. He feels so guilty that Karen died. He can't hear anything negative about his precious kid without getting mad at me." She sighed. "I think this is going to be a long process. And I'm going to need all the help I can get."

Working Skillfully with Our Emotions

We all experience difficult emotions, but many of us haven't been taught how to handle them effectively. We often deny them, become numb, or pretend that we're not feeling sadness or anger, especially if we grow up in a family where these emotions are taboo. Like Chrissie, Dylan was trying to find a different way to be with difficult emotions.

Avoiding Default Positions

When an opportunity arose for Jan to take a new, exciting job, she and Dylan decided it was her turn to focus on her career. So Dylan works at home while she's away. But he finds it lonely—and finds being the primary parent challenging. Their older child has always been pretty "rough and tumble" in Dylan's words, but third-grader Nathan is "a quiet, sensitive kid," and Dylan isn't sure how to respond to him with sensitivity of his own.

The annual school concert is coming up, and all the kids are excited about it. Nathan "isn't exactly musical," his dad reports, but he loves singing to himself while he's playing or in the shower, and he doesn't seem to care that he can't carry a tune. Unfortunately, the music teacher apparently does care, and at one point she stopped the music and said, in front of everyone, "Nathan Johnson, I think it will be better if you just mouthed the words."

It took a while for Nathan to tell Dylan the story, because he was absolutely devastated and embarrassed. At first he just moped and didn't want to talk. Once the problem came out, as Dylan recalls, "I tried to get him to cheer up, told him it wasn't a big deal, to forget about it, but he couldn't. I didn't know what to do. But telling him to cheer up just made it worse. Not only did I feel totally unequipped to help my son, but I didn't really have any idea what he was feeling. In my family, my dad would have told me not to have a sad face, and that would have been the end of the discussion. I was raised not to feel anything that was uncomfortable. My mom was the type of woman who, when asked how she was after having surgery for cancer, replied, 'never better'—I feel unprepared for parenting Nathan.

"I hate the fact that the teacher silenced him. And I hate the fact that I feel so useless. I think he misses his mom. I started to feel worse and worse, brooding that my wife is the better parent and that I'm incompetent. Other dads aren't at the playground, they have important jobs at offices; they don't work at home. And then I got angry at the teacher for shutting him up and shaming him, and then I started hating myself for being such a loser of a dad. My thoughts just took off and I was this angry, bitter mess. And then, after the kids were asleep, alone with Jan away, I got out the gin and poured myself a few drinks." He winced. "All that got me was a hangover."

We all have default positions we take when faced with uncomfortable emotions—we run away, escape to TV or our smartphone, drink or snack.

> ## Reflection: What Is Your Default Position?
>
> • *Grab some paper and a pencil or take notes on your phone. (No, don't check your messages or social media or return a text. That can wait.)*
> • *Spend a moment taking a few breaths, coming into the moment, putting your hand on your heart, or giving yourself a hug.*
> • *Ask yourself this question: When emotional discomfort comes up, what do you do?*
> • *Most of us distract ourselves, finding solace in things like food, drink, Netflix, or recreational drugs.*
> • *What is your default position of choice? Jot it down.*
> • *Notice it, with kindness and without judgment.*
> • *Give yourself some compassion. Yes, it is hard to feel this, to have this happen. Be with it, even if it is just for a minute.*
> • *Try saying to yourself, "It's OK, let me be with this. Let me feel it, even for a moment."*
> • *Take a few soothing breaths, and when you're ready, return to your day.*

Dylan knew that the ways he was trying to handle emotions he didn't fully understand and wanted to get rid of were not making him feel any better, so he was open to learning new ways to deal. Before he was ready to learn how to be with difficult emotions, however, he needed to learn how to be kind to himself when he was in pain.

When I was in training, Prozac and the other SSRIs were just coming out, and one of the psychiatrists on the unit started calling them "ego glue." We all liked the metaphor because it described the benefits that folks were experiencing. People felt like the medication helped them function more effectively, which made them feel better about themselves. Mindfulness can help as well, and for some people it is as effective as medication.

One of my meditation teachers once quipped that there is only a one-letter difference between meditation and medication. There are many classic practices that use the breath as on object of meditation, taught in one form or another by almost every teacher, but the following practice is a version with self-compassion, designed just for parents.

Dylan and I did this together in a session, and then he practiced it during the week, setting aside five to ten minutes a day.

💟 Ego Glue for Parents

- Start by sitting comfortably on a chair or a cushion.
- If you are too exhausted to keep your head up, feel free to lie down. (No guilt; I've been there.)
- If you need to curl up in a ball or move into a fetal position, it's OK.
- Take two to three deep breaths, letting yourself settle, letting yourself stop.
- There is nothing you need to do right now, no one to care for. This is time for you to rest.
- Really. Aaaaaahhhh . . .
- If you like, put a hand on your heart or another soothing place as a reminder to bring some kindness to yourself.
- Notice that your body will breathe without your doing anything. Let your body breathe you.
- You don't have to micromanage your breath. You don't have to control it.
- Just feel the breath, feeling the natural rhythm of it flowing in and flowing out.
- Distractions will arise—thoughts, emotions, worries, discomfort, plans. Just let them go and return to your breath.
- If you doze off, don't be concerned. We are all exhausted.
- Be aware of what has come up without judging yourself; just notice the thoughts *I'm terrible at this, I can't even rest,* or *I'm a hopeless idiot, I'm such a stress case.*
- Don't get mad at yourself for having a thought or a feeling. Acknowledge it and let it go.
- Let yourself have a new response, rather than beating yourself up or criticizing yourself. Let yourself begin again.
- Starting again with kindness and warmth, not staying with your breath, is the essential practice. This is what we are trying to cultivate.
- Let your whole body be moved by the breath.
- Allow yourself to be rocked, held, even internally caressed by your breathing.
- For the last few moments, just feel the comfort of your breathing.

- Your breath has been with you since you were born. Think of it as a friend.
- Release the attention to your breath, sitting in the quiet of your experience. Let yourself feel what you're feeling and be just as you are.

Dylan had tried breathing practices before but hadn't liked them: "I always thought that the point was to stay with your breath and not let your mind wander, which is why I hated it and found it boring and stupid. However, I really like the idea of learning to start again and not constantly chastising myself when I screw up. Now that could be useful. I'm used to building an arsenal of rage at my wife, the teacher, my kids, my life . . ."

"Exactly," I said. "You are learning how to get out of your own way."

This practice is an adaptation of a core practice in the MSC course. It is something that can be used in the heat of the moment, when you are feeling an onslaught of difficult emotions. Used daily, as I suggested for Dylan, it will help you build your self-compassion muscle and increase your resilience and your ability to deal skillfully with difficult emotions.

Self-Compassion: A Way to Stay Afloat

A client mentioned a meme she found online. It goes something like this: Parenting is saying the same things over and over and expecting different results. Oddly enough, that is also the definition of insanity. Is this a coincidence? Maybe not.

For most of us, life can be hard. In fact, it can be *very* hard. And having children often makes things harder. It makes us vulnerable and anxious in ways we weren't before. It increases stress exponentially. Suddenly, we are responsible for another person, who is totally helpless and dependent. It takes our time and attention away from our relationships, our work, and our needs. Formerly well-ordered lives become chaotic and overwhelming. Most parents, not just new ones, feel inadequate and unprepared. We suddenly find ourselves trapped with endless obligations, noise, anger, resentment, and financial pressure. And this isn't only when our children are young. When we have children, there is so much that can go wrong. In fact, giving birth can feel like we're just asking for trouble.

How do we react when things don't go our way? Like Chrissie and Dylan, we worry that we are at fault and become critical of ourselves: "I was beginning to feel that something was wrong with me. That I was somehow missing an essential parenting gene or a software chip that dads need to have." We often embark on a mission to fix things, to change ourselves, or, most likely, to change our children. We tell ourselves we need to "toughen up" or "get a backbone," or "be authoritative," or that they need to listen, to behave and follow the rules, to "learn a lesson." However, while we may try to change ourselves, or usually our kids, the results are rarely what we seek.

But we can learn to parent in a new, healthier way. Instead of fighting difficult emotions, we can learn to respond with kindness and understanding—learn to respond to ourselves the way we would treat someone whom we love deeply. And, once we learn to tend to ourselves, we find that we can respond to our children, and our partners, with the same warmth and kindness. It is a common misconception that self-compassion is a form of weakness, but the research on the topic shows just the opposite. For example, imagine that your daughter comes home one day with a failing grade on a math test. How motivating would it be if you say to her, "I'm so ashamed of you. You are a total loser. You'll never get into college." How does that feel? You can imagine that she would become afraid of failure, develop "math anxiety" (as it is called), and be likely to give up on math entirely. What would it be like if she heard, "Yes, you failed on this one test, and I love you anyway. How can I help? How can I support you so you can achieve your best?"

In study after study, researchers are finding that people who are compassionate with themselves are less stressed, less depressed, less anxious, and have better coping skills. They have a better relationship with their bodies, are less afraid of failure, and have more rewarding relationships with others. We model self-compassion for our children so they can learn to treat themselves kindly when things are not going well. This then becomes a resource that they can call upon throughout their lives, helping them become more resilient and resourceful.

So, instead of blaming and criticizing ourselves (or our children or partners) when things go wrong, we can practice self-acceptance. In an MSC class that I was teaching, Lorraine spoke up: "I've noticed that when I give myself compassion after blowing up at my teenager, it can shift the day. Rather than fuming and raging for hours or days, like I used to do, and listing all her faults and everything she ever did wrong, I simply stop and say to myself, 'Yup, difficult moment, let it go.' And when I'm in a better place, it helps her as well. It has gotten me out of these 'ruts of rage' as I call them. You know, it's funny, but my mother would hold on to slights for years, decades. Kind of amazing, isn't it?"

And this isn't just about you. Self-compassion can be contagious. It's the foundation of compassion for others.

If you have been having a hard day, a hard time, a hard year, a hard decade, try this exercise:

Reflection: When You're Struggling

- *Think about a time when you had a close friend who was struggling with some aspect of parenting—something that happened, some misfortune, some failure or difficulty, some inadequacy. And, on the other hand, you were in a pretty good place at the moment. How would you respond to your friend in this situation? What would you say? What words would you use? What tone? Any nonverbal gestures? What would be your posture? Facial expression?*
- *Take a few moments to jot down your responses.*
- *Think about a time when you were suffering in some way around parenting. It could be something that happened—a misfortune, a failure, a difficult interaction, or a time when you felt inadequate. How do you usually respond in these situations? What do you say to yourself? What words do you use? What is your tone of voice? Are there nonverbal gestures?*
- *Take a few moments to jot down your responses. What do you notice? Are there differences?*

When we teach this practice in the MSC course, or when I use this with parents who want some support around parenting issues, most people are stunned by the difference between how they speak to a friend and how they speak to themselves. Maya, a struggling single mom who was a nurse, found that she used this practice when she would berate herself for not having a larger income: "I would never tell a friend she was a loser or a stupid idiot." Brandon used the practice to ease up on himself: "I used to guilt myself if I was tired at the end of the day and didn't feel like going out to play catch. Now I can find an activity that works for both of us, rather than feeling that I have to do everything my son wants to be a good dad." And Jess couldn't believe the difference between how she treated herself and a friend. "If I talked to a friend like that, I wouldn't have any friends. Hell, I don't even treat the dog like that! I say to him, 'What a good dog!' I don't say, 'You stupid bird-brained animal!' It's helped me feel more peaceful with my kids. And I'm nicer to them as well!"

Most of us often find it easier to be kind to others than ourselves. But being kind to ourselves is a skill that we can learn. Kelly McGonigal, a research psychologist at Stanford, argues that our brains are wired to be critical of ourselves and compassionate toward others. The trick is to learn to turn our natural compassion inward as well as outward. But this can often be a challenge. Many people find that they can't start right off with compassion. If you never had it as a child, and your family never modeled it for you or treated you with compassion, it can feel awkward and foreign. It can be a process to develop compassion for yourself, so please be patient with yourself. If this is your experience, try starting with mindfulness and building toward compassion. Anton shows us one way this can be done.

Anger Management

Anton had a stressful job working for a tech startup. Money was tight, and his temper was hot. The long hours, constant travel, and lack of sleep were taking their toll on the marriage and his relationship with his kids. "When I get home, OK, I admit it, I'm irritable. I'm exhausted, totally fried, and I'm a bundle of nerves. I know I'm not pleasant to be with. I snap at my wife and yell at the kids. I have a hair-trigger temper. I know I shouldn't lose it, but they set me off."

"What are your thoughts about what triggers your temper?" I asked.

Anton was willing to reflect on what got him angry.

"I think it's the constant bickering. It's endless, ceaseless. My two boys, they are seven and nine, are constantly fighting, challenging each other, picking on each other. I just want some damn quiet when I get home.

"I put up with bickering all day and all night and all weekend at the firm." He smiled a genuine smile and laughed. "Ah, I'm constantly dealing with bickering boys. Yes, that's it. I hadn't seen the connection. No escape." He paused. "So, how are you going to help me? I'm a busy man. I want to fix this problem."

Anton was not going to be receptive to the language of mindfulness, and he would certainly be allergic to even the *idea* of self-compassion.

"Anton, I want this to be effective, and I don't want to waste your time. My suggestion is that we start with stress reduction. It will help you at work, at home, with your kids. And, it'll help with your health. I notice here in the chart that you have high blood pressure."

"Yeah, yeah," Anton acknowledged, "my doc wants me to relax and destress, but there is no time for that."

"Got it. Let me teach you something that you can do in three to five minutes. You can do it in a meeting, on the phone, at dinner, even driving. These practices can increase your well-being and improve your physical health."

The following practice can help stressed-out parents find some calm in the midst of a crazy busy life. In this exercise, we bring awareness to the places where the body is "touching"—such as the eyes, lips, hands, legs, and feet. It is a way to shift attention away from the racing mind and to anchor and ground attention in the body. Research shows that bringing awareness to the body in turn helps calm the mind.

Touch Points for Stressed-Out Parents

- Start by sitting comfortably. No matter how frazzled, exhausted, or stressed you are, see if you can assume a posture of dignity. Getting in touch with your essential worth, that you are deserving, which is often lost in the fog of parenting, is a good way to "reset."
- Let your body rest. Let your face relax, your shoulders drop, head, neck, and back come into an easy alignment.
- Take three or four breaths to let the body and mind settle. Come into the present moment.
- Notice the places where the body is "touching" and bring some kindness to each touch point—the eyelids touching, the lips touching, the hands touching, the sitting bones touching, the backs of the knees touching, and the feet firmly touching the ground.
- Find a comfortable rhythm, repeat the sequence, and bring some appreciation to each part—notice the eyes touching, the lips touching, the hands touching, sitting bones touching, knees touching, feet touching.
- You can note these points silently to yourself to help you keep focus.
- If your mind wanders and you get distracted, it's not a problem. Don't criticize yourself; just start again.
- When you are ready, take a deep breath, stretch, and find some movement in your arms and legs. Try to bring this focused, kind attention into your next activity.

This is a very practical and grounding practice that can be used in the midst of daily life. The order can be reversed as well, as many people like to start with the feet touching the ground. Maria finds it helps keep her steady when she is trying to make dinner and her children are fighting for her attention. Richard uses it at the end of a long day when he is tired and the chaos of his four kids playing grates on his nerves. He was looking for a simple practice that would help him keep it together when his three-year-old spilled his milk all over the kitchen table. When the inevitable accidents happen, rather than yelling at his son to be more careful, he spends a moment noticing his feet touching, knees touching, sitting bones touching, and so on, until he can say to himself, "This is a mess, life is full of small messes, if you have kids you have messes. It isn't the end of the world."

Food Fights

The next week, Anton reported the following challenge. "I've been too busy to practice, and I got distracted by the constant food fights at home.

"The kids are fussy eaters, especially the youngest. All he wants to eat is plain, boring white food. I hate that. I'm sick of rice, pasta, chicken, white fish. It drives me crazy. And my wife caters to him, and then we fight. Not good. So my wife makes white fish with white pasta and I forgot, I put some pepper on the dish before bringing it to the table. You would think it was a tragedy. The end of the world! Samir refused to eat it. I was not in the mood for defiant behavior. I'm sick and tired of how picky he is.

"'Go to your room without dinner,' I yelled. But my wife gets in the middle. 'Let me scrape it off; he just doesn't like pepper,' she pleads.

"I yell at her to stop spoiling them. She yells back. So I take my plate and eat dinner in the living room watching TV. Everyone was mad at me. I'm the bad guy, at home and at work. Tell me, what is so bad about a little pepper?"

"What does your son say?" the therapist asked.

"He says it burns his mouth," Anton responded.

There was silence.

"Look, Anton, I understand that your intention is to raise children who are respectful and well behaved. But I wonder, how would you respond to being forced to eat something that burned your mouth?"

"I don't want him to be soft; I don't want a wimp for a son. I won't tolerate a spoiled brat. And my wife just indulges him."

I didn't want to get caught in a struggle with him, so I tried another angle. "I get your point. So many parents and children fight about food. Almost as much as couples fight about who takes out the trash."

Anton laughed.

"And I know you are busy. I don't want our session to devolve into a discussion of the merits of pepper. I'm interested in you. What is happening for you? If we put the pepper aside, what is happening for you?"

"Can't dinner just be peaceful? There is constant fighting at work, constant bickering. Why is there always a problem with everything? Nothing is ever good enough!" He paused. "I guess this is the story of my life."

"I think we hit something big. Let's stay with this for a few minutes." Anton had begun to get curious about his reactions. The Touch Points practice was allowing him some perspective and over time was helping him slow down enough to notice where his mind was going, but could he learn to bring some kindness to himself?

Sometimes it is good to combine or layer practices, just as we add some layers when it is cold or we are in a place with air conditioning. I suggested the following practice, irreverently called What the Hell Is This? These two practices, in combination, help us sort and manage difficult emotions. Once we begin to develop some friendly curiosity about our experience, compassion can follow. This practice is an adaptation of a classic Zen koan called "What Is This?" It was originally designed as a way to work with anger and worry. The following version is specifically for parents.

What the Hell Is This?

- Start by sitting comfortably, finding a position you can assume without strain. As always, it is fine to lie down.
- Take a few moments to ground and anchor your attention. Try Touch Points for Stressed-Out Parents or Ego Glue for Parents as a way to start.
- Bring your attention to what you are experiencing right now in relation to parenting.
- It could be anger, self-doubt, worry, sadness, or fear. See what it is for you.
- Notice what you are feeling with a warm curiosity. If it gets too intense, return to feeling the body touching or being with the breath.
- If you like, put a hand on your heart, noticing what is present with kindness, with interest, and without judgment.

Anton came in the following week and reported on his insights.

"Well, I practiced What the Hell Is This?, and it helped me get a grip.

I found I could do it in three minutes. I realized that I was getting really intense and rigid about food. Really holding on. For me, it wasn't about pepper. Of course it wasn't about pepper. But it was the story behind it. It's the principle of it. I'm working so hard, busting my ass, putting up with all sorts of shit so my kids can have a better life, and what do I get? The lack of gratitude pains me. And then I start to spin out. I start to worry that they don't respect my authority, that my colleagues at work don't respect my authority, that my wife doesn't respect my authority, and I go into a sort of rage. I worry that I'm not a good parent. I'm not around enough. That my kids will reflect badly on me. And suddenly, I'm having all these battles in my head—with everyone. The kids, the wife, the colleagues. It was huge."

"Sounds like you could see what was happening underneath the story," I noted.

"Yes, exactly," Anton responded. "And I found myself saying, in a voice that was new for me, 'Anton, it's just pepper. It isn't a tragedy.' And I realized that I don't like garlic. And I hate beets. So I could relax a little. We all like some foods and don't like others. It doesn't mean much of anything. It was just a thought. I didn't have to let it spin out of control." He paused. "Maybe, just maybe, you've helped me avoid a heart attack."

What shifted for Anton was that he was able to see that he was spending his precious time with his children getting into fights about inconsequential things. In fact, he realized he was getting in fights with almost everyone in his life. It wasn't productive or effective for him to constantly lead with anger. His colleagues were avoiding him, and his family didn't want to be around him. By bringing some mindful curiosity to his behavior, he understood that his knee-jerk anger was interfering with his ability to enjoy his children. When he stepped back about his son not liking pepper, he could acknowledge that he didn't like certain foods either. Once he could allow that he had certain preferences, and that wasn't the end of the world, he could let his kids be kids and smile at their likes and dislikes, making room for them to be human. As he practiced, he began to get in touch with humor and inner resources he didn't know he had.

You may also want to try combining the practices if it is one of those days when you need a little extra help. Dylan added *What the Hell Is This?* on days when his wife was away and his patience and reserves were low. "It feels like adding some more extra-strength glue or getting some reinforcement troops to come and help hold down the fort—guess we're watching a lot of old movies these days," he smiled. Chrissie added this practice when she had a hard day with Jenny. "It feels like combining them gives me a little more space or some more daylight. And if it's a 'single parent' week, it feels like a friend is there for me, saying 'OK, girl, now what is happening here?' It slows me down and helps me feel less alone."

I Can't Adult Today

Alex entered my office one day wearing sweatpants and a T-shirt that announced, "I Can't Adult Today." It turned out that her external appearance reflected her internal state: "I was sorta keeping it together until my third child was born. Now I joke that she's a career killer. Once upon a time I was a lawyer, but that was a long, long time ago." She paused, noticing her choice of words. "Do you think I've been reading too many children's books?" she joked.

"So, I was trying so hard to do it all. Function without sleep, keep everything going, get the kids to daycare. But it wasn't working. I couldn't keep it up. I started taking naps at my desk. My friends at the office were really supportive. 'Alex, you just need to lean in,' they would say. Forget that. As they say, 'I just need to lie down,' she laughed.

"My third is only six months old, and I have a three-year-old and a seven-year-old, and I'm so tired I can't see straight. My oldest wants to do youth soccer; not sure how I'm going to fit in all the practices and the games. Can't believe that I'm about to become a soccer mom."

"Not what you envisioned?" I asked.

"Nope. I wasn't going to be a stay-at-home mom, no way. I was going to be different from my suburban, boring, cookie-baking, apron-wearing mother. Ha. I wish someone would bake me a cookie," she said wistfully. "I've taken a leave from work. And now I'm feeling so angry, resentful, and discouraged most of the time. Am I depressed, or is this what being a mother is about?" she asked plaintively.

Alex is hardly alone. For many of us, the overwhelming stress of parenting young children is hard to foresee and even harder to handle. Especially in hard times. Money is tight for many families today, and there are other pressures, including the responsibility for aging parents.

Reflection: What Is Overwhelming for You?

Take a minute and reflect on what is stressful for you right now, in addition to parenting young children. Are you worried about:

- *Health issues?*
- *A recent or impending loss of a job?*

> • *An ill parent or sibling?*
> • *An unsafe living situation?*
> • *A recent loss or death?*
> • *Conflict at work?*
>
> *Write down what else you are dealing with.*

Rarely are we just dealing with the stress of parenting. It is usually parenting plus the stress of all the other things that life throws at us. No wonder you feel exhausted and overwhelmed.

"Sometimes being a parent mimics the signs of depression," I suggested and asked Alex to tell me more about what she was going through.

"I'm often irritable and grumpy," she explained, "and I snap a lot at the kids. Hell, I just snapped at you! And I'm crying a lot, more easily than ever. I was reading to Alyce the other night—she's the oldest. And I've been waiting to read her *Alice in Wonderland*. We just started the book. I've been looking forward to this; I was a huge reader when I was a kid. So I start the first chapter and I read about Alice falling down the rabbit hole. They say Lewis Carroll was a drug addict, and clearly he was on *something* strong when he wrote it, but it felt so real this time. I was reading about Alice falling and falling and falling and I started to cry. When I was a kid I thought it was so cool, and I kept looking for rabbit holes so I could discover another world. I wanted to escape the one I was in. But the other night, it seemed terrifying to me. My daughter noticed I was crying and asked if I was OK, and I felt I had to lie and protect her from my sadness— 'Oh, it's nothing, just the sniffles.' But it isn't. The reason I'm here today is that I'm in free fall. I'm worried that I'm falling into a bottomless pit and that I'll take my family with me."

Am I Depressed or Is This Parenting?

In times of exhaustion and fogginess—what Alex calls "parenting brain"— mindfulness and compassion can help us get a grip and get some balance. Therapist and mindfulness teacher Sylvia Boorstein has one of the best explanations of mindfulness and compasion that I know. She calls it "awake attention to what is happening inside and outside so we can respond from a place of wisdom." And if we know what we are feeling, we are less likely to lash out in anger—or fall down a rabbit hole.

One of the most important uses of mindfulness and compassion with parents is helping us deal with difficult feelings. It helps us find the possibility of a pause between a challenging situation, such as a child refusing to eat, and our usual conditioned response—yelling, threatening, or punishing. We can use that pause to collect ourselves and consider a different response. Rather than strike out when we are tired or frustrated, we can take a moment to try to respond from a place of wisdom instead of reactivity. Working with these difficult feelings in mindfulness practice can help us recognize a feeling as it begins, not days, weeks, or years later. Turning toward difficult feelings can help us not lash out at our children or partners, not ignore these feelings out of fear or shame.

In the following practice, the body provides a way to ground and anchor difficult feelings so we can work with them effectively, with some more perspective, rather than becoming overwhelmed. This practice can help establish greater balance during the storms of parenting.

The Winds of Parenting

- Start by sitting comfortably, or lying down, eyes either closed or half open. Spend a few moments listening to the sounds around you, noticing the touch points in your body, or being with the comfort of your breath. Whichever "anchor" you choose, let this be your home base, a place of rest and comfort.
- Notice any tension, discomfort, or tightness in the body. No need to fix anything; just notice what is present.
- Check in on the "weather" in your internal landscape. What are you feeling right now? Are there feelings of anger . . . sadness . . . disappointment . . . anxiety . . . fear?
- Return to the anchor of listening to sounds, touch points, or the breath. Then watch, see which "winds" carry you away. Make this the object of your attention.
- Notice where the feelings are residing in your body. Tune in—is there tightness in your chest? Are you clenching your jaw? Is there tension in your shoulders? Is there a pit in your stomach? Does your head ache? Is your pulse racing? Bring a kind curiosity and interest to whatever you are feeling and noticing.
- Be gentle with whatever feelings or sensations you notice. Parenting stirs up a lot. Notice if you start to berate or criticize yourself. Have you started to think about what's for dinner? Notice what takes you away.
- Try bringing the warmth of your hand to the place where the feelings are most intense. Invite this place to soften and relax. You might want

to try breathing into the discomfort. Don't struggle or resist. Just
notice the feeling and allow it to be.

- Sometimes just becoming aware of the emotion in a friendly and
curious way can help. If you start to feel overwhelmed, distracted,
or agitated, simply return to the anchor of the sounds, touch points,
or breath.

- Notice any judgments or criticisms you add on, then let them come
and go. Don't feed them or get behind them; they will pass.

- When you are ready, take a breath, find some movement in your fingers and toes, arms and legs, and open your eyes. Try to bring this
kind curiosity into your next activity.

When Alex tried this practice, she reported that her response was
complicated: "Sometimes I'm having so many feelings I feel blown around.
I just feel so overwhelmed at times. And then at other times, I look at the
baby and she is just beginning to smile and I feel so happy. And then other
moments, I'm crying. And then other times I'm just bouncing off the wall."

Sound familiar? This is the territory of being a new parent. Alex had
had the same experience with her first two kids, but now, she said, "It
just feels like it's exponentially more. And sometimes I feel disoriented.
'Where am I? How did I end up with three kids? What day is it? Whose
life am I living? This is my life!?! Huh? Can I take a break from all this and
go to a tropical island?'"

A friend once said to me that parenting is like driving in the dark.
Things look different, you're not sure where you are, and you can only see
a short distance ahead of you. For Alex and maybe you too, it can feel like
losing the life you had—and you may not like that feeling. But, as Alex
noted with chagrin, "I can't tell anyone, I can't say that, 'cause people will
just tell me I should be grateful that I have three healthy kids. And then I
feel guilty and ungrateful. A first-world problem."

It doesn't help to beat yourself up, and it's not self-indulgent to think
about it, talk about it, and work it through. As psychiatrist Dan Siegel says,
you have to "feel it to heal it," and "name it to tame it." In other words, the
only way to manage difficult emotions is to allow yourself to feel them and
to know what feelings you're experiencing. This is particularly important
for people like Alex, who says, "Growing up, we weren't supposed to feel
much of anything. And we certainly couldn't talk about it." Likewise for
Dylan, who was generally scolded to just stop being sad or angry or whatever painful feelings he was having. We can get so caught up in trying to
parent well and making our children our priority that we often don't allow

ourselves the time to accept and identify our emotions. Here is a simple practice of labeling that can help.

Naming Difficult Feelings

Labeling feelings is a well-researched meditation practice. In 2007, J. David Creswell and colleagues found that in the process of labeling what we are experiencing, we deactivate the alarm center of the brain (the amygdala) and activate the prefrontal cortex, which is often called the brain's control or CEO center. It helps us move out of a place of reactivity and upset into a place where we can reestablish balance and perspective. In an essay, Matthew Lieberman compared this practice to hitting the "snooze button" on an alarm clock. And what parent wouldn't want to hit the snooze button?

 Hitting the Snooze Button

- Start by sitting comfortably, eyes either closed or slightly open. Or lie down if you prefer. Take a few soothing breaths, just letting yourself settle.
- Spend a few moments connecting with an anchor—this could be the touch points of your body, the sounds around you, or the comfort of your breath.
- When you are taken away by a feeling, simply note what that feeling is. Do this with warmth and compassion. For example, note "fear, fear, fear." Don't agonize about getting it exactly right.
- See where you feel it in your body. No need to fix it. Allow it to be.
- Notice the attitude you're bringing. Are you chastising yourself when you notice "anger, anger, anger"? Are you telling yourself that you're a bad parent for having this feeling?
- Allow a large spectrum of feelings to be acceptable. All feelings are welcome. See if you can label with kindness, acceptance, and warmth.
- If the feeling becomes too intense, and you start to feel disoriented or overwhelmed, simply return to your breath, the touch points, or the sounds around you.
- There is no need to analyze the emotion. No need to create a story around it. Don't delve into the history. You don't need to say, "My mother was angry with me, I'm angry with my kids, this will never end."

- Label it and let it go.
- Bring as much kindness and compassion as possible. If you feel that negative feelings don't deserve compassion, note this as well.
- Be open to pleasant feelings and label these as well.
- Alternate between labeling the feelings and grounding with your anchor.
- When you're ready, take a deep breath, find some movement in your fingers and toes, arms and legs, and stretch. Open your eyes if they've been closed.
- Try to continue to be aware of your emotional reactions as you transition to your next activity.

The next time I saw Alex, she was wearing bright-green socks that read "Parent in Training." I couldn't help joking that her clothes were very articulate. She laughed along with me: "I know this is very silly, but a friend gave them to me. And she just gave me a onesie for the baby that says, 'I'm a Baby. What's Your Excuse?' They help me laugh and feel that I don't have to have my shit together all the time. It takes some of the pressure off. And I guess I beat myself up thinking that I should have an excuse if I have a bad day or I cry or have a tantrum. Sometimes it's just hard and I miss grown-up conversation. I'm thinking of Parent in Training as a new job description."

I was reminded of a comment from a Zen master, that "life is just one mistake after another." I think the same is true of parenting. It's on-the-job training. We're constantly making mistakes. We're constantly falling down. We weren't taught to do it. And our culture rarely helps us parent. No wonder so many parents feel alone and depressed.

"The 'Snooze Button' practice worked for me," Alex reported. "I'm feeling less agitated and hating myself a little less when I have 'bad feelings' or I get angry at the kids. I feel like I have this archaic image of what a mother should be. That I shouldn't yell. That I shouldn't lose it. That I should be loving and kind 24/7. That every damn dinner should be made from scratch. And that the kids should have homemade cookies when they get home." She shook her head. "This gives me a little space, a little latitude between my mom with her immaculate home and perfect meals and me, with my mess." As Alex learned to be kind to herself, paying attention to her own feelings and tending to her needs, she turned to some practical measures as well to ease the daily external pressures of the stress imposed by the kids. She found that driving the kids around town like some "underpaid chauffeur" was taking its toll.

"Generally I'm feeling better—on some days, I should add," Alex reported. "But the kids are still themselves. And they aren't about to become peaceful Zen masters. The constant fighting is wearing me down. I looked into adoption, but it's not that easy," she joked.

There are mindfulness educators who teach that children, by learning to take a moment, focusing on their breath, and noting their emotions, can learn not to lash out at others. One of my favorite stories about what mindfulness is comes from a kid. His school launched a program to teach the kids mindfulness and compassion, with very positive results. When asked to describe mindfulness by a reporter, this boy responded, "It's not hitting someone in the mouth."

This is the practice we developed for Alex's family. It's a bit of a riff on the old car game of noticing license plates from other states or naming what you see—trucks, billboards, birds, or cows and horses if you are in the country. While the labeling portion works best for children who are verbal, younger children often like to feel the breath.

Mindfulness and Compassion in the Car

- At home, perhaps at bedtime, help your child find his or her breath.
- One way you can do this is for both of you to put your hands on your child's chest or belly to feel the breath rising and falling. With young children, it is often easiest to feel a hand on the belly.
- Some children like the image of the belly rising like a balloon. See what images work well for your kids.
- If (when) an argument starts while you are in the car, try out the following suggestions, adapting them as you see fit.

The following scenario was common in Alex's family:

"Mommy, Mommy, Alyce pinched me."

"Alyce, stop it."

"She kicked me."

"Did not."

"Did too."

"STOP IT, NOW. I'M DRIVING" [said with increasing anger]. "I can't break up this fight. Do you want me to get into an accident?"

"But she hit me!"

"If I have to pull over and stop the car, everyone is in BIG trouble!"

Alex tried to adapt the Name It to Tame It practice when driving. This is what it often looked like:

"Mommy, Mommy, Alyce pinched me."

"OK. guys, everyone find your breath."

"Ah, Mom, she pinched me."

"I heard you. We are trying something different."

"But it hurts. I don't want to find my breath. This is STUPID."

"Let's try being quiet for 30 seconds. Try hands on the belly."

"I don't want to."

"This is SO DUMB!"

"I'm MAD."

"Great, let's try naming it. So far I hear Stupid, Dumb, and Mad. Any other words?"

"But it hurts."

"Keep those words coming. We have Stupid, Dumb, and Mad. We have Hurt. Let's keep going. What else do we have?"

"This is unfair."

"And we have Unfair. Now we have Stupid, Dumb, Mad, Hurt, and Unfair. Anything else?"

"This is boring. I hate this. This is for idiots! This isn't a GAME!"

At this point, Alex's kids would often be laughing. Sometimes they would shout out what they were feeling. But usually the fighting would stop and Alex would be able to drive. She found that having healthy snacks in the car cut down on the fighting as well.

One important caveat is to keep the naming warm and kind and to keep a sense of humor. Yes, we all get mad, think things are dumb and stupid, and feel hurt. This is part of what the self-compassion researchers call common humanity. While the kids sometimes protested about the practice, Alex found that it interrupted their fighting and got them laughing.

So, the next time you are driving to soccer practice or to school and the kids start fighting, try some mindfulness and compassion in the car. And play around with it to see what works in your family. There isn't one right way to do it. Try to have some fun with it.

The practice can also set the stage for learning about how to manage difficult emotions. It is a natural opportunity to hear another's point of view, to listen to what someone else is feeling and experiencing, and to communicate your own needs and desires. And on a good day it can open the door to learning about negotiation, compromise, and even forgiveness. While it may appear to be a game that gets you to soccer practice without a splitting headache, it can also serve the larger aims of teaching cooperation and communication. You might want to think of it as a secret or hidden ingredient, like the grated zucchini that you surreptitiously fold into the chocolate cupcakes.

Reflection: What Works for You?

As you've watched Chrissie, Dylan, Anton, and Alex learn to bring some self-compassion to their daily struggles, what do you think will work for you? Spend a few moments reflecting on what you've learned and how it can help you stay afloat. What would you like to incorporate into your daily life? Could you use the Self-Compassion Life Saver for Parents when your children are being impossible? Would you like to learn to sit with emotions that get evoked when the kids fight and learn to accept them even with they are painful and difficult? Are you dealing with a stressful situation in your family or at work? Do you want to try labeling the confused emotions so you don't feel that you are moving through a parenting fog? And how about being kind to yourself as you learn these new skills? And why not be kind to your family by helping them tone down the chaos by using the same tools?

Of course there will be challenging moments that will arise, but think of these as tools for life. We are working on building a core of self-compassion that will help you be resilient and learn to navigate whatever life throws your way—without going under. "On a good day," Alex said, "and mind you those don't come that often, but sometimes when I go down a rabbit hole I learn something. I've started to say to myself, 'Alex, this is a new hole. It's a new world. Get interested. What's happening here? What the Hell Is This?' And that helps me keep engaged and curious, at least for that particular rabbit hole. And it helps me not freak out as much," she smiled, "at least until the next one."

3 "Where Did *That* Come From?"

DEALING WITH THE BAGGAGE WE BRING TO PARENTING

How we relate to our childhood impacts how we parent our children. Some days it feels like an alien (or an angry mother) has taken over our bodies when we suddenly respond to our kid with an angry "Because I said so!" We might be taken aback by our sudden and automatic response. "Where did that come from?" we wonder, feeling ashamed at our sudden outburst. And other days we feel that we can channel the best of our parents, like not going into major road rage when a jerk cuts you off in rush-hour traffic while your kids are hungry, screaming, and punching each other. You remember your kind, calm, and generous dad saying years ago in a similar scenario, "Let him go, not worth getting into a tiff, maybe he has a sick child and is rushing to the hospital." In this chapter, I will explore how understanding our lives in a deeper, more thoughtful way can help us build more effective relationships with our children and our partners. As we grow and extend compassion to ourselves for our difficult experiences, we can begin to create a foundation of care, kindness, and security that will allow our children to thrive.

Recent research in the field of human development has shown that a child's ability to form a secure connection with his or her parents is connected to the parents' understanding of their own life experiences. While we used to believe that childhood events irrevocably influenced our destinies, the good news is that isn't the case. If you had a complicated, difficult, or traumatic childhood and work to understand those events, you are not bound to re-create those interactions with your children. It's never too late to make sense of your life to help your children, and when you do gain such insight you can avoid perpetuating harmful styles of interacting in your family.

Becoming a parent gives us a chance to grow by attending to old wounds, including many that we may have forgotten. As parents, we return to an intimate parent–child relationship, but in a different role and with a different perspective. So many parents I work with have been shocked by what comes out of their mouths. Brian commented, "When I found myself yelling at my kid for no reason, my blood ran cold. I felt like my father, who has been dead for years, had returned from the grave and was suddenly yelling. Where the hell did that come from? What happened?"

As parents, we often find ourselves trapped in unproductive patterns that we had not imagined would arise when we first held our precious newborns but that happen in spite of our best intentions. The aim is not to reject our upbringing, since we can't erase it (though there are times when we wish we could), but to understand it and develop a new relationship with it, bringing self-compassion to ourselves in those moments when we lose it. We also want to embrace the positive and draw on the many good moments of parenting we experienced to sustain us during rough times. When Sharon was feeling exhausted tending to her son while he had a high fever during a bout with the flu, she remembered her mother patiently reading *Goodnight Moon* over and over to her when she was ill. She found the memory gave her strength and some needed grit at a tough time. I hope that the following stories and practices will help you better understand your own challenges and, more important, find a way to respond to yourself and your child with more compassion.

I Hate My Body

When we met her in Chapter 1, Amy was struggling with loneliness and stress as the mother of an infant and a three-year-old in a new environment with a frequently traveling husband. Five years later, the baby is in kindergarten and Sophie is eight, and Amy has put on weight—"cookies, doughnuts, ice cream, cupcakes, we all love to cook and eat!" she said, laughing—but she seemed reconciled to carrying a few extra pounds. "I don't have my 20-year-old waistline; that's gone forever." She smiled wistfully. "It's Sophie I want to talk about. She's heavy, and the other girls have started to tease her already. It starts earlier these days," she sighed. "I guess everything starts earlier these days." She shook her head. "I never thought about my weight when I was her age.

"She started taking swimming lessons at the local Y. And she's a good, strong swimmer, has always been. At this point she can beat most of her classmates in a race. I think it was jealousy, but one of her classmates looked at her in the locker room, made a face, turned up her little nose, and taunted her: 'Fatty, you are a faaattttyyy.' And the other girls laughed and some joined in. Since then she has refused to go to swim lessons, and she used to love it. She had such potential. It's hard for me to see her give it up. I gave up some activities, and now I regret it."

When asked how Sophie was dealing with this, Amy said her daughter refused to talk about it but had taken up basketball, where her height and weight were an advantage and she didn't have to wear a swimsuit. Then she paused and said, "Now that I think about it, I'm the one who's having a hard time. She's doing OK. I feel so guilty. I blame myself. I wish I had given her a graceful, willowy body. I wish I had instilled better eating habits. I feel like an inadequate mother." She smiled. "Guess some things don't change."

"You're not alone with that," I said. "None of us feel like good enough parents. And we can't control the bodies our children get. But we can help them learn to respect and care for them."

"Yeah, yeah, I know, but I still hate myself," Amy said dismissively. "One of her thin friends eats spinach pancakes made from egg whites and wheat germ for breakfast. Duh? We eat waffles with syrup, eggs, and bacon." She shook her head. "Do you know that one of her classmates has parsley and raw kale for a snack! Really! I'd be starving all the time."

I laughed with her. "I'd be hungry too."

What was really going on for Amy was that she hated her own body, and not having known about healthy eating when her kids were little made her feel like a bad parent, even though "stick to your bones" food was how her family had eaten for generations.

We all carry baggage from our parents and grandparents. And often we're unaware of what we have inherited from them. It's not just eye color, hair, weight, and ways of seeing the world; it's deeper issues as well. It's worth getting curious about what you are carrying. Are you feeling weighted down by baggage about your body? Try this practice and see what comes up for you.

 The Baggage We Inherit

🎧 *Audio Track 3*

- Sit comfortably, finding a place where you can be uninterrupted for at least 10 minutes.
- Take a few minutes and let yourself settle in. If you like, spend a few

moments listening to the sounds in the room or feeling the inhalation and exhalation of your breath.

- Ahhh, let yourself relax; this is time just for you.
- Think back to your grandparents, if you knew them. (If you didn't, skip these instructions and move to your parents.)
- How did they treat their bodies? (*Pause.*) What did they teach you about food? (*Pause.*) About taking care of your body? (*Pause.*) What comments did they make about your body?
- Feel free to jot down notes on the things that come to mind.
- When you're ready, focus on your parents. How did they treat their bodies? (*Pause.*) What attitudes did they convey about food? (*Pause.*) What comments did they make about you?
- If your parents had divergent perspectives, focus on one and then the other.
- Write down the ideas and insights that emerge.
- Now take a moment to reflect on what you are carrying. What are the common threads that you see here? How are you treating your body? What attitudes have you retained? How are you eating? What beliefs about your body have you internalized?
- Write down what you have discovered about this "inheritance."
- Pause for a moment. Spend a moment reflecting on what you have learned before returning to your day.

Amy found this practice revelatory, describing how she had forgotten that her family celebrated weight as a sign of good health, in large part because her grandparents had a farm and everyone needed strength and energy to keep the place going. "On a farm," Amy said, "you're up before dawn and you work all day long. You couldn't get along just eating a spinach egg-white pancake!"

The next generation, Amy's parents, had desk jobs, and they resorted regularly to fast food, frozen food, whatever was fast and easy, to feed the family. Amy's mom also had a sweet tooth, so the house was full of candy, cookies, and ice cream. Ironically, she remembered, her own mother hated her body and constantly criticized herself.

"When I became a teenager, after years and years of fast food, I was heavy as well. She turned her criticism on me, and it was constant and destructive." Amy began to cry. "I felt so fat and ugly, and at a time when I was so insecure and vulnerable. And she was mean, I remember she called me a 'fat pig.' Ouch. And here we go again. I'm passing it on to Sophie, and I wasn't aware of what I was doing. I'm hopeless."

"Amy," I replied gently, "you're not hopeless. We all do this. It's how we have been treated, and we often pass it on, usually without thinking. And you aren't calling her names or berating her."

"You're right; that is an improvement. I'm not vicious, at least most days, and I'm glad Sophie has the good sense to get out of the way and go with her strengths.

"But how do I stop hating my body? I don't want her to have a mother who is constantly dieting. In my lifetime, to be honest, I have tried just about every popular diet of the last 25 years. It was how my mother and I bonded. But the weight comes back, no matter what I try."

If you found in the preceding practice that your relationship with your own body isn't always kind and supportive, try the following practice and see if it can shift your relationship to your body and help you stop beating yourself up.

Bringing Kindness to the Body

The body scan was popularized by Jon Kabat-Zinn in his mindfulness-based stress reduction training. Germer and Neff's variation introduces compassion, and helps us cultivate an attitude of warmth and goodwill toward our bodies. As you move through each part of the body, try to bring gratitude, a loving inclination, and compassionate language, even adding soothing touch as needed. Try to allow 20 to 30 minutes for this practice.

- Find a comfortable position, lying on your back. Place one or two hands on your heart as a reminder to bring kind awareness to yourself during this exercise. Take a few slow, relaxing breaths to help yourself settle, and if you like, return your arms to your sides.
- In this exercise, we will be bringing kind attention to each part of the body, discovering how it is to be with the body in an affectionate way. We will be inclining our awareness toward the body, in the same way we would pay attention to a young child.
- If there are judgments or unpleasant associations with a certain part of the body, or if there is pain or discomfort, you may want to put a hand on that part of the body, perhaps imagining kindness flowing from your hand into your body.
- Let this exercise be as gentle and comforting as possible. There is no need to stay with an area of your body if it is too difficult.
- There is no need to change anything in the body; allow it to be just as it is.

- Begin to bring attention to your toes, noticing any sensation, perhaps giving your toes an inner smile of appreciation.
- Then move to the soles of the feet, giving them a little appreciation. They work so hard to hold up your body all day long.
- If there is any discomfort, allow that area to soften. Address the sensation with kind words, noting the sensation and allowing it to be.
- Now feel both feet. If there is no discomfort today, extend gratitude for the discomfort you *don't* have.
- Bring attention up your legs, one part at a time, noticing whatever sensations are present. Send kindness if there is discomfort. Move slowly, bringing attention to your

    Ankles
    Calves and shins
    Knees
- When your mind wanders, return to the sensations in that part of your body.
- Move on to your . . .

    Thighs
    Hips
    Abdomen
    Groin
    Buttocks
    Lower back
    Upper back
    Chest
- As you move from one part of the body to another, return your awareness to the sensations that are present, making sure to bring kindness and gratitude to each part of the body.
- Continue to bring your awareness to your

    Shoulders
    Upper arms
    Elbows
    Lower arms
    Hands
    Fingers
    Throat
    Back of the neck
    Back of head
    Forehead
    Eyes

Nose

Cheeks

Lips

Chin

Whole face, perhaps appreciating how your eyes, nose, and ears guide and inform you all day long.

Crown of your head

- When you have paid loving attention to each part of your body, put your hand on your heart again and give your *entire body* a final shower of affection.

- Take a few deep, slow breaths and when you are ready, open your eyes.

The Mother in My Head

For Amy, the practice made her realize that it was as if her critical mother was lodged in her head and she couldn't get her out.

"I realized how much self-hatred I have carried, for almost every part of me. My feet are too big, my legs are too short and fat, I have thunder thighs, cellulite everywhere, my ass is huge, my hips are too wide, my sagging belly needs a tummy tuck, and after nursing two kids my boobs need a reduction. You think it would have been depressing, but it wasn't. I felt like I shifted my perspective. I've never stopped to appreciate all that my body does every day—running after the kids, hugging them, caring for them, carrying them, soothing them, driving them to school and sports and playdates. My body does so much, and it's strong and powerful. And all that I was seeing is that I'm not a supermodel."

"Exactly. And so many of us have critical mothers and fathers in our heads, and we join in with the criticism. It can be a relief to see it and stop it."

"But what can I do in the moment, when I see a young woman running by and wish I were her? And I start blaming myself for my body? She's not all stretched out and flabby from having kids and eating for two, as I did when I was pregnant. Sometimes I will see other moms at school or practice and I hate myself again. I'm just a fat pig. Sophie is going to be a fat pig. If only I'd known about spinach pancakes," she quipped. "I can't stop. I'm constantly comparing myself to others, and I lose every single time."

"You and most mothers," I agreed. "Our bodies are rarely the same after childbirth and nursing."

"I read an essay a while back that was inspiring, by a scholar and translator, Thanissaro Bhikkhu. He argued that we internalize the gaze of others and get lost in comparison. We get caught in objectifying our bodies, in thinking that what we see in magazines is what we should be, when that isn't even real, or possible for most ordinary human beings."

Jill Soloway, the writer and director of the TV show *Transparent*, commented in a 2017 *New York Times* interview that *being seen* stops us from *being*.

Try this reflection when you start hating your body. For you this might happen when you see your body reflected in a mirror or store window, you see yourself in a photo, or when you see a younger, thinner, or sexier person and you start spiraling down into envy and comparison.

Reflection: Resetting the Image of the Body

- *Find a moment to pause, or take a moment to stop, even if you are walking.*
- *Take a moment to get in touch with your assumptions.*
- *Are you believing that your body's worth is measured by outward beauty or its appearance?*
- *If so, bring some kindness to yourself; you're not alone.*
- *As a parent, can you do what therapists call a "cognitive reframe," which is to affirm that your power and worth are not in your appearance, but in your ability to nurture?*
- *Beauty is fragile and temporary. No matter how much we try to ward off signs of aging, they arrive anyway.*
- *Shift your focus to the subjective experience of your body, noticing warmth, sensation, the rise and fall of the breath.*
- *Bring your attention to the good your body can do, to the ways it supports your child/children every day.*
- *Reflect on the way it supports and sustains others.*
- *Think about your body as a vehicle to express kindness and generosity.*
- *The wrinkles, the cellulite, the sags are not a threat to your goodness, to your essential worth.*
- *Try to rest not in the imagined gaze or judgment of others, but here and now, in your experience of presence.*
- *The more you can free yourself from the internalized gaze of others, the more liberated you will feel.*

The Unlived Lives of the Parents

When we met Lionel and Kyra, their son Tyrone was an infant and having lots of problems with sleeping. Since then he's had some developmental delays from his premature birth, but with therapy for him and support for his parents at their local hospital clinic he was doing well by age five, keeping up in school, talking a mile a minute, and beginning to read. Now he's seven, and his parents have a new challenge: He's at the age where he can start playing Little League, but he can't run as fast as the other kids, doesn't have great hand–eye coordination, and rarely connects with the ball or catches it. "He just likes to be part of the team, he likes to play, and he loves wearing a uniform. It makes him feel like he belongs," his dad said wistfully. "We don't have any other kids, and he's lonely much of the time. It's tough when his teammates make fun of him for not being quick enough."

Lionel looked sad. "His goal in life is to play Major League Baseball. He's passionate about it. When he comes home from school, Kyra will hear this noise and commotion upstairs. The other day there was a crash, and she ran upstairs to see if he was OK. 'Mom, I just stole a base and I'm safe!' He was ecstatic. He had knocked over a lamp, but he was just smiling so big Kyra couldn't yell at him.

"But the fantasy is coming up against reality in a way that really isn't pretty—that's why I'm here. I don't know how to handle my own reactions. With kids this age the games go on forever, and the scores are something out of basketball, 'cause no one can throw a strike. I leave work early so I can watch him play. It's important to him that I'm there, and I come whenever I can. One game was actually close. Our coach is an amazing man, loves the kids, loves the game, and for him, it's about sportsmanship, getting along with others, working together as a team. But the coach for the opposing team had a win-at-all-costs approach.

"So, the game is tied. One hit and Tyrone's team would have won 'cause it was getting dark. The other coach looks at the lineup. There are two outs, and the coach sees Tyrone as an easy out. So the bastard decides to intentionally walk the kids in front of him. Now the bases are loaded. Then Tyrone is up. High ball, he swings blindly and misses, strike one. Next pitch, low. He swings anyway, strike two.

"'Take it easy, eye on the ball, wait for a good ball,' the coach says. Third pitch, he doesn't swing, and the ump calls it a strike. He's out, the game is over. He's in tears. He's heartbroken. I've never seen him look like that—so dejected. His teammates mutter and give him dirty looks.

"The coach keeps it all in perspective, but I'm livid. I want to kill the other coach, punch him out, curse at him. 'How could you do that? How could you treat my kid like that?' Steam was coming out of my ears. Kyra had to calm me down.

"The worst part was that I wasn't the dad I hoped I would be. I was pissed, and for a short but horrible moment, I turned into my father. Rather than say, 'It's OK, son, you gave it your best,' I yelled at him. 'You need to keep your eye on the damn ball, pay attention! You need to try harder!' I vowed I would never behave like that. I'm so ashamed." Lionel hid his face in his hands. "I couldn't sleep all night. I've been really down since then."

"How do you make sense of what happened to you?" I asked.

"We never talked about my childhood when we came in years ago. There wasn't time. We focused on our marriage and getting Tyrone to sleep. I was the youngest of seven kids, the runt of the litter, and my father never let me forget it. My dad and older brothers would pick on me, beat me up. They were all big men, well over six feet. They played basketball, hockey, football. I couldn't compete.

"Baseball was my game. I was small and fast. It was my ticket out. I was hoping to get a college scholarship, but I got anxious when the scouts came to watch us play. When I was up at bat, guess what happened? I struck out. Here we are again." Lionel shook his head. "My dad was disgusted with me, called me a loser, a runt. I never forgave him for that.

"It broke my heart to see Tyrone strike out. I felt that old shame. There was something about seeing his face collapse. I couldn't bear to see his sadness. I don't know what happened; I just lost it. And here I was, becoming my father. I never thought that could happen, never!"

"Let's take a look at this, for you and your son. And let's talk about repair after a rupture like this. What was happening for you?"

"I had some dreams for him. I was hoping that he'd be the athlete that I wasn't. That he'd hit the home run or make the amazing catch and be the star. I mean, I knew it wasn't realistic for Tyrone, but I just wanted things to be easier for him. Is that too much to ask? Guess I had my baseball fantasy as well."

"We always want things to be easier for our kids. They rarely are," I said. "And we all have our fantasies for our children."

"My dad was an angry man. He was always facing into the wind. And it was a harsh wind. But he taught us to survive. He had a sadistic side, that can't be denied. After work, he loved to come home, take the spare change out of his pocket, and throw it on the floor. 'Fight for it,' he would yell, and then laugh as we fought for pennies. Got bloodied sometimes. It was like a cockfight. We became like animals. And he would drink his beer and laugh and laugh.

"Any good ideas, doc? What can I do not to kill that coach? Or humiliate my kid? Or end up in jail for assault?"

"There was a Swiss psychiatrist named Carl Jung who said, 'The greatest burden a child must bear is the unlived life of the parents.' What's unlived in you?" I asked. "What happened when you saw his face collapse? Did something get triggered in you?"

"Yeah, yeah. That's it. I had hopes that he would be all that I'm not. That his life would be so bright you'd need sunglasses. That he could do what I couldn't. And damn, he's another flawed kid with his own set of problems. He's no star. I wanted so much for him. So, so much."

"I know, I'm with you. This comes up for almost all parents. I think of it as the underbelly of parenting. It is hard."

We were both quiet for a few moments. "If you're ready, let's try a reflection together and then I'll teach you some practices that will help you deal with what comes up for you."

Reflection: What Is Your Fantasy?

- If you are like most parents, you might be feeling something now. Perhaps a longing, a twinge of sadness, an emptiness in your gut. See what you notice in this moment.
- Take a moment, let yourself settle, find an anchor in your breath, the sounds around you, the sensations in your body, or the touch points.
- Bring some kindness to yourself right now.
- Add some soothing touch if you need a little extra comfort.
- What fantasy did you have about your child? Did you dream that your son would be a Major League Baseball star? Your daughter a prima ballerina?
- Did you dream that your child would be an Olympic gold medalist? A Pulitzer Prize–winning journalist? A wildly successful entrepreneur? A tech genius? A movie star? A brilliant film director? An amazing scientist who finds a cure for cancer?
- Don't hold back. We all have dreams of what our little ones could become. Don't chastise yourself.
- Rarely do our kids fulfill our fantasies.
- Take a moment, jot down your dreams for your child. You don't have to show this to anyone.
- Gently, kindly, take off the rose-colored glasses.

- *Let the stardust fall from your eyes.*
- *See all the good in your child. See his or her gifts.*
- *Try to see your child clearly, without the burden of the dreams and fantasies you carry.*
- *See if you can let your child be himself (or herself) without adding your unlived dreams.*
- *This isn't easy. See your fantasies and try to let them go.*
- *Let yourself sit for a moment for two.*
- *Be kind to yourself as you let go and return to your day.*

Lionel found this practice challenging but helpful. "I had a dream for him that didn't fit with reality," he reported. "And I knew it. I'd been telling myself my dreams were harmless, but I realized I wasn't seeing him clearly. I wanted him to do more than he could do. And that was hard. He probably won't ever hit a home run, even in Little League. And it'll be hard for him to ride a bike. That hurts. But I think I'll get less angry at him. And less demanding. My expectations weren't in line with his abilities," he said, looking down at the ground. "But I guess the bright side is that I won't punch out the coach of the opposing team."

Lionel was right. Our fantasies can distort our expectations for our children, causing suffering for them and for us. And Lionel is not alone.

Alison and her daughter Cate were fighting about ice skating. Alison loved watching the winter Olympics and wanted Cate to have the grace, strength, and coordination of an elite athlete. Cate was a strong skater, but she didn't have a fiercely competitive spirit and had trouble mastering the jumps and spins. She wanted to be with her friends and didn't want to spend hours and hours and entire weekends at practice. When Alison saw that this was her dream, and not Cate's, she could let go of being "a crazy skater mom driving my kid all over the state to competitions." "I guess," she said sadly, "this was my dream, not hers." With this understanding, both Alison and Cate felt less stressed out and the relationship became less combative. Cate, given that she was a strong and fast skater, took up ice hockey, which met her needs to be with her friends and play with a team.

The following became Lionel's go-to practice during Little League games. He began to use it at work as well, when a client made him angry. Alison used it when Cate's hockey team was losing and she got upset and overinvested in winning. Try it anytime you need to get a grip. Next time you are sitting in the bleachers and getting more and more agitated, having thoughts of punching out the coach, or a player, or another parent (or having angry thoughts about your kid), try this practice. It's a quick way to help parents (and kids) feel more grounded. It is especially useful when you are working with aggressive or impulsive feelings. It can be done sitting or standing. Use it whenever you need it. This is a great all-purpose practice.

 Soles of the Feet

🎧 *Audio Track 4*

- Start by moving your feet back and forth, from the heels to the toes, then from side to side. Circle your ankles and wiggle your toes if you like.
- You can raise one foot and then the other as if you are marching. Notice the sensations.
- Feel your feet resting firmly on the ground. Observe all the different sensations. Feel the soles of your feet.
- If you like, imagine that there are roots underneath each foot, anchoring and grounding you. Let yourself feel held and connected to the earth.
- Rest here and wait till you feel less agitated. Allow the aggressive feelings to rise and then pass away.
- You don't need to act; let the urge to harm or act go.
- Stay in this moment; no need to fix anything.
- Let things be as they are.
- You can return to the soles of your feet whenever you need an anchor in life.

"That's good," Lionel said. "Focusing on the soles of my feet was surprisingly helpful. I feel like I've come back to myself. Sometimes, when I get really pissed, I feel like something takes me over."

Many parents experience that. Therapists call it being hijacked. And often it happens when we hit a past wound or something painful that isn't resolved. It's one thing to know that we have past unresolved wounds, and entirely another to begin to heal them. The following reflection, inspired by Mark Coleman, is helpful.

> **Reflection: The Wounds We Carry**
> - We often recoil from our pain. Try, even for a moment, to turn toward it. What does it take to get curious about your pain?
> - Try to find a place where you can be uninterrupted for 10 minutes.

- *Close your eyes and bring your attention to the sensations of your entire body.*
- *Take some time and get interested in a hurt you may be carrying from the past. When did it happen? How old were you? Was it from childhood? Adolescence?*
- *Stay with yourself. Notice what is happening in your body. What emotions arise?*
- *What are you defending? What are you trying to protect?*
- *How do you respond to these vulnerable feelings? Do you turn away? Get lost in thoughts about dinner or your favorite TV show?*
- *As you connect with this painful wound, imagine that you can greet it. Say hello. Even shake its hand.*
- *Bring some kind attention to this wound.*
- *If the feelings are too intense, return to the breath or the soles of the feet.*
- *Try to create some space to be with this wound. You might want to use some words that express a healing and kind intention, such as "May I hold this wound with kindness" or "May I care for this wound."*
- *Rest for a moment, perhaps putting a hand on where you feel the pain.*
- *During the next few days, make a practice of checking in on the pain and repeating the words.*
- *When you are ready, slowly open your eyes and stretch.*

The Fears We Carry

Fear of Flying

"I'm ashamed to talk about this, I feel like such a wimp, but I'm terrified of getting on a plane," Anjali told me at our first meeting. But it wasn't her fear of flying that had brought her to me. It was that she was afraid she was passing on that fear to her six-year-old son, "creating a neurotic kid." On a recent flight to visit her parents, the plane had hit a pocket of turbulence and her son panicked. Anjali couldn't comfort him because she was just as frightened. "He could tell I was panicked," she said. "I was clutching the armrest and clenching my teeth during takeoff. I know I turned absolutely pale when we hit the turbulence. I started to hyperventilate. He turned to me and asked, 'Are we safe, Mommy? Are we going to crash? Am I going to die? I'm scared,' and he started to cry loudly. I don't want Sudhir to have these fears as well. I want him to have a fuller, less restrictive life."

When I asked Anjali whether she'd ever had a bad experience flying, she said she couldn't remember one herself but had heard stories from her brother about flying through a storm on a small plane with high winds, thunder, and lightning when she was three and he was seven. Apparently something went wrong and everyone started screaming and crying, and the pilot had to make an emergency landing. Anjali said her mother thought they were going to die and was screaming at the top of her lungs. While the pilot landed safely, Anjali's mother never flew again, and neither has her brother. But her mother never talked about it.

"Well, you come by this anxiety honestly!" I said. "There is a saying I learned in my training that resonates here: 'If it's hysterical, it's historical.' This is historical."

"Well, it might be, but I don't remember it," Anjali said, challenging me.

"Yes, but the body remembers. What you are experiencing is what we call a body memory. The dancer Martha Graham put it elegantly when she said 'the body never forgets.' "

Anjali reflected. "I have this visceral experience that I didn't understand. When I get on a plane I feel this tightness in my body, this tension in my throat, and it's like I want to scream, 'Help, help, get me out of here.' I was thinking I was crazy."

After assuring her it didn't sound crazy at all, I mentioned that the whole incident was likely banished from consciousness since she was so young and no one talked about it. But when I proposed some mindfulness and compassion she could use when flying, she instantly rejected the idea as "too touchy-feely, weak, and sappy." She had come in for drugs.

"OK," I said. "I can respect that. I certainly don't want to push therapy if you aren't interested. We can give you some Ativan, which will help when you fly."

"Thanks," Anjali said, packing up her things. "I need to get back to work."

"But before we stop, what about Sudhir? No one is going to give him drugs, and knowing how to help him calm down is a good skill to have, for all sorts of circumstances."

"If there is something that you can teach me in five minutes, that I can share with him, I'm open to that. I want to be a good parent, especially since I'm doing it all alone." She looked me straight in the eye. "Nothing silly."

"Got it," I said, smiling. "But let's do it together or it will be hard to teach him."

I call the following practice Fierce Compassion. Many of us think of compassion as weakness or passivity. That it means saying yes to everything, not standing up for yourself, or allowing others to be treated unfairly. But compassion doesn't mean shirking our responsibility or being a doormat, or losing our powers of discernment. Stepping outside our familiar patterns of reaction is an act of courage.

This practice is helpful for many types of fears, not only fear of flying.

 Fierce Compassion

- Start by sitting comfortably, letting your body settle as much as possible, letting go of any unnecessary tension.
- Feel your back. Feel the strength of your back. Imagine all the vertebrae lining up. Connect with your backbone. You may want to say to yourself, *Strong back.*
- From this place of dignity and strength, where do you notice the fear?
- No need to exile the fear or demand that it disappear. Try to turn toward it as if it were a young child.
- Find it in your body. See if you can put a hand or two hands on that place.
- Tune in to what type of touch you might need. Maybe it is crossing your hands over your chest in a protective embrace.
- Try out or audition different ways to hold or comfort yourself.
- Give yourself a moment to let this land.
- Tune in to your breath.
- Are there words you might need to hear?
- What would be comforting?
- On an airplane, they always tell parents that if the plane loses altitude they should put their oxygen mask on first. The same principle applies here.
- Once you have tended to your fears, turn to your child.
- Once your child can feel the strength of the backbone, see what type of soothing touch he or she might need.
- What words might be helpful?
- What does he need to hear from you? It is fine to offer phrases such as "I'm here, I'm with you" or "You're not alone."

Anjali said what she liked about his practice was starting with strength: "I'm afraid of losing my edge, of becoming weak or fragile. I don't want to uncover all those memories and events. I don't want to get overwhelmed. I'm alone; no one takes care of me."

"Of course you don't want to go there," I said. "And that is a common misunderstanding of therapy. We don't have to go back and examine everything that has happened. But we can heal what's blocking our way."

There is a line from Hafez, the 14th-century Persian poet: "Fear is the cheapest room in the house. I would like to see you living in better conditions."

Like Anjali, many of us find ourselves living in rather cramped quarters. How might the Fierce Compassion practice provide better living conditions for you?

Parenting has a way of encouraging us, not always gently, to face disowned parts of ourselves—whether we want to or not. One friend of mine talks about her young kids as Zen masters who are saying, "Mommy, wake up, wake up." And sometimes it's not just in the morning.

Most of us haven't grown up in families who welcomed our wounded parts or our anxious feelings. We've all been told that we're weak or self-pitying for having them. And we learn to put on a brave face, pretend we are just fine, and compensate. But in fact it's an act of courage and compassion to care for those parts of ourselves that have felt overwhelmed or vulnerable. We all have leftover issues from childhood that impact our parenting and cause us, and our children, needless pain and suffering.

Please Don't Leave Me

Remember Meghan from Chapter 1? If you've struggled with the demands of a new baby while trying to do your best for a first child, her story probably resonated with you, especially if you too suffered from postpartum depression. Meghan's depression lifted with the help of therapy, medication, and meditation, but a few years later she is struggling with new issues, namely separation anxiety. But not her children's—her own.

"When we go on playdates or to birthday parties, I'm the one who doesn't want to leave. I worry that something might happen to the kids, that they'll get hurt. Johnny rolls his eyes when I find excuses to linger, and my husband just gets annoyed. But Lila picks up on my worries, she clings to me, and I worry that she doesn't feel safe."

Meghan's parents weren't psychologically attuned to her needs when she was young. She was high strung and nervous, and had been sick as a child as well. She became too upset when they went out, so they tried to skip the drama by slipping out the back door and disappearing without saying good-bye. When she realized that they were gone and she had been left with a sitter, she'd become hysterical and inconsolable. She remembered standing on the couch, looking out the window, and just sobbing and sobbing hysterically.

The child psychoanalyst Donald Winnicott called this terror of being abandoned when you barely have words to express it a "primitive agony." We just don't feel safe. And we carry this subconscious fear for the rest of our lives.

"That's just what it feels like—I have these recurrent dreams of falling and falling and there's no one to catch me," Meghan continued. "I think my mother never read any parenting books or talked to anyone about how to raise kids. I can't believe some of the shit she did."

"My brother and I would fight, like most kids. But sometimes we just couldn't stop. Neither of us would back down, and it would just escalate. My mother didn't have the sense to separate us, set limits, or give us a time-out. She had no parenting skills. So what she would do, if you can believe it, was announce that she was leaving and not coming back 'cause we were such horrible children. She would get in her car and drive away, sometimes for what felt like hours. And I would just lose it, that old terror would return, and I would get hysterical. Of course, the fighting would stop. My brother would try to comfort me. He was a good kid, he cared about me; we were just fighting. 'Don't worry, Meggie, she'll come back. She always does,' but I'm sure he was scared as well. And I never trusted that she would return. Things never felt stable. And they still don't. I don't trust that people will stay. And it isn't just neurotic. My dad left us, my brother died in a car crash a few years ago, my mother died when I was pregnant with Lila. People leave, and I feel so vulnerable. Sometimes I get so panicked and worried that I can't think straight or even see straight." To illustrate this point, she told me that on the way to my office she mistook a garbage truck for an ambulance. "At least I can laugh about it, but I'm always anticipating the next disaster, even if there isn't one. I'm realizing that I consistently imagine the worst-case scenario."

Because of past traumatic experiences, we often see danger where none exists. For our ancestors, it was important not to mistake a poisonous snake for a stick. Fortunately, for us the dangers aren't as dramatic, but our brains are still scanning for danger. This is what scientists call the brain's "negativity bias."

If you have suffered losses or trauma, your negativity bias may be fairly severe. One thing that can help is a practice that combines mindfulness and fully coming into the present moment with compassion. The following meditation is inspired by the work of neuroscientist Rick Hanson. Meghan can use it when she takes Lila to a playdate and it's hard to leave, or when she doesn't want to leave Johnny at a sleepover. You can use it whenever you feel panicked, while parenting, when driving during rush hour, in social situations that make you nervous, in crowds, if you have a fear of heights, or other situations that might stress you out, such as riding on elevators or escalators, or driving on bridges. You can even use it when you feel down and lonely.

In This Moment

- Start by letting go of any stress or tension you feel in your body. See if you can let it drop.
- Let yourself be here, just now, in this moment. Let go of any dialogue in your head, any commentary, any arguments. Drop into the present moment. Just here, just now.
- Look around. Ask yourself, *In this moment, right now, am I safe?*
- What arises? If you find yourself saying, *Well, I'm safe now, but maybe not in the next hour, or later today, or tonight, or tomorrow,* come back to the present moment, realizing that in this moment, right here, right now, you are safe.
- See if your body begins to soften and relax.
- Bring some compassion to yourself, and maybe even some supportive touch for the stress that you carry.
- Keep returning to the reality of the moment.
- When you are ready, return to your day, but come back to present-moment awareness as often as you can.

When Meghan tried this practice, she realized that she spends a lot of her time in catastrophic scenarios and in a constant state of alarm, spinning out all the time. "I think Johnny will fall in the playground and break a bone. He hasn't fallen yet, but he might fall and then I'll need to take him to the hospital, so I have to watch him like a hawk. And then I yell, 'Johnny, be careful, don't climb too high' And then, OMG, if I have to rush him to the hospital, who will take care of Lila? What will I do? How will I cope?' and on and on." She laughed. "I spend so much of my day creating disasters that don't happen. My mind is such a mess!"

Meghan is hardly alone. Even if your overprotective negativity bias has not reared its alarmist head before, becoming a parent has a way of calling it to the fore. There's a great saying that I love from the writer Anne Lamott: "My mind is a dangerous neighborhood. I try not to go there alone."

So many of us are trying so hard to avoid the next disaster, trying to make sure that the stick on the ground really isn't a poisonous snake, that the spider in the rented cottage isn't a tarantula. Maybe you've heard that wonderful Mark Twain line that goes something like this: I'm a very old man, and I've had many hardships and tragedies in my life, most of which never happened.

We Can Reparent Ourselves

With mindfulness and compassion, we can reparent ourselves. We can create an inner sense of security, even if we never had it as children. But it involves learning new skills and training the brain. The attachment researchers have a name for it that I like, which is "earned secure." It is something that we can achieve, something that we can learn, and something that feels earned. We can give ourselves the tools and the skills that our parents weren't able to offer us when we were children. And finding ways to soothe yourself, and your child, is a great way to start.

Mindfulness in Daily Life

Tantrums

All parents have experienced tantrums, not just those of our toddlers during the "terrible twos" but, let's be honest, our own as well. (Yes, common humanity again. Don't tell me that your tantrums stopped at age two.)

The next time you sense a meltdown coming, either yours or your child's, see if you can interrupt it with the following practice of soothing (or supportive) touch. This informal practice is part of the MSC curriculum. I find that it works best if you experiment with touch that works for you before the meltdown. I also suggest teaching this to your child, and toddlers respond well to this exercise. You can have a favorite doll or stuffed animal join in, mirroring the touch to make it more playful.

Often our bodies respond to self-care more quickly than our minds, so this is a good practice to do in the heat of the moment. The following are some of my favorite forms of supportive or soothing touch.

- Hand on heart
- Two hands over heart
- Hand on heart and belly
- Two hands on belly
- Hand on cheek
- Holding face in hands
- Stroking your arms
- Crossing your arms and giving yourself a squeeze
- One hand holding the other

If you need more support, add the Self-Compassion Life Saver for Parents (Chapter 2).

Soothing Touch in the Heat of the Moment

It's late afternoon, you and your child are tired and hungry, but you need to run to the grocery store to grab some things for dinner. Your child sees some candy that she wants. "No, honey," you say, "I don't want you to spoil your appetite for dinner."

"I want it, I want it NOW!" she screams.

Other customers begin to look at you.

"No, honey, it's not good for you."

"Waaahhhh!" Your child starts to scream, throws herself on the floor of the grocery story, and starts to kick and pound her fists. Oh no, a full-blown tantrum. People are watching. "I WANT CANDY NOW!" she screams at the top of her lungs. If you don't do something fast, all the candy boxes will soon be on the floor. And can you believe it, someone has taken out his phone and is recording this! Will you be flamed on the internet? Arrested for child abuse? Help!

- Pick up your child, even though she is thrashing and screaming. Hold her tight.
- In the most soothing voice you can muster, start with labeling. "Yes, honey, I know this is hard, really, really hard."
- If possible, move away from the candy so she isn't distracted by it.
- Bring in soothing touch that you have practiced together. Oops, no time to practice yet? No problem. Try a hand on her chest and a hand on her belly.
- Using a soothing voice, help her begin to label what she is feeling, "Yes, you're upset. Yes, you're mad. I get that."
- "Sometimes we get mad. It's hard."

- "It's OK, I'm with you, I love you."
- Perhaps put a hand on your heart if you can. You can label your feelings as well.
- Keep trying to maintain perspective, "It's OK, honey, this will pass."
- "I'm with you, I love you."
- As you hold and rock your child, try singing her favorite song until the storm subsides. Trust me, this tantrum will end.
- When it is over and you are safely home, and the child has calmed down and been fed, pour yourself a double martini. Parenting isn't easy.

The Rainy Vacation

You've waited months for a break. And you've been scrimping and saving for the special beach vacation splurge with your partner and kids. You find a cute little cottage right on the water. For the past few months your dreams have been filled with sunshine and warmth, the smell of sweet ocean breezes, images of the kids happily building sandcastles, all of you watching stunning sunsets together, and then going out for dinner and letting someone else cook for a change, and yes, a margarita or two. But it doesn't always turn out that way.

One year our vacation started out fine. The weather was great, the kids, who were about three and six years old, were delighted to play in the water, catching tiny minnows in their colorful plastic buckets and finding hermit crabs hidden in snail shells. It was the magical vacation that I dreamed of having. For about one day.

Then, suddenly, the weather turned and rain moved in. For days. Lightning, thunder, heavy rain and wind. The rustic cottage didn't have TV or internet. And it began to smell like mildew. All our clothes were damp. My husband had a work crisis and had to drive back to the city. I was alone with two kids who were getting bored and starting to fight with each other. Constantly. I was running out of things to do.

One bleak morning I began to feel sorry for myself, and my negativity bias began to kick in. Somehow the weather seemed like a personal affront: "Why is it raining on my vacation?" I wondered. "But I really need a vacation," I started to whine to myself since there was no one to listen. I began to spiral down into what I call my "Eeyore state of mind." I'd been reading a lot of Winnie the Pooh books to the kids those days. "Oh bother," I thought, "it never works out anyway. Nothing ever goes the way you want it to. This vacation is going to be a wash. Nothing to do. I shoulda stayed home. All that wasted money . . . " (At this point I think I was chan-neling the more negative traits of my family of origin.)

My mood began to plummet, and I started to get more and more upset, dejected, and irritable.

But then someone called my name. I looked up. And there on the sand flats was a dad who had rented a neighboring cottage. He was a painter and was out in the wet, shallow flats with his easel and paints, happily painting away. We had just met his family the previous day, and they also had young kids.

"Look!" he said. "Look at this magnificent sky. It's like Rembrandt or Vermeer. Seventeenth-century Dutch landscape painting. Isn't it amaz-ing!"

I realized that all I'd seen were the rain clouds and the dark sky. I only saw the problems. I'd been so focused on how I would entertain the kids, I hadn't noticed how beautiful the sky was. I walked out to the flats in the drizzle, looked at the sky, and he was right. It was magnificent. It changed my day. His words have been an inspiration ever since. Although my friend wasn't a therapist, it was one of the best "cognitive reframes" I've ever encountered. His enthusiasm made me realize there was another way to experience both the external and internal weather. And the con-stant storms in our lives.

We got all the kids together, pooled our games, resources, and food, and they played and painted together for the rest of the vacation, happy as clams (sorry, couldn't resist that pun). The take-home for me was that dark clouds aren't always bad news; sometimes they can be seventeenth-century landscape painting with a silver lining. And we stayed good friends for years.

The following are practices you can try, with your kids (or without), when you are feeling trapped by life (or the weather, or a moldy cottage, or parenting alone, or the kids constantly fighting, or a vacation that isn't what you hoped for).

Silly Walks

Kids love to be silly and goofy and often take delight when their parents get silly as well. This practice builds on the foundation of Soles of the Feet, which is found earlier in this chapter.

- Start by feeling your feet on the ground.
- Feel the weight of your body.

- You might want to bend your knees slightly, feeling your connection to the earth.
- Try rocking back and forth, from the heels to the toes and then from side to side.
- Try raising one foot and then the other, as if you are marching.
- Feel the sensations in the soles of your feet.
- You might like to imagine that you have roots underneath your feet that connect you to the earth.
- Now let yourself play as you walk. You can take huge, dramatic steps. Or try walking sideways, like a crab on the beach. Experiment with walking backwards. See how that feels. You can even jump, skip, hop, or twirl. If you are doing this with kids, try jumping like a frog, or hopping like a bunny. Be silly, have fun.
- See if you can be fully in your body as you do these silly walks. Notice the sensations as you let yourself go. Don't worry about how you look. The goal is to have a good time and fully inhabit your body.
- Enjoy moving and having fun.

I've seen this practice used by yoga teachers, Zen masters, and therapists alike. When you or your child are feeling tired, down, bored, or in a negative place, this is a good pick-me-up. And, if you really want to get silly, you can find the original version in the Monty Python "Ministry of Silly Walks" on YouTube.

Another practice that is fun to do in daily life is inspired by my friend who found beauty in the storm clouds. This can be done with kids on the beach, at a lake, in a park or playground, in your garden, or on a street in your neighborhood. In this practice, look for something that makes you smile.

Finding Beauty

- Take an adventure walk with your children, or by yourself if you need some downtime.
- Start by seeing what you notice around you: the ground, the animals and insects, the grass or sidewalk.
- What do you hear? The singing of birds, the chirping of cicadas, the sounds of cars or buses? People talking on their phones? Be attentive to all sounds. Try not to privilege one over another.
- Notice the sky, the clouds.

- Breathe in the air; notice the temperature. Is it warm? Is it cool? Humid? Dry?
- See what it feels like on your skin.
- As you walk, keep your eyes open for something that you find interesting and that makes you smile. It could be an acorn, a flower, a shell, a stone, a twig, or even a weed. It could be a baby bird or a butterfly. An ant, a slug, a beetle.
- For this practice, it is fine to have your phone. Feel free to take a picture. One of my students found beauty in a hydrant that had mottled shades of red and blue.
- See what speaks to you. Spend some time with your object; really look at it.
- You may want to spend three to five minutes really looking at one thing.
- Let this connection bring you back to earth.
- If you are doing this with your kids, help them find objects that they like—ants, earthworms, and puddles are fine (see if they can look for 30–60 seconds—great for developing attention and concentration).
- If you can find something that you can take home—an acorn, weed, rock, or shell—take it with you and use it as an anchor when you need to remind yourself of some beauty or joy.
- Let this help you keep perspective.

I've tried many variations on this practice. When my daughter was young, she found beauty in weeds (which I was pulling out because they were "weeds") and even had a favorite weed, which was beautiful, and which I had never really noticed. Now, whenever I see the weed I smile. Once, in a meditation class, we were given an assignment to go outside and look at something for 15 minutes, which at first seemed like an eternity. I looked at a petunia for that period of time, something I thought of as an ordinary, rather boring flower. But I was astonished at how complex, intricate, and beautiful it was. I now see petunias in a different light.

Whatever we find can help us gather our attention, get perspective, and help shift our state of mind. Pia was having a hard day. A coworker had been rude and dismissive, and she began to worry about her job security. At dinner she snapped at her daughter, who was setting the table, because she wasn't doing it fast enough. "Hang on, Mom," the daughter said, trying to help, and ran out of the room. She returned with a moon snail shell that Pia had collected on their walk together. "Here's your beautiful shell that we found at the beach. Maybe it will help."

"It wasn't the shell itself that made a difference; it was more symbolic," she said." It helped me remember the closeness I felt when we had our walk together. And I was touched that my daughter noticed I was having a hard day and tried to help. That little bit of love and care was what turned things around for me. It made me realize that there wasn't a rush about setting the table. Snails move so slowly! It put things back in perspective. I didn't need to yell at her. I didn't have to take out my work worries on her. And at least I don't carry my home on my back," she laughed.

It isn't only family burdens and emotional baggage that we all carry. We can also carry reminders of our strengths, our parents' wisdom, as well as our own inner toolbox of mindfulness practices that help us keep perspective, be resilient, and stay grounded in the present moment.

4 "I'll Never Be Good Enough"
AVOIDING THE COMPARISON TRAP

In many cultures, there is tremendous pressure for children to succeed. Because we mistakenly feel that our worth as parents is measured by our children's achievements, it's easy to get caught up in competition and comparison, which often start before our children are born. In an attempt to give our children an advantage, we often go against our better instincts and inclinations. Julie absolutely hated classical music but began playing Mozart, Beethoven, and Bach when she became pregnant, hoping her baby would develop an appreciation of great music. Charles, wanting his son to have the head start he never had, purchased a collection of Baby Einstein videos, dreaming that his boy would become a computer whiz. Lei, exhausted by the pressure of the race to get her daughter into a prestigious college, joked there was a "parenting virus" that she was trying desperately not to catch. At times it seems impossible to resist, and it can certainly feel contagious.

When my kids were young, we had a wise, rather crusty pediatrician who practiced well into his eighties. In our last meeting before he retired, he reflected on the changes he had seen in his 60 years of practice. One thing that stayed with me was a comment about the increased anxiety that parents have about having a perfect child. "Fuhgeddaboudit," he joked in his Boston accent. "No one excels at everything, and that's OK." He lamented that parents were having less fun and less joy because they were trying to tailor their child's life (and their lives) to maximize success. "It's only one factor in life," he told me, "and not the most important thing." His advice has helped keep me a little saner on the roller coaster of parenting and has helped me soothe parents when they are caught in the throes of the "virus."

The goal of this chapter is to help you put competition in perspective so you can worry less and enjoy your child, and your life, a little more.

But there are times when achievement feels like the most important factor. When a child is struggling to learn a new skill and not succeeding, it's easy to get bent out of shape. At times we feel embarrassed and ashamed, and we often blame ourselves.

"What If He Can't Make It?"

Valerie came to my office in distress about an incident at her son Matt's preschool. Now almost five, Matt had been held back due to the illness described in Chapter 1 and was just starting his second year of nursery school. Valerie's daily ritual was to walk Matt to school and then hang out in the classroom for a while to help him get settled while the kids started on the project—coloring, building with blocks, finger painting—that the teacher put out to engage them right away.

On the day in question, the children were supposed to draw an animal and then cut it out with scissors. Valerie was a little embarrassed to report how she reacted when Matt simply didn't have the motor skills for the task. "It doesn't seem like a big deal," she said, "but he can't use scissors, and when he realized he couldn't complete the activity, he looked upset and froze, and his chin quivered. I was pretty sure he was going to cry and went into a panic. I literally started to sweat, I felt so anxious. So I grabbed the scissors and started to cut out the blob Matt had drawn when the teacher came over and said, in a scolding schoolteacher voice, 'You need to let him do it himself.'

"I felt so stupid. Here I was being a micromanaging, intense, bad mother again. You know that I worry about everything. Now I was on the verge of crying, and Matt was right there, so I couldn't say 'But he can't.' The only thing that saved me was that it was time to switch activities, and the teacher let me know it was time for me to leave. I was so angry with myself. It ruined my day.

"Matt seemed fine once the kids formed a circle and the teacher started to read a book. Not me, though. I really started spinning out. I decided that the teacher hated me, had decided that I was a neurotic helicopter parent. I agonized that maybe the other parents didn't like me. I wondered if Matt was happy that I had left, if I was suffocating him. But I'm still afraid that he won't be able to keep up.

"I know it's silly, as there aren't many adult jobs where you need to wield scissors, but my fear is that this is just the beginning. He'll get chosen last for sports, he won't achieve in high school, he won't get into a good college, and then he won't be able to get a job and support himself."

When we're worried about the welfare of our children, it's easy to get swept up in an avalanche of worries and catastrophize way into the future. Instead of seeking the remedial scissors class that Val jokingly proposed, I suggested she try a reflection I had devised that was inspired by self-compassion researcher Kristin Neff.

Reflection: Putting It in Perspective

It's very hard to see ourselves clearly. Most people feel they need to be above average on the skills and traits that society values. This exercise helps us gain some perspective (and humor) and learn to accept ourselves (and our children) with all our imperfections.

Take a few minutes and try this reflection on your own:

1. List a few things you do at which you are above average.

   _____

   _____

2. List a few things you do at which you are just average.

   _____

   _____

3. List a few things you do at which you're below average.

   _____

   _____

This exercise helped Valerie remember that a lot of her skills involved doing things with her hands and that she was really good at arts and crafts. Therefore, she realized with chagrin, she was assuming that Matt needed to have this skill and had been unintentionally putting pressure on him to catch up on a task he couldn't care less about. Valerie realized she was also "just average" in social relationships. "I can be awkward, shy," she reported. "I can be out of it. I often say something clumsy, or I miss some social cues. And as I reflect, Matt is naturally friendly and outgoing, kids like to be with him, and parents like him too; he's always getting invited to playdates. He's fun and goofy and has a natural joy about him that's contagious."

Valerie's expression relaxed into a smile as she thought about her little boy's great qualities, and she was able to look at her own shortcomings with a little humor, calling herself a klutz ("I never learned how to ride a bike or ski"), and laughing about the extra miles she would drive just to avoid highways because she was such a "wimpy driver."

Val—and you—can boost self-compassion by crafting and repeating to yourself statements about the myriad imperfections that everyone has. These are the ones that Valerie liked:

Achievement Isn't Everything

- No Olympic gold for my skills as a marathon runner
- No Tour de France medal for my bike riding, or for Matt's
- Not going to be in the Hall of Fame for hitting home runs
- No Super Bowl championship ring
- The Louvre will not display Matt's artwork
- So much for landing a triple axel on ice skates in the Olympics
- Life goes on; it isn't the end of the world

What statements could you adopt for you and your child?

As Valerie learned to step back from her own fears and preoccupations, she was able to begin to appreciate Matt for who he was, seeing him clearly rather than trying to make him into a "mini-me." And it helped her not chastise herself for being imperfect. "I'm a fallible, flawed human being, and that is OK. I can stop beating myself up and driving my son crazy," she joked.

> ### Reflection: What Are Your Worries?
>
> *We all have them, and we often don't talk about them because we feel neurotic or embarrassed about our concerns. But remember, this is a judgment-free zone. Take a moment to reflect:*
>
> **What do you worry about?**
> - *That your child won't survive in the rat race?*
> - *That he or she doesn't have enough grit to make it in the world?*
> - *Not enough drive or ambition?*

> *Spend a few moments looking at your concerns. Jot them down on paper or in your phone if you like.*
>
> **Do you worry that your child is ...**
> - *not athletic enough?*
> - *not attractive enough?*
> - *not socially skilled?*
> - *not outgoing enough?*
> - *not smart enough?*
> - *not brave enough?*

Sometimes our worries about our child's perceived failings and inadequacies can keep us up at night, and we can blame ourselves, our partner, or our children because they are not conforming to our notions of how things should be. This is where compassion can come to the rescue.

The ABCs of Compassion

Meditation teachers have a saying that we don't see things as they are—we see things as *we* are. And, by extension, how we see our children is colored by our experience. We want them to do well, we want them to succeed, and we want them to have the advantages that we didn't have. Given the way our society is structured, we often worry, as Valerie did, that our children need to be special to be worthy of love and acceptance. But as the reflection above helps us realize, we can't be superior in everything. That doesn't mean we want to acknowledge it. The fictional town of Lake Wobegon, popularized in a radio program, is a place where "all the women are strong, all the men are good-looking, and all the children are above average." And that tag line speaks to a deep American vulnerability. We push our children to succeed and achieve, but often at a price. In fact, psychologists use the term "Lake Wobegon effect" to describe the need to think of oneself (and one's child) as superior.

The research speaks to the irrational need to be on the top. Ninety-four percent of college professors think they're better teachers than their colleagues. Research also shows that people tend to think they're funnier, wiser, more attractive, more logical, more trustworthy, and more intelligent than others. And ironically, people also believe that they're above average in the ability to see themselves objectively.

No wonder that when things are difficult, or go wrong, we don't want others to know and we often withdraw. As much as we try to deny it, we are all flawed and all imperfect. But we often feel the need to keep up the appearance that we, our marriages, and especially our children are just fine, "never better." And with this social pretense, we create a distance from others and an illusion that ultimately doesn't serve us.

In the urban public elementary school my children attended—even though it was an "inclusionary" school (children with severe disabilities were included in the classroom), which diminished the sense of competition—many parents wanted to believe that their children were gifted. While we joked about this, and knew all our children were not gifted, parents hated to see their children not chosen for the "advanced" reading or math group and would often complain and get pushy about making sure their kid had the "best" teacher or was getting "challenged" enough.

Other parents thought their kids needed to learn to compete early, so there was pressure to join Little League, youth soccer, ice hockey, swim team, and the like, often juggling two to three sports a season in addition to academics. It was surprising how intense parents became in "T-ball" (which prepared children for Little League) when their four-year-old wasn't connecting with the ball. As the years went on, not only were the moms exhausted from driving all over the city (and yes, it was almost always the moms) and surrounding towns for practice (and multiply that by two or more kids), but it created a division between the kids who were athletic and their less talented peers, a dynamic that continued into high school and college, especially with the competition for athletic scholarships at top schools. It created a distance between the parents as well, particularly those who didn't appreciate that everything became a competition. The result was that many parents felt needlessly isolated instead of supported.

How Compassion Can Help

The word *compassion* means to "suffer with." It has a relational quality. And it comes from the deep understanding that we are all imperfect and we all suffer. The pain that one parent feels in challenging times is essentially the pain that other parents feel. We often feel helpless in our inability to control outward circumstances—to have the lives we want to have, to be who we think we should be, to have our children be who we think they should be. We cling to our vision of the way we want our lives to be.

However, when things don't go the way we want, we often feel ashamed and blame ourselves, feeling inadequate. Rather than seeing events in the light of shared human experience, we're likely to feel isolated and disconnected. LaTonya, one of my patients, whose son Isaiah did not make friends easily in his small school, put it eloquently: "He feels different and feels separate from the other kids. It's hard for him to feel that he belongs. He's not a jock, will never be. He's working through his identity right now. It's become a vicious cycle: the more of an outsider he is, the more isolated and vulnerable he feels."

Because Isaiah was becoming increasingly depressed and despondent, refusing to go to school, his parents took action and found another school for him. Although it was a longer commute, Isaiah didn't feel like as much of an outcast in the larger and more diverse school. This community was focused on coming together and not excluding any student. LaTonya made new friends as well. She and other parents didn't judge their kids' athletic awkwardness from the bleachers at basketball games and supported each other, taking any mishaps with warmth and humor. Isaiah joined a theater group, finding his voice and new forms of expression.

Why Is This Happening to Me?

When things don't go the way we expect them to, we often feel that something is wrong, somehow imagining that this isn't the way it should be. It is as if we think our lives are supposed to go smoothly, that it is somehow our fault if they don't. Few of us are immune.

A number of years ago, when our children were in preschool, we purchased an old run-down house that needed major renovations. While the construction crew uncovered one new problem after another, we lived in a cramped apartment and then, due to numerous delays, had to move into the house with a nonfunctional kitchen and one working bathroom. We lived in survival mode on microwaved hotdogs and bad takeout.

After months of disruption, we were finally getting settled, the workmen were mostly gone, and it seemed that life was going back to normal. Then one morning our daughter woke up with a bloody nose. No big deal, we thought; it must be because of breathing the dust from the renovations. But the bleeding wouldn't stop. Finally, after an hour, we called the pediatrician. I assumed she would suggest a new technique to staunch the bleeding or ask me to bring her in. "You need to take her to the Children's Hospital ER and they'll cauterize it," she said.

"Great," I thought, "just what I need." I canceled my patients, bundled her up with lots of tissues, and raced to the hospital through rush-hour traffic. And then we had to wait. When she was finally seen, the attending doctor looked at her and then at me. Her eyes narrowed. "Why does she have all these bruises?" she asked. "Bruises—what bruises?" I answered. She pointed out many bruises on her legs. "Oh, I think she's bumping into things at nursery school." She shot me a look, perhaps thinking I had been abusing her.

"And this rash, how long has she had this rash?" the doctor inquired.

"What rash?" I asked, not having noticed and feeling like the most negligent mother in the world. "These red spots all over her body." I shook my head. I thought it was just exposure to the sun. I hadn't looked closely. The doctor pressed on the rash. "She's bleeding under her skin. We need to do blood work immediately."

By this time, my husband, whose dad was an oncologist, had joined us. When he heard what was going on, he turned white and his eyes filled with tears. "This isn't good," he whispered in my ear.

After hours of waiting and more tests, they determined that our three-year-old had a rare blood disease. The course was uncertain. She needed to be hospitalized. I blamed myself for being so preoccupied. Why hadn't I noticed? Why had I dismissed the bruises as normal? Why did I think the rash was due to the sun, just because she is fair and burns easily? How could I have been so stupid?

After a number of days on the oncology and hematology unit, she stabilized and we were allowed to take her home, being told that it would be months or maybe over a year before the illness fully resolved, that is, if we were lucky.

"She can't fall," the doctors told us. "No swings, no monkey bars, no running. The sandbox is OK," they warned sternly.

How do you explain to a three-year-old, a budding gymnast, that she can't do what she loves and that she needs to have her blood drawn every week? Our pediatrician had a wry sense of humor. "It'll be like a Victorian childhood," she quipped. "Lots of painting and reading books." She paused and gave me a measured look. "Susan, you don't have a choice. This is a dangerous disease. Let's hope she gets better."

I had hoped that when she returned to nursery school, the other parents would support us. I was so happy to go back to our life again and expected a warm welcome from the small community. Instead, the other parents were concerned that the illness might be contagious, and many of them turned away, treating us like pariahs, keeping their distance. When one of my friends came over and gave me a hug, saying kindly, "This must have been so scary for you, sounds like it's been awful," I burst into tears. I had no idea that parenting could be so lonely. And while I had a mindfulness practice at the time, which helped me manage the stress, I wish I had known about self-compassion during the long, seemingly endless months that followed.

The illness finally resolved almost two years later, but during the nights in between I frequently woke up in a cold sweat, wondering how things would play out and realizing that I had absolutely no control over my child's illness. In those dread-filled moments the hug and warm words from my friend were like a balm. When I remembered my compassionate friend acknowledging how frightening the experience was, I could stop and acknowledge it as well. In feeling her compassion, I could give myself permission to feel compassion for what my family was going through. And feeling it didn't mean falling to pieces.

Many parents tell me how alone and isolated they feel trying to raise children. Families are not around or are estranged, partners can be preoccupied with work, the demands of supporting a family, and their own issues, and friends can be competitive, transient, or judgmental. Many people are single parents and don't have someone to share the trials of the day. At some schools, things are so competitive you feel you can't let your guard down. If you do, you might worry about gossip or the vicious rumor mill. It is hard to feel that others really have your back. There are many reasons you might need to supply your own compassion rather than expecting others to extend it to you. This is where self-compassion can be a life saver. And as I've mentioned before, compassion isn't all warm and mushy. There are times when it needs to be fiercely protective of both you and your child.

Reflection: How Has It Been for You?

Take a moment and jot down what comes up for you.

- *When have you felt lonely parenting?*
- *Were you new in the neighborhood, or new to the school?*
- *Perhaps you didn't have friends yet?*
- *Are you shy? Not very outgoing?*
- *Do you feel different?*
- *Are you not from the dominant culture? Of another race?*
- *Do you not feel welcomed? Do you not fit in?*

Look at what you have written down. These are moments when we need self-compassion all the more.

Drawing on my experience with my kind and empathic friend, and the challenges of my daughter's illness, I put together the following self-compassion exercise. Try it when you or your child is going through a challenging situation and you feel that you could use some additional support.

♥ Having Your Back

🎧 *Audio Track 5*

- Think of a time when someone was protecting you—a parent, a sibling, a friend, a teacher, or a relative.
- Remember what this felt like in your body—in your jaw, your spine, your shoulders. Remember what you were feeling—strong, determined, grateful, relieved, maybe fierce.
- Now, knowing what this felt like, try this for yourself. What is it like to be on your side, to be an ally to yourself? Being someone who has your own best interest front and center, who looks out for you, who protects you. You matter. Your needs matter.
- Other reactions may come up as well, perhaps embarrassment that you need protection or support, perhaps a sense that you shouldn't need help. Just notice these feelings and step back from them, allowing some daylight between you and these feelings of unworthiness or embarrassment. Come back to standing up for yourself. Stay with it, let it deepen. Pause. Take a few breaths.
- Remember times when you were there for yourself. When you were supportive of yourself during a difficult time—during an illness, speaking up to someone who put you down or hurt you. Feel this in your body and stay with it.
- Know what it feels like to have your own back. Feel what it's like to really care for yourself. Let this land in your body; let it sink in.
- Let this be a resource, even a "superpower" that is there for you whenever you need it.

Making Space for Your Feelings

When my daughter was ill, there were days when I felt very sad and alone. It seemed like everyone else had a healthy child. At times, sitting in the sandbox while other children were running and swinging on monkey bars, she looked at them wistfully. My heart ached for her, and I began to feel self-pity as well. "Why me? Why does my child have this rare illness? Will she ever recover? Will she ever be able to run again?" At times I felt isolated, cut off from the world of "normal" families.

There are so many issues we struggle with—anxiety, depression, drug addiction, eating disorders, being bullied, serious illness. All parents have their worries and sorrows. When I started to feel sorry for myself, I tried to open my heart to all parents who were trying to do their best, to realize that parenting was rarely easy for anyone. And our weekly trips to the hospital to check on my daughter's blood count were a stark reminder that I wasn't the only one having a hard time. But we don't need a major illness or catastrophe to feel very alone. Disagreements on how to parent and how to discipline a child can create a divide between partners. We are rarely on the same page with our partners and often disagree about how to raise our children. Our kids, looking for opportunities to meet their needs, or cause some drama, often seize on the differences between parents and play them. All the more reason to be kind to yourself.

Recognizing our inherent connectedness can transform our relationship to parenting. When we make mistakes, or when our children struggle, when things go "wrong," we can remind ourselves compassionately that this too is part of the human experience, so that difficult moments can become part of our connectedness. When we realize that others have undergone similar hardships, we feel less alone. Of course it still hurts, but we don't have to multiply it by adding feelings of separation, inadequacy, and self-hatred. We learn not to turn away from pain and suffering.

Janelle, someone I have worked with for years as she struggled with her son's opioid addiction, was surprised and grateful when other parents at her son's school came through for the family. "You know," she said, "we come together when we are hurting and vulnerable, not when we are at the top of the heap, not when we're 'killing it and making a million.' People have let my struggles touch them. Every kid can be reckless and irresponsible; and most adults have been as well. We are more alike than we are different."

Comparisons and competition don't play out just in schools and neighborhoods—but they can be especially insidious and damaging in our families. Sibling rivalry is hard enough to endure when we're growing up, but it often continues into adulthood, increasing the feelings of being trapped, alone, and inadequate. The frustrations and putdowns that often marked our childhood relationships, and that we thought we could escape, unfortunately are not contained in childhood but can continue into adult life, especially during the holidays.

Holiday Madness

Alex's father died suddenly in the past year. Her mom usually hosted Thanksgiving but was not up to entertaining. Even though she had a new baby, Alex offered to have everyone over for the holiday. The only problem was that Alex didn't cook, nor did her husband, and she had no idea what was involved in having 20 relatives for dinner.

As Alex later described it, it was "THE. WORST. THANKSGIVING. EVER. . . . I had no idea how much work it is, but I figured it's time to step up, be an adult, and make dinner. How hard could it be, right?

"So my brother and sister-in-law arrive over an hour late with their perfect, well-behaved, beautifully dressed, not-a-hair-out-of-place monsters, oops, I should say kids. He brings a store-bought pumpkin pie and a six-pack of beer. So generous. Can't be bothered. And then the aunts and uncles arrive, everyone bringing alcohol. The most important food group in my family. Dinner isn't ready yet, so they all start drinking. Things get noisy and chaotic, and the turkey still isn't done.

"So William goes into his big-brother critical routine. 'Hey, sis, I'm hungry. When's dinner?' I explained the turkey was taking longer than expected, and he makes some nasty crack about trying out recipes before serving them to company, and all at once we've regressed 25 years. My husband hears us yelling and steps in, offers him some crackers and cheese, escorts him out of the kitchen, and they start talking football. And, BTW, my brother was a football star in high school.

"I start to sob, feeling so alone, really missing my dad, upset that I'm the one who is hosting. My mom doesn't notice, or at least pretends not to. She never stood up for me. My brother was always perfect. Luckily, my aunt, my dad's sister, comes in to help. She serves the soup and then helps me carve the turkey. As we carve, I notice that I never removed the plastic bag with the innards—the heart, the lungs, the liver, the gizzard, all that gross stuff. I can't believe that I didn't think to take them out. 'OMG, will I poison everyone?' I whisper. 'Will we all end up in the ER?'

"'Don't worry, dear, it'll be fine. The same thing happened the first time I made Thanksgiving,' and she gives me a wink. I guess I looked horrified. 'Remember that story about Julia Child dropping the turkey on the floor on her TV show?' She puts on a stuffy British accent, 'Don't worry, no one will know.'" Alex began laughing through tears. "She really saved the day for me. And no one got sick."

> **Reflection: What about Your Family?**
>
> In my experience, most people have a "complicated" family, or at least a complicated relative or two. What about you?
>
> Think back to your holiday adventures. What pushes your buttons and makes you go ballistic?
>
> - Drunk relatives who start political or other (fill-in-the-blank) fights?
> - Relatives who make jokes that you won't tolerate (racist, sexist, ethnic, homophobic, etc.)?
> - The turkey (or whatever) burns?
> - No one brings food?
> - You have to do it all and don't feel appreciated?
> - No one helps clean up?
> - Dinner starts two hours late and you and the kids are starving?
> - The kids are rude and are too busy to help?
> - Your mother-in-law yells at you in front of everyone because you are scraping dishes while you help clear? (Who knew there were rules about that? You were raised by wolves.)
>
> What is your family's flavor of dysfunction? (Oh, the stories I wish I could tell you . . .) Jot it all down. Practices to help are coming up soon.

A Perennial Problem

Alex's aunt may have saved the day for her, but she couldn't be there in the middle of the night when Alex found herself so revved up she couldn't sleep. Staring at the ceiling, she brooded over the humiliation of her brother's disgusted looks as her kids acted out after dinner, bored with hearing the long litany of accomplishments that made up William's monologue about his own wonderful children. When the comparison game that William always won in Alex's mind was in full swing, she tried watching her breath, but that didn't help, so she started the practice of labeling and was surprised to see clearly how angry she'd been for years. With sadness in her voice, she related that she finally took an Ambien to sleep, saying she thought mindfulness might just make things worse for her.

It can be upsetting to get in touch with buried rage, and its intensity can be unsettling. If you have an experience like Alex's, know that it's OK to notice the anger you've been holding. It can be a relief to talk about it rather than stuff it, which is what many families, including Alex's, do. Mindfulness is good for becoming aware of emotions and underlying patterns—it can help us settle—but compassion is what helps when we need some warmth and comfort as we begin to face the shame that we hold.

The Nuts and Bolts of Mindfulness and Compassion

Mindfulness is the foundation of self-compassion. We need mindfulness to notice that we are in pain before we can attend to it with kindness. It helps us get some distance from the drama of the story and helps us to not ruminate about what someone said or did. If we aren't aware of what is happening in the present moment, and what we are feeling, we are more likely to numb out with another beer or two, or an extra slice of pumpkin pie with a scoop of ice cream, rather than attend to what is making us upset.

However, during emotionally difficult times mindfulness alone may fall short, and like Alex, we might feel like it isn't enough. But when we think about what a good friend, or a benefactor, might offer during a hard time—such as the hug and the kind words from my friend when my daughter was hospitalized—it can help us see what we need and give us an insight into how to comfort ourselves. Compassion is especially useful if we have a harsh inner critic (see the You Are Not Your Fault practice in Chapter 1 as well) as it helps us develop the capacity to meet our history, and our shame, with warmth. When we go through challenging experiences and feel like we have lost our ground, regressed, or fallen apart, we need to be put back together. The practice of loving-kindness meditation, or LKM (which is translated from the Pali *metta*, or "friendliness"), is designed to do just that.

Mindfulness meditation primarily uses the power of *attention*, where loving-kindness uses the power of *connection* and relationship. The practices are closely related, but there are essential differences. Both can transform the way we relate to the events of our lives, but loving-kindness specifically attends to the *person* who is in pain. With practice, this type of meditation teaches us how we can become a better friend to ourselves.

Just as mindfulness is a way to train the mind to bring awareness to the present moment without judgment, loving-kindness is a way to train the mind and develop our innate capacity to be more loving and compassionate. Research on both mindfulness and compassion shows that it is "dose dependent," meaning the more you do, the more stable and reliable the effects are. What is exciting here is that there is growing evidence these practices can help rewire the brain to be more resilient.

♥ Rewiring with Loving-Kindness Meditation (LKM)

- Let yourself settle, either sitting or lying down. Feel free to put your hand on your heart or any other place that feels comforting. Try to bring not only awareness, but loving awareness, to yourself.
- Think of a living being who makes you smile. It could be a grandparent, a child, a supportive relative, or a beloved pet. Whoever brings happiness. If many beings arise, choose one.
- Let yourself experience what it's like to be with this person. Allow yourself to relax in this person's presence. Ahhhhhh. Create as clear an image as you can in your mind's eye.
- Notice that just like you, this person wants to be happy and free from suffering. With warmth and kindness, repeat the following words:
    May you be safe.
    May you be healthy.
    May you be peaceful.
    May you live with ease.
- Repeat these phrases two or three times.
- While these are the classic LKM phrases, feel free to add your own words if you like, or continue with these phrases.
- If you notice that your mind has wandered, just return to the phrases. No rush; take your time.
- When you're ready, add yourself. Create an image in your mind's eye of you being together with this being who makes you smile.
- Now try these phrases including yourself.
    May we be safe.
    May we be healthy.
    May we be peaceful.
    May we live with ease.
- Let go of the image of the other, letting your attention rest on yourself.
- Notice what is happening in your body, being aware of any stress or discomfort, and offer yourself these phrases.

May I be safe.

May I be healthy.

May I be peaceful.

May I live with ease.

- Take a few deep breaths and just rest quietly, noticing what you're feeling.
- When you're ready, stretch, open your eyes, and find some movement in your arms and legs.
- Know that you can return to this at any time.

People resist the practice of loving-kindness because it sounds, well, hokey. My initial impression, almost 20 years ago, was that it was a practice for people who wore rose-colored glasses. I prided myself on seeing the dark underbelly of life, and my clinical practice was comprised primarily of trauma survivors. I didn't want to lose my edge. One friend joked that I was doing all trauma all the time, and I was beginning to have nightmares from the intensity of the work.

I was also in a difficult relationship with a colleague, and I kept blaming myself for a host of problems we were having. Friends told me that LKM had made a big difference in their lives. I was bored with following my breath during meditation and was ready to try something new. When I started the practice, it didn't seem to make any difference. Useless, I thought. Too much hype. But I kept it going for a number of weeks. One teacher suggested that I think of the phrases as a healing and irrigating rain that was reaching the dry and arid places in my being. That seemed to help. There were more dry and arid places than I realized. I had been so focused on taking care of my patients and my family that there was nothing left for me. I felt exhausted and angry much of the time.

The teacher then suggested that I think of the phrases as a vitamin that I needed to stay healthy. I tried that as well. I hadn't realized I felt so depleted and burned out. Over a few months I slowly noticed a gradual difference. I wasn't as short-tempered with my kids when they fought or my husband when he came home late, delaying dinner. When my son spilled milk on the floor, I used to "hit the roof," as I didn't have the bandwidth for something else to go wrong. But of course things always go wrong. I was spending time and money shopping for things I didn't really need. I began to think of this preoccupation as "angry shopping" to soothe my frustration.

It wasn't that I became a different person. I was often irritable with my recently widowed mother, who insisted that I call her every night. It wasn't that I never yelled at the kids or got angry at my husband or bought things I didn't need. It was just that I had developed a sense of what I really needed. "Hmm, do I really need that chocolate bar?" Could I let that desire pass? "Will I still want it as much if I work in the garden for a while?" Did I really need a new pair of earrings? That extra glass of wine with dinner? Yes, it had been a stressful day, but I'd been feeling foggy when I got up in the morning. I began experimenting with putting a pause between my desires and my need to fill them immediately. And after a number of months, it was subtle, but I began to be a little kinder to myself. I realized how much I had been yelling at myself and berating myself when I screwed up. When I was running late, burned dinner, yelled at the kids, forgot something, became angry at my husband, felt let down by a friend or a coworker, it wasn't the end of the world—it just went with the territory of life. It didn't feel so personal. Kids would fight, my husband would run late, my coworker would continue to disparage me—and I didn't need to take it all so seriously. Plus, I didn't need to spend hours thinking about what I would say or do, what action I would take. I began to notice my fantasies and the ways I would spin out and began to shift to things that were more sustaining.

Alex and I worked together to develop a loving-kindness practice for daily life. As she practiced, she began to see the distinction between the actual experience and the story she was weaving from it. The practice helped her change the story she was creating and find a different response, besides making her feel less alone. She imagined her aunt, and it was comforting to feel her love and support, but she also started to see that she played a role in the confrontations with William, becoming instantly enraged when he baited her, as he'd done since they were kids.

"But there was something else I hadn't seen before," she said, "which is there is another possibility for how I can respond. If I hadn't been so freaked out about cooking, and my dad being dead, and dinner being late, and me being a failure compared to my brother, I could have responded in another way that would have shut it down. I could've had a sense of humor about it, saying something like 'Yeah, I know. Did I tell you I was just thrown off a reality cooking show where they humiliated me and said, "Take your knives and go. This is the worst turkey ever! No one would want to eat this. You don't deserve to be alive!"' And then, without missing a beat, I could have smiled and said, 'How 'bout some crackers and cheese?'

"Oh well," she added with a wry smile, "there's always Christmas."

Mean Girls

Rob got a job as an accountant, which is where he's been working for the three years since we met him in Chapter 1. He appreciates the stability and has more time to spend with his kids, but as tends to happen in a parent's life, he now has a new problem. He's worried about his daughter, 13-year-old Heather, who has been coming home in tears every day.

It took a while for Heather to open up to her parents about what was going on, but it turned out that the girl who was Heather's joined-at-the-hip best friend last year had dropped Heather at the beginning of this school year. Having acquired an older boyfriend and a new crowd to hang out with, Deb apparently not only had no need for Heather anymore but felt she had to cement her new social position by rejecting her former friend cruelly. Rob felt his own heart break when Heather described how Deb would stand up and smirk if Heather tried to sit at her lunch table, say, "Let's go, guys, smells bad here," and walk away.

The indignation and hurt grew when Heather's mom tried to talk to Deb's mother about the problem. The four parents had, after all, spent the summer having cookouts together while their daughters hung out. Surely once she knew what was happening, Deb's mom would help. Unfortunately, that wasn't the case. Rob fumed, "All the mom says is 'Well, Deb just wanted to move on. She's so mature, but Heather is still so *babyish*. Deb got tired of talking about her damn hamster. But Heather will catch up one of these days. Deb is just farther along. Did you think they'd be friends for life? Deb just wants to meet new people. Nothing wrong with that!'

"My wife has a temper," Rob went on, "and things got really heated at that point. They haven't spoken since; they don't even acknowledge each other on the street. And we're neighbors. It's really awkward."

Luckily for Heather, her school has an antibullying policy, and Rob was relieved to find that they took the situation seriously, especially considering that Deb's new clique seemed to take daily pleasure in taunting Heather, which lots of other students witnessed. And Heather had found other friends. But as he toted up these positives, Rob still looked sad. "My wife says 'Let it go; this happens all the time.' But it breaks my heart to see her come home in tears every day.

"The worst thing is that I can't protect her. It's so hard to see her suffer. And of course I got teased in middle school. Who doesn't? I remember kids making fun of me for being hardworking, for being a good student, for playing in the school band. You can't win.

"The other day," Rob continued, "Heather came home and took out some drawing paper. And she draws a ladder and puts each girl on a rung in terms of popularity—who's on top, who's on the bottom. And she's close to the bottom. She's questioning everything about herself and feeling that it's her fault. 'There must be something wrong with me,' she says, and she just cries and cries. 'Why are they so mean to me?'"

Rob and his wife responded the way any parent would—by assuring their daughter that there's nothing wrong with her, that her parents loved her and were there for her, and by acknowledging that life can be hard sometimes. They encouraged Heather to keep focusing on the new friends and activities that made her feel good and to remember that she didn't need to buy into an artificial hierarchy set up by those she didn't like.

Sometimes you reach the top of the ladder, a useful saying goes, only to find it's up against the wrong wall.

Of course what's tough about the mean-girl culture is that often there's little the parents can do that is effective, other than standing by their child and making sure she has support. And letting the child know she isn't alone. Rob and his wife got additional help from Heather's school and felt fortunate that their local schools took bullying seriously. Even today, not all schools do. And not everyone is able to find new friends as Heather did. If you notice that your child is not able to bounce back, has signs of depression or an eating disorder, or is cutting or hurting herself, please seek professional help (more on this in Chapters 6 and 7). If you, like Rob, are feeling helpless and impotent, the practices on needing to control (Chapter 5) might be helpful as well.

When children bring home experiences like Heather's, many parents are surprised to find that their child's experience opens old wounds of their own that they thought had long been sealed off by tough scars. It seemed clear that Ron could soothe those old wounds using the loving-kindness meditation, but he bristled at the phrase until I told him he could change the name and tailor the phrases to suit him—and you can too.

After trying the practice and finding it useful, Rob named it his "Oxygen Mask." "You know, when you're on a plane and they tell you to put on your oxygen mask first so you can help your kids if the air gets thin. This has made it easier for me to breathe."

 Oxygen Mask for Turbulent Flights

Set aside 20 minutes where you can have some quiet and not be interrupted. The exercise is designed to help you discover loving-kindness and compassion phrases that speak just to you. If the classic phrases work for you, try this as an experiment but don't feel obligated to switch.

If it feels comfortable, put a hand on your heart, allowing yourself to become receptive. While meditation teachers will encourage students to find words that speak to them, this variation of finding your own phrases is adapted from Neff and Germer.

- Ask yourself the following question, letting the answer arise spontaneously. What do I need? (*Pause.*) What do I really need?

  Let the answer be a deep need, a universal human need, such as the need to be peaceful, connected, free, or kind.

  Let this be a need to help you feel complete, full.

- When you are ready, open your eyes and write down what arose for you.

- The words you discovered can be used in meditation, or they can become new phrases for yourself, such as:

  May I begin to be kind to myself.

  May I live in peace.

  May I be free of anger.

  May I be free of hatred.

  May I feel connected to others.

- Now close your eyes again and reflect on a second question: If I could, what do I *need to hear from others?* What words do I really need to hear? It could be:

  "You're a good parent."

  "I'm here for you."

  "You're not alone."

  "I love you."

- Stay open and wait for the words to come.

  What words would I like whispered into my ear *every day of my life* that would make me say "Thank you, thank you," every time I hear them?

  Allow yourself to be vulnerable; listen with courage.

- Now gently opening your eyes, write down what you've heard.

- The words can be used in meditation, or they can be wishes for yourself. For example:

  "You're a good parent" can become "May I know my own goodness."

  "I'm here for you" can become "May I be here for myself."

  "I love you" can become the wish "May I come to love myself."

- Now review what you're written and choose two to four words or phrases that you'd like to incorporate into your meditation.

- These words or phrases are gifts you give yourself.
- Now close your eyes one more time. Try saying your phrases over and over, whispering them into your ear as if in the ear of a loved one.
- Try hearing the words from the *inside*, allowing them to take up space.
- Let yourself rest in this experience.
- Consider this the beginning of a journey.
- When you're ready, open your eyes.

Rob found that getting in touch with his own worth as a parent was like "pushing a reset button." When he felt more centered, he got less pulled into Heather's drama and felt that he could be a steady and loving presence for her. He realized that he wanted his daughter to develop some of the grit and resilience he and his siblings had built when they were teased, but that he couldn't help her weather the turbulence if he was back in the past, reliving his battles with high school bullies.

Undoubtedly all adults are grateful that seventh grade doesn't go on forever. And sometimes seemingly irreparable rifts are healed and friendships renewed. At Heather's age, everything changes, and everything is uncertain. To help Rob and his wife stay ready for those changes, I suggested another way to use his Oxygen Mask practice: "You might want to think about what Heather really needs to hear from you and your wife. What words might help *her* get through her day and this year?"

If your child is in distress, you can do this too. First put on your own oxygen mask, but then be sure your child has one too.

While mindfulness can give us perspective and help us see the story we are creating about our experience, when we add loving-kindness, we can shift our default story. So often the story we tell about our lives is motivated by anger, rejection, and fear, and we keep adding fuel to this fire. When we add loving-kindness, and especially tune in to what we need, it can make a huge difference. Rather than our first response being one of isolation, rage, and alienation, it can become one of connection, understanding, and kindness

The Brain on Meditation

What happens to us when we meditate? Most of us have read the headlines in the news that claim that mindfulness can help decrease anxiety and depression, can lower blood pressure and stress, and can help increase memory as we age. Yet one of the most consistent findings is less well known but of key importance for parents. In 2001, Marcus Raichle and Deborah Gusnard identified a region of the brain that is active when the mind is at rest and inactive when the mind is engaged in a specific task. It's called the default mode network, or DMN (some call it "damn" for short). And depending on which study you read, it turns out that our minds wander between 46.9% and 80% of the time. In short, a wandering mind is an unhappy mind. But where does the mind go? What is it doing?

Try this reflection yourself, setting a timer for five minutes.

> ### Reflection: Letting the Mind Wander
> - *Sit comfortably and just let yourself relax. Feel free to lie down if you like, but try to stay awake (I know, it's hard).*
> - *Let your mind wander. No need to be productive. No place to go, nothing to do.*
> - *It's fine to let yourself daydream. No need to control anything. Just rest.*
> - *Pay gentle attention to where your thoughts go. Are you thinking of your child? Reliving your past? Worrying about the future?*
> - *When the timer goes off, jot down a few notes about what you noticed.*

Most people notice that the mind goes to thoughts about the past, to concerns about the future, or to resolving problems. There is usually a preoccupation with I-Me-Mine. This is the DMN, which plays an important role in maintaining an "autobiographical self," which supports our identity. The mind wanders to something about ourselves—our emotions, work, status, our children—so that we become the center of the universe. We create a movie in our minds where we star, replaying distressing scenes, sometimes triumphs, but often bad memories, over and over.

Our minds are often drawn to what is troubling us. When we're in the DMN, we tend to look for something that is wrong, either with ourselves or with our children. We find things that need to be fixed. Psychologist Kelly McGonigal has compiled all the recent studies on the DMN and analyzed them. She finds that in the DMN there is a social focus. We think about other people in relation to us: What did someone say about us? What do they think about us? We make social comparisons: How am I compared to my siblings? My coworkers? How do my kids stack up compared to their peers? We tend to judge, big-time: My life should be different. Why am I this way? Why is my child this way? Self-criticism is a powerful activator of the DMN.

An important effect of mindfulness and compassion meditation is that all forms of meditation deactivate the DMN. And scientists are now finding that even a small dose of mindfulness can change what the brain does by default, even when we're not meditating.

So what does this mean for us as parents? Most important, we realize that we don't need to be held hostage by our comparing minds. When we notice that we are judging and finding fault with ourselves, our children, our partners, or our standing in the social pecking order, we have a choice—we can change the conversation in our heads. We can stop ourselves from going down the rabbit hole of anguish if our child can't wield scissors, if a sibling (or parent, or in-law) puts us down, or if we find ourselves the low woman on the totem pole in the middle school rat race.

The Dreaded Potluck Dinner

As Rob so poignantly described and you may have experienced personally, it's incredibly painful to see your child rejected by or otherwise negatively compared to his or her peers, and it can open old wounds from your own childhood. The last thing we need on top of this reality is being drawn into the comparison game with our own peers. Shouldn't we all be above this as adults? Shouldn't we have learned better? Possibly, but it often doesn't happen. We carry a lot of baggage with us from childhood (see Chapter 3). Alex still gets ambushed by her brother's guise of superiority, Rob still feels the sting of being teased in school, and many adults—William, perhaps?—got into the comparison game at a young age and have never stopped trying to climb the wrong ladder against the wrong wall.

"If I have to attend another 'Parent Get-Together,'" Anjali said, "I'm going to lose it." Describing these events as not just tedious but often torturous, she said she thought that as the kids get older the parents get more competitive:

"Sudhir is in sixth grade—but it feels like things are ramping up on every level. More homework, more attention to extracurricular activities, more emphasis on team sports. And as a single mom, I feel more alone and more inadequate. I don't have anyone to accompany me. I'm aware of status, how people are dressed, how successful people are, where they live, what their houses are like. And I feel like I'm being judged. It's a hierarchy at the potlucks and the parent–teacher meetings. I try to ignore it, but I can't. I notice all these groups. There are the power couples, the professional moms with high-powered jobs, the volunteer moms, the moms who spend their days working out—doing yoga, or running, or Pilates—and have bodies to die for. And then there are the stay-at-home moms with lots of kids. And people spend a lot of time getting dressed for these events. It's important to wear the right thing—can't be too sexy, too tight, too formal, or too casual, and it is a lot of pressure. And this is a public school. It shouldn't be a big deal.

"There was this class party over the weekend, at someone's big, beautiful house. I found it intimidating. The women were dressed up, made up, not what you see at drop-off in the early morning. There was so much attention to appearance. It was potluck, but even the food was competitive. It's so silly. Who made the most elaborate entrée?? The best cake? The best chocolate chip cookies? I hadn't expected food to be another venue for comparison.

"What I noticed was that the parents were in the same cliques as their children—the popular kids, the superstars, the athletic kids, the nerds, the artsy ones. And I felt like I was excluded, so I was pretending to be an anthropologist. Because I'm not married, the women are a little wary of me, and the men don't want to be seen flirting with me, so it was lonely.

"I started feeling like I didn't belong. Like people didn't want to be talking with me. They kept looking elsewhere to see if they could talk with someone who had more status. And I know I'm sensitive about having brown skin and being different, but I do try to blend in. I don't wear a hijab. I don't advertise that I'm a Muslim. But lately I'm assuming the worst about people, which I don't like.

"I feel like I've shut down. And the potluck brought that home. It's hard for me to open up to people. I feel suspicious. Guarded. I think they are judging me, I'm judging them. Anything I can do?" she asked.

Robert Thurman, who is a professor of Buddhist studies at Columbia University (and yes, the actress Uma Thurman's dad), tells a story about what living compassionately might look like. "Imagine you're on the New York City subway," he says, "and these extraterrestrials come and zap the subway car so that all of you in it are going to be together . . . forever." How do we respond? Suddenly, through no choice of our own, these are our own people. We may not like them. We may not approve of them. In fact, we may dislike them. But if we're going to be together, we need to find a way to get along. If someone is hungry, we feed them. If someone is having a panic attack, we help them. Whether we like it or not, our lives are connected.

The following meditation allows us to extend the practice of loving-kindness to everyone at the potluck, the school, the neighborhood. Even without the aliens zapping us, our lives are linked, whether we want to acknowledge it or not.

So, playing with the image of the subway car, imagine that the dreaded potluck (or the PTA meeting) is zapped by extraterrestrials and you are all together . . . forever.

Reflection: The Zapped Potluck Gathering

- Let yourself sit comfortably. See if you can have some fun with this practice.
- Take a few deep breaths.
- Allow yourself to have whatever feelings you might have about spending more time with the group of parents. Don't feel the need to censor your feelings. Notice what is present.
- No need to try to manufacture any specific emotions. No need to pretend that you like certain parents. You can send loving-kindness even if you don't really like them. All we are doing here is acknowledging a connection.
- For people who rub you the wrong way, imagine what they might be dealing with—alcoholism, infidelity, financial worries, aging parents, illness.
- The traditional practice is to start with ourselves, but if that is difficult, begin with someone who has been supportive and then repeat the phrases for others.
- The classic phrases are **May I be safe, May I be happy, May I be healthy, May I live with ease**—in other words, may daily life (and parenting) not be so difficult.
- The **May I** is said in the spirit of generosity, blessing ourselves and others. **May I be safe, may you be safe.**
- If your attention wanders, don't worry. You can always begin again.
- As you go through the collection of parents (and don't pressure yourself to go through everyone right now), call to mind someone who has been kind to you, someone who has helped you. Picture the person, say the person's name, and offer the phrases. Wish this person what you've wished for yourself: **May you be safe, May you be happy, May you be healthy, May you live with ease.**

- *For this practice, don't worry if the words aren't perfect. The point is to connect and to wish this person well.*
- *Think of someone who is having a hard time right now—a sick child, a divorce, an ill parent, a job loss. Picture this person, say the person's name, and offer the phrases to him or her.* **May you be safe. May you be happy. May you be healthy. May you live with ease.**
- *Expect that your attention will wander. Remember, this is what the mind does. Don't beat yourself up.*
- *Call to mind someone you don't really know. A parent you see sometimes, in passing, but you've never talked to. You may not even know the person's name. Not a problem. Picture him or her, get a feeling for the person, and know that he or she also wants to be happy, worries about a child, and is vulnerable as well.* **May you be safe. May you be happy. May you be healthy. May you live with ease.**
- *Now call to mind some parent whose words or actions or behavior has been difficult for you. Maybe this person has been rude to you or disrespected you. Try sending loving-kindness to this person. If you find this is too hard, don't force it; just go back to sending loving-kindness to yourself. In that instance, you're the one who is in pain, so send yourself some warmth and kindness.*
- *Finally, offer good wishes and loving-kindness to everyone at the potluck.* **May you all be safe. May you all be happy. May you all be healthy. May you all live with ease.**
- *If you like, extend these wishes to all parents, even all living beings:* **May all parents be safe. May all parents be happy. May all parents be healthy. May all parents live with ease.**
- *When you're ready, open your eyes. See if you can continue to bring loving-kindness into your day and maybe practice when you drop off your child in the morning or pick up your child at the end of the day, or at the next school gathering.*

After practicing the Zapped Potluck exercise for a few weeks, Anjali began to see the other parents more clearly. For example, she remembered that another single mom, who was also struggling, had been very kind and invited them over for dinner. She'd been too busy to reciprocate. Then there was a mom who was going through chemo for breast cancer and had lost all her hair but was there almost every day to pick up her child: Anjali realized she could bring dinner for her. And then of course there were "the assholes," including one couple who wouldn't have anything to do with Anjali and her son because of race and religion. She had tried sending them kindness, but it was too hard, so she redirected it toward herself. She was reminded of how hard it is to be marginalized. "But mostly," she said, "it made me feel like I could soften and relax a little around the other parents. They aren't against me, and some of them I wasn't even seeing or thinking about. This has helped me open my eyes a little."

When we are going through difficult times, our world often constricts. We turn inward and become protective. The practice of loving-kindness can help restore us to our best and kindest selves, both as parents and as individuals. It can help ground us in what matters to us and realign with our core values. Psychologist and meditation teacher Jack Kornfield puts it succinctly: "The point isn't to perfect your body or your personality. The point is really to perfect your compassion and your love."

Mindfulness in Daily Life

It's a Jungle out There

After recent experiences with her middle child, Alex came up with a new phobia, called Fear of Playgrounds. "It feels like no one is playing," she explained, "but everyone is competing. Really, it sometimes feels like a competitive sport. So my daughter really likes colors, and she's three and pointing out the colors on her ball—blue, red, green, yellow. So last week this other mom comes up and says, 'How'd you get her to do that?' As if she is a trained seal.

"So I reply, 'I didn't get her to do anything; she likes colors.'

"She goes, 'Wow, that's really advanced. How old is she?' I give her a WTF-is-your-problem look. And then this week, I see the mom with her son, and she's quizzing him. 'Now what color is this? And what color is this?' as if it's a race to recite the colors. Where's that gonna get you? So crazy.

"But that isn't so bad, I could let that go. Competition is in the air we breathe here and we don't even notice it, like fish don't notice water. But my daughter is on the top of the slide, and this big aggressive kid comes up, right behind her, and tries to push her out of his way. She's hesitating about going down. So I'm standing on the ground with the baby in the carrier, and I yell up to him, 'Don't push; wait your turn,' and I talk her down. She does it but very slowly. The slide was high, and she is tiny and fearful. And I can't climb up with her now that I have the baby.

"So the mother comes up to me and says, 'You should direct your own child!' Like how dare I say anything to her precious bully son.

"'And you should direct yours. He tried to push her off!'

"'My son isn't aggressive!' she retorts.

"I gave her the evil eye, and we just got up and left, but I couldn't believe it. I wasn't going to get into her face and start a fight about whose kid was more aggressive. Somebody would videotape the fight. I don't need that. But her denial was amazing to me."

"Did anything about that feel familiar?" I asked.

"Bingo," Alex said and smiled. "You called that one," she nodded. "My brother is everywhere! And my mother is too!" Sometimes it feels like the world is a neglectful and indifferent mother.

"I feel like I see it everywhere. It feels like the other parents aren't paying attention to their kids. People pushing their children on swings engrossed in their phones, not making eye contact with the kids, not talking to them. Letting them play alone in the sandbox while they check Facebook. Instagram. Whatever is in right now. Changes every day. I just wanted to get the hell out of there.

"I know people can be difficult and aggressive and competitive, and I don't want my kids to have that as a model. But I can't move to a refuge on a mountaintop. I don't want them to see me try to take down a mom who is twice my size because her kid tried to push my kid. That irony is not lost on me, but I do want to model some mature adult behavior. Not that I know what that would look like."

Loving-Kindness at the Playground

One of my favorite sayings when people are being aggressive toward me and I get angry and reactive in response is from psychologist and meditation teacher Tara Brach: "This is not an enemy," she intones in her soothing voice. "This is another soldier in a foxhole having a hard day." What might this look like in action on the playground when other parents are pushing your buttons?

Try this exercise the next time you visit a playground:

- As you enter the playground, look around at all the parents and children.
- You might want to start with emphasizing your common humanity and interconnection with these loving-kindness phrases.

  I, like every parent and child here, want to be free from inner and outer harm.

  I, like every parent and child here, want to be happy.

  I, like every parent and child here, want to be healthy.

  I, like every parent and child here, want to live with ease.

- As your child runs off to play, remain present; don't reach for your phone to distract yourself. This time with your child is precious. It will pass before you know it.
- Continue to make eye contact as you push your child on the swing. Don't interrupt the interaction by looking at your phone and checking messages.
- To deepen the connection with your child, try wishing your child well as you watch him or her play.

  May you be free from inner and outer harm.

  May you be happy.

  May you be healthy.

  May you live with ease.

- Let's say a conflict arises with another child or another parent. Before engaging, start by wishing yourself well—*May I be safe, May I be healthy, May I be happy, May I live with ease.*
- Pause; take a breath or two.
- Listen to what is happening with the other child or parent.
- Rather than reacting, see if you can respond by saying to yourself, "This is not an enemy; this is another soldier in a foxhole having a hard day."
- See how this perspective can help you manage or deescalate the conflict.
- Repeat in the various playgrounds of your life as often as needed.

These practices of mindfulness and compassion can create enough space in your head so that when you're irritated or upset with someone you're less likely to act in ways you might regret. Rather than getting lost in those endless loops of the DMN, about who we are and how others treat us—"how dare they," "I'll show them," and so forth—we can practice the art of responding, rather than reacting. There is a great line in *The*

Philadelphia Story that can help keep us compassionate: "The time to make up your mind about other people is never."

As we try to keep an open mind and an open heart, to be awake and alive, we can disentangle from our worries and anxieties and see things more clearly. Living in the present unburdens us from the constant comparing and judging mind. Mindfulness teaches us that we can train our minds in revision and see other beings as being like us, having the same needs, wishes, and vulnerabilities. And this can help shift our experience of parenting, moving from a competitive sport of us versus them, or winning and losing, to a deeper experience of human connection.

But above all, be kind to yourself. We all get caught at times. When I notice that I have fallen into "comparing mind," I think about what the Dalai Lama once said in an interview. "What was the happiest moment of your life?" the interviewer asked. He paused, looked around, and smiled. "I think this one."

Try applying that in your life. Notice the sunshine on your child's hair as you push him on the swing; notice her joy as she runs, laughing, in the playground. Stop. Take this in. Let this be enough. Let your child be enough. And you are a good enough parent. Let yourself be grateful for the small things in this moment. The smell of the air, the flowers, the moist earth, the birds singing. Savor these sweet and precious moments.

5 "What Should I Do?"

WORKING WITH THE INEVITABLE UNCERTAINTY OF PARENTING

As we saw in Chapter 2, Chrissie's second marriage came with an evil stepmother role she hadn't anticipated. Four years later, her relationship with stepdaughter Jenny had improved, but she was worried about Steven, now eight.

"He's always been high energy and is in constant motion. So am I. I can't sit still, so I didn't think anything about it. He's also a natural athlete, like me, and he loves to run. However, he can't sit quietly at his desk like the teachers want him to do. So he's been having trouble in elementary school. We just had a meeting with his teachers and the guidance counselor. They say he's can't stay focused on his work. So the school has come up with an IEP (individualized education program), and he's getting special services. It's not that I mind him getting help, although it was hard at first—of course you want to think your kid is perfect—but what is really upsetting is that they think he should try medication. They say it will help him concentrate and help him sit still. It makes me furious. Giving a kid drugs in elementary school to calm him down? I think it is just to make things easier for the teachers.

"I don't want to be one of those difficult, arrogant parents who think they know everything. They say it would help, and my friends have kids who are on meds, and it has made things easier for them. But I don't want him to be a dulled-down medicated version of the exuberant child I love."

There is no simple answer to this quandary, which I hear from many parents. Should a child be medicated for problems with attention? Anxiety? Depression? Behavior? Aren't we becoming an overmedicated nation? Isn't it all too much? Since I'd never met Steven, I didn't feel qualified to weigh in on what his treatment should be. However, I did connect Chrissie with a child psychologist to help the family sort out the best plan of action.

When we are feeling battered by life, compassion is a reliable antidote. As Maya Angelou wrote in her book *Letter to My Daughter*, "You may not control all the events that happen to you, but you can decide not to be reduced by them." If we think about it, we are challenged daily to act on our own behalf and on behalf of our children and loved ones. Chrissie was so upset that she had stopped taking care of herself. She wasn't sleeping, she was staying up late drinking gin and tonics to calm down, and bingeing on her favorite TV shows accompanied by ice cream and cake.

When things spin out of control and we don't know how to proceed, we have a choice about how we respond to the difficulties and uncertainties that inevitably arise. Like every other parent in the world, you might feel rage, shame, and embarrassment when things go south, but you can work on holding these inevitable difficult emotions with care and compassion.

Take a moment to reflect on what you are dealing with.

Reflection: Working with the Uncertainties of Parenting

- Put down the drink, turn off the TV, set aside your phone, and put the ice cream and cake away (at least for the moment—but don't worry; it's your choice). Things can get messy and tough sometimes. Every parent has hard times.
- Take a few deep breaths, put a hand on your heart, or try some soothing touch.
- What is uncertain in your life right now? What are you struggling to control?
- Is your child having trouble in school?
- Have the teachers identified a problem? Are you being asked to take action that doesn't feel right?
- Are you waiting to hear how your child performed on an important test? If she or he got into a school or college?
- Are you managing health issues in your family?
- Are you struggling with difficulty in your job? Or your partner's work?
- Have you experienced an economic downturn?
- Are you dealing with loss?
- Has your child been struggling with addiction? With the law?
- Are you dealing with the uncertainty of a separation or a divorce?

- *Write down all the things that feel uncertain or out of control in your life.*
- *Pause. Stop. Bring kindness to yourself.*
- *All parents struggle; all parents suffer and fail. You are human. Don't blame yourself, don't criticize yourself.*
- *Try to look at the problems and uncertainties clearly, not ignoring or denying them—but try not to beat yourself up.*
- *No matter what they are, you still deserve kindness and compassion.*
- *Finish by putting your hand on your heart and taking a deep breath. You can return to this practice whenever you need it.*
- *See if you can bring this practice into your day as you return to your daily activities.*

Chrissie felt that this reflection helped her feel a little less isolated. "It's not something that you can talk about in casual conversation. I've kept it to myself. It's hard to talk to other moms about Steven's problems; they don't want to hear about them. They start to look anxious, like there might be something wrong with their kid. That he is having trouble too. Like it should be a big secret. But when I think about how everyone struggles with something, even if they keep silent about it, I feel better. We all struggle, but most of us don't talk about it."

While the reflection was helpful, she needed more. The dilemma with Steven was keeping her up at night. Chrissie found she was having nightmares where Steven morphed into a robot and she would wake up screaming for him to come back. "I think I'm the one who needs meds right now," she quipped, only half joking.

I introduced her to the classic practice of RAIN, which stands for recognize, allow, investigate, and nourish/nurture/natural attention (the N representing different words depending on the teacher) and is one of the most useful exercises that I know of for dealing with the roller-coaster emotions of parenting. The beauty of this practice is that you don't have to sit still to do it (unless you want to) and it can be done in the chaos of the moment. It can also be practiced in a more formal and reflective way to work with something that has happened and is upsetting you when you want to spend some time writing down your thoughts and reactions.

Often people turn to meditation seeking calm, but we can't bypass emotional distress, no matter how much we try. And as parents, it is virtually impossible to avoid. Self-compassion helps us cultivate new tools so that we can relate more effectively to our difficult emotions when they inevitably arise. Developed by meditation teacher Michelle McDonald, RAIN is an effective way to welcome and work with difficult emotions. Almost every teacher has a variation of the practice, and I have experimented with versions by Sharon Salzberg, Tara Brach, and Rick Hanson. I developed this composite version especially for parents. It was renamed by Chrissie, who said she felt like the practice got her out of the "hurricane-force winds" of her conflicting emotions.

Try it sitting, standing, walking, lying down—whenever the winds of life knock you down.

The Rain/Hurricane of Self-Compassion

• *Recognize.* To face an emotion, and have some resilience, we need to acknowledge that we are feeling it. Bringing the skills of mindfulness to bear, we notice what is happening. Let's say you've had an interaction with a child that leaves you feeling raw and upset. Don't try to ignore it, sweep it under the rug, or deny it. Saying, "Oh, it's nothing," can actually make it worse. Look at it. You might label it if the practice of noting has been helpful. "Ah, this feels like anger." See if other thoughts follow, such as irritation, sadness, thoughts about not being respected. You may notice that you want to cry. It might be that you are criticizing yourself for being angry: "Good parents don't get angry." Whatever it is, you are not the first parent who has ever felt this way. Just let yourself recognize it with some kindness.

• *Allow.* Allow the emotion to be there, even if it is unpleasant to do so. Don't try to control it. You are giving yourself permission to feel it, even if you think you shouldn't be feeling it. Remember, we don't invite our emotions to arise; they just do. You might say, "I should only have loving feelings about my child" or "This shouldn't upset me," but let things be as they are. Some teachers have us imagine that each feeling or thought is a visitor knocking at the door. Greet the feeling, acknowledge it, then let it go. Rather than dismiss difficult feelings as "bad," rename them as painful. This opens the door to increased self-compassion. With this framework, you can create space for your emotions to arise even if they are uncomfortable. See if you can bring self-compassion rather than self-criticism to what you are experiencing.

• *Investigate.* The steps of recognizing and allowing help us bring curiosity to the investigation of our emotions. This is different than being caught in a reaction against them. We are not trying to analyze an emotion or construct a story about it, which can distance us from the immediacy of it, but to get closer to it. See if you can get curious and interested in what you are experiencing, with an attitude of friendliness or tenderness. We can begin to explore how it manifests in our bodies, and what the emotions might contain. Anger, for example, can also contain fear, hurt, helplessness, and sadness. See what the soft feelings might be under the rage. Here we can focus on gaining insight. Progress doesn't mean that we no longer have negative emotions—that doesn't happen, especially as a parent. It is just that we become more open to insights and understanding about what is arising.

• *Nourish (with Self-Compassion).* Self-compassion arises readily when we recognize that we are suffering. Tune in—what does the part of you that is suffering need? What is most comforting to you right now: reassurance, companionship? Try out the loving-kindness phrases from the last chapter. What words might feel comforting? "I love you," "This is not your fault," "I'm listening," "I'm here for you." "Parenting can be painful and difficult." See if any of the gestures of soothing touch will settle you. Even a small gesture of offering love to yourself can be nourishing. Notice that you are having a feeling without being it. You are more than your anger. Don't spiral down into recrimination or judgment. "I'm an angry terrible parent and that will never change. This is just who I am." Try instead a friendly "Oh, I'm suffering right now." See if you can disentangle from the experience. This is just a small part of all that you are. Let this experience pass.

This is what came up for Chrissie as she worked with the practice of RAIN during the week:

"In the **Recognize** step I realized not only how angry I was, but how scared I was. I realized I was worried that I would lose Steven, that he would become someone else. And I worry that I won't be able to protect Steven from hurt—not that we can ever protect our children from hurt. It felt like someone had punched me in the gut.

"I'm always trying to fix everything. So I was spending all this mental energy trying to figure out how to fix Steven. I came up with all these plans: I would enroll him in a karate boot camp to help him learn focus and discipline. That would cure him. Or get him into gymnastics since he loves to jump and do backflips and fancy turns on his skateboard. I'm always trying to solve problems. Ha. And I was feeling like such a bad and inadequate parent, and even imagining that my genes were defective. So

I just stopped and let all the feelings be there, allowing them, the whole shitty mess of them. I just let myself stop and pause for a few minutes. 'OK, Chrissie, you can't control this one. Chill.'" That helped.

"With the **Allow** step, I acknowledged that he is struggling in school, which I was denying. I was blaming the lazy teachers, the principal, the large classroom, my husband, my ex-husband, my genes. And then I could acknowledge that I'm upset and that it isn't my fault. I was feeling like everyone else was at fault. That wasn't getting me anywhere. I was telling myself I shouldn't be so emotional, or so sensitive, or be upset. Lot of good that was doing. I just made everything worse, and the school thought I was a bitch on wheels. I was acting like everyone was an enemy to be conquered—the school, the teachers, the guidance counselor, the ADHD if that is what we want to call it. I've been fighting with the diagnosis. Now I'm letting myself feel the hurricane of emotions. I was trying to eat my way out of the feelings.

"With the **Investigate** step, I started to feel what was in my body, which was a huge mess, a knot of fear and anxiety in my belly. A sense of 'Oh no, not this again.' And there was a sense of shame, that I'm not a good mother. That I did something wrong when I got divorced. That it's all my fault and that I've screwed Steven up for life. So rather than spinning and trying to fix it, deny it, or hate myself, I just felt the mountain of pain and hurt and worry that I was carrying. Usually I yell at myself and berate myself. This time I worked on caring for myself.

"And the **Nourishing** and self-compassion ending helped. I'm so critical of myself, and the only way I nourish myself is with wine and cocktails and chocolate. I know, not the kind of nourishment that goes anyplace other than my waist and butt. I got in touch with a part of me that is really terrified for him. I was able to extend some kindness toward myself, rather than the usual loathing, saying, 'Chrissie, hang in, be there for yourself, you're a good mom.' And then I was able to feel some of that kindness for Steven: 'Oh, my sweet baby, I love you, I won't turn away. I'm here, kiddo, you aren't alone.'

"I feel like I'm settling a little, not fighting so much about this, not raging as I was last week," Chrissie reported. "I'm in a saner place."

Compassion to Go

I like to think of the "Hurricane" practice as "self-compassion to go." It isn't a practice that you need a quiet space for. You can use it whenever you need a shot of compassion, rather than that extra shot of espresso (don't worry, sometimes we need that as well). How have other parents used this practice? Samantha had a fight with her son about carpool arrangements for soccer practice, and he yelled at her and was disrespectful. It didn't work for her life to take him and pick him up for every game, but he wanted her to be there. She was furious that he didn't respect her needs, but there was no time for quiet reflection to calm down. She was in the car and on the way to work where she had to give an important presentation and not be a mess. Although she was driving in rush-hour traffic on the highway, she was able to recognize what she was feeling, allow it to be there, even though it was unpleasant, investigate what she was experiencing with some curiosity and friendliness, and then nourish herself, gently observing that this was painful rather than beating herself up. "It got me out of that ruminating rage I get into, where I spiral down into a funk. And I get that he wants me to be at every game, but I'm only human, and my needs matter too."

Hiroto used the practice when he and his ex-wife were going through a bitter and contentious divorce and custody battle. The kids were getting caught in the cross-fire. Whenever he felt overwhelmed with anger and bitterness, he turned to RAIN. "It helps me feel a little less crazed and work with my feelings in a constructive way rather than being afraid of their intensity. I'd started drinking again, I was so upset. Downed a whole bottle of wine myself the other night. I just wanted to numb out. It's been so hard. I have a broken heart, a fear of the future, and the desire for revenge. But I need to put the kids first. Now I feel that I'm a little more understanding of how much this hurts. I'm not drinking every night, taking things out on my colleagues, or yelling at the kids. I'm learning to relax in the midst of all this chaos and change."

The Illusion of Control

In our fantasies about the children we will produce, we often dream that our best qualities will live on. For many parents, it comes as a shock to realize that their child has a distinct personality, with needs and desires and wishes of his or her own. Our children are not us. And often, the more different the child is, the more difficult it is for the parent. Many parents blame themselves when their children are not in line with their fantasies of what the child should be. In the privacy and safety of the consulting room, parents often complain that they have been catapulted into a permanent relationship with a stranger. It is not what they imagined, not who they imagined. And often they don't even like the stranger. They worry that something is wrong with them: Was it their failure to bond? Could it be the result of a Caesarean section? Can they blame their unemotional mother or father?

While many of us take pride in how different we are from our parents—more emotionally attuned, more open-minded, more balanced, more successful, more enlightened about politics or the state of the world—we often despair when our children are different from us or when they decide to live according to their own values, which often conflict with ours. We often believe that not only should we control our own destinies, but we should control those of our children.

This false belief is often a major cause of stress and anxiety. When we begin to question it, we see how delusional it really is. Before we start beating ourselves up, we might want to ask, "Now how could I have controlled that?" More often than not, we could not have prevented the difficult situation for which we are nevertheless blaming ourselves. Our children are biologically different. They carry recessive traits and genetic material and are subject to environmental conditions that are beyond our control. As Chrissie began to realize, the task is to learn to love our children as they are and not for the reflection of ourselves in them.

The next time you find yourself wanting to change your child, or have him or her behave a certain way, or be someone you want him or her to be, try this reflection:

Reflection: Letting Your Child Emerge

- *For much of our lives, especially before we had children, we were used to being the center of our universe, feeling we could control at least some aspects of our world.*
- *Our culture reinforces that—social media encourages us to have others "follow me," "like me." Our phones show us "our" weather, news, stocks.*
- *Let that drop away. Center with the breath, the sounds around you, the sensations in your body.*
- *When we have children, everything shifts. The universe expands, and we lose our sense of mastery and control. Suddenly we feel more vulnerable, things feel shaky, the future becomes uncertain.*
- *See what it feels like to stop trying so hard to have it all together.*

- *Let yourself rest. Stop pushing. Relax your striving.*
- *We often assume that we should be different, and that our children should be different, and it is our job to fix them.*
- *The more fear and worry we have, the more frantic we are about trying to manage our lives, and the lives of our children.*
- *It's exhausting to be trying to manage everything 24/7. To feel that we have to perform, that our children have to perform.*
- *What if you didn't have to try to make your child be anything? If you could just allow him or her to be? To enjoy? Not to have to do so much or achieve so much?*
- *Imagine Michelangelo in front of a beautiful piece of stone, waiting, listening to see what the stone wants to become. Can you imagine bringing that kind, gentle, loving attention to your child?*
- *Do not force. See if you can guide, support, let this child unfold.*
- *Try saying silently, "I see you. I'm listening. I care about you and your needs."*

Mindfulness encourages us to see the whole web of conditions, influences, and factors that come together to create any given moment. We are part of a greater whole. Much as we might want to (or think we do), we don't orchestrate the universe. On a good day we might have some control over ourselves and our children, perhaps getting them to eat a healthy dinner, do their homework, and not hit their siblings, maybe even connect with you in a meaningful way, but beyond that our powers are sadly limited. The awareness of a bigger picture and a vaster universe can help ease our self-blame or guilt when our children have problems, don't behave, meet our standards, or perform as we think they should.

"I Can't Get Off This Treadmill"

In Chapter 2 we saw how Anton felt compelled to micromanage his kids, even to the point of dictating what they ate. This urge stemmed from his worries about the future and his desire for them to have secure lives. But he was feeling exhausted trying to run a business, manage his kids, and keep his wife happy. "I feel like I can't stop, and I worry that if I do everything will fall apart. I know I put them under a lot of pressure to perform. The more fear and uncertainty I have, the more I try to manage and control everything. And I know it isn't good, and I'm embarrassed to admit this, but I often resort to guilt and threats to get the results I want. And I blame them for making me stressed. I know it's a vicious cycle, but sometimes I feel I don't have any choice."

Clearly Anton needed to relax a little. I thought a story might help:

Once there was a little boy who noticed some white hairs on his father's head.

"Why do you have those white hairs, Daddy?" the son asked.

"Well, you know how sometimes you misbehave? And sometimes you won't eat your dinner? Or you fight with your brother? Or you make me mad? Or you make your mother cry? Well, every time you do something bad, I get a white hair."

The little boy thought and thought. He was quiet for a while.

"But Daddy," he said, seeing the contradiction in his father's argument, "why is Grandpa's hair totally white?"

Anton broke out laughing. "That's a good one, that is very good," he said, slapping his knee. "In fact, I want to talk today about Samir. The issue is that Samir is being defiant again. He makes a big stink when I ask him to do the extra daily math problems I assign him." I raised my eyebrows.

"The public school isn't preparing him sufficiently. He's in a large class of about 30 kids, and he's not being challenged. And he tends to be lazy. Strong math skills are the key to success in this world. The teacher is too busy and too overwhelmed to give him special attention, so I need to make sure he is working to his capacity. I've stepped in to supplement to make sure he's acquiring the skills. And I know math. I can teach him better than the teacher, who is a sweet young woman, fresh out of school, but not a mathematician.

"The problem is that he fights me every time. It's disrespectful. I'm doing this for his own good. He sulks, sometimes he throws a tantrum. I'm sure you can imagine how well I take to that."

"What does he say?" I asked.

Anton relaxed a little. "He says it's boring; he doesn't care."

"What does he care about? Playing video games?" I asked.

"Yes, like most kids his age, he likes games of skill. And he's good at them. But he loves animals."

"Being around animals?"

"Everything about them. Watching them, reading about them, watching TV programs. He's obsessed."

"Sounds like he's found a passion."

"There's this old dusty museum that he loves, it's connected to one of the schools nearby. And they have these ancient displays of animals of every type from all over the world. It's a natural history museum. He's in heaven when he's there. My wife takes him, often with friends or with his brother. They have classes where they learn about science, the animals, and old skeletons. Sometimes they sketch them, build models of the animals, sometimes do some research. And he has a good sense of humor. 'Dad, we saw a *man-eating tiger* today. It looked scary. Wouldn't want to meet him in the jungle! And there was a bird that was all colorful and they named it a *secretary bird*. Isn't that silly?'

"How do you respond?" I asked.

"I joke with him. 'That's nice. Now do your math problems. The man-eating tiger will not get you a job, my son. This is a dog-eat-dog world, and you need to be able to survive. Get to work. I don't want that tiger to eat *you*.'"

"What if, after the math problems, you spend an hour at the museum with him, as special father/son time?" I asked.

"He would love it, but I *really* don't have the time."

"You can disagree with me if you like, but my bet here is that if you spend an hour with him at the museum and get to see what he loves, he might not fight you as much."

He rolled his eyes. "I guess I could give it an hour, but it's not going to help him get a job or survive in this world," he challenged.

"Look, Anton, I get how busy you are, and how leisure activities seem like a luxury. We can't control the job market, but you do have some control about how you relate to your son. It might help build a stronger relationship with him, which you want. And remember, we don't know what the economy is going to be in 15 to 20 years. Those skills of classification, observation, and analysis can translate into many things. OK?"

Anton heaved an irritated sigh.

"Anton, I know you want him to achieve. We all want our kids to achieve and do well and be successful. And it's important for kids to find some balance. And for parents to support their interests. I'm just asking you to spend an hour. Deal?"

As Anton walked out, glancing at his smartwatch, I wondered if I would ever see him again.

Bigger, Better, Faster

We dream that our children will be improved versions of ourselves— smarter, more athletic, more attractive, more successful. We often go to great lengths to make this happen. Over my 30 years of practice, I've watched parents with limited means use precious savings to pay for exam tutors and college consultants to provide their children with every advantage, only to feel bitter and enraged when the investment of time and money makes a minimal difference, if any.

There is a story that when Jean Piaget, the Swiss developmental psychologist, came to America in the 1960s to lecture on his ideas about the stages of child development, someone would inevitably ask, "How can we speed these stages up?" The question became so ubiquitous that he came to call it "the American question."

His reply embodied some Zen wisdom: "Why would you want to do that?" He didn't see any virtue in pushing kids ahead of their limits, feeling that it was neither healthy nor desirable. He trusted that children would reach the developmental milestones in their own time. We tend to think that the better we are at parenting, the faster our children will develop. What gets lost here is a sense of fun and of play.

At the core of the question is a basic desire that is so human, one that both Anton and Chrissie share—how can my child have a happier life, or a life with more ease, than I've had?

Yet the underlying truth is that the more we try to control and micromanage, the more our children will push back. I think back to the woven finger puzzles I played with as a child—the more you struggle to free yourself, the tighter the grip. In seeing the underlying innocence of Anton's wish for his son, even though it manifested with a fierce intensity, I remembered my mother's attempts to teach me to write. She'd been a talented journalist and had dreamed of moving to New York City to achieve her dreams. In the story she told, she had given up a job at a prestigious magazine after being diagnosed with a heart condition. She put aside her dream, became a schoolteacher, married, moved to the suburbs, and had two children. But dreams die hard. Her restless unfulfilled ambition surfaced when I was in middle school and became her new focus. However, I had no talent and no interest. The more she tried to get me to write, the more I resisted and became defiant, producing work that showed a total lack of style or creativity. I was more interested in visual arts and the theater, and the unlived life of my mother didn't engage me. In fact, I ran as fast as I could in the opposite direction. I just wanted to act. She eventually gave up on that project to improve me.

Anton didn't cancel his appointment for the next week. "I have to give you some credit," he said sheepishly. "We went to the museum together. I don't think I remember seeing Samir so happy. He ran around all the rooms, with all these cases of ancient specimens, pointing out the bears, the birds, the blue butterflies, the skeleton of a dinosaur, a prehistoric fish embedded in rock. He knew so much. I have to say, I was impressed. He knew all these animals. And he was so happy that I was there. He gave me a big hug as we were leaving. He never does that anymore. I think I was so caught up in my fears that I wasn't seeing him. I'd look at him and just see my own anxieties reflected."

If you find you're getting caught in your own needs and worries and losing sight of your child, try this reflection. If you like, grab some paper and pencil (or your phone) and write down what comes up for you.

Reflection: Seeing Your Child Clearly

- *What makes him come alive?*
- *What does she love to talk about? (Even if you usually tune out.)*
- *Where is she most creative?*
- *What does he like to play with?*
- *What are her passions?*
- *What do others appreciate in your child?*
- *Reflect on what your child loves to do. Make a list:*
    Building
    Drawing
    Cooking
    Art
    Sports
    Dancing
    Experimenting
    Being in nature
    Writing
    Organizing
    Being with other children
    Dreaming
- *How can you help your child express his or her gifts?*

"Anton, I'm curious. Do you ever play together, do things that are fun together?" I asked.

His eyes narrowed. "Sometimes we play soccer together. It's important for him to be agile and athletic."

"Anything else? Just spending time together hanging out?"

"Sometimes, but I try to be productive," he responded. "We don't watch TV much. I don't want him to goof off."

"Before you go, can I tell you about some research on brain development?" I asked.

Play Is Not Frivolous: A Touch of Science

Some parents erroneously believe that their children shouldn't waste their precious time on aimless play as it doesn't achieve concrete goals. But it turns out to be necessary for health. Recent research shows that the absence of play contributes to depression and anxiety. Playing can help our children build more resilient brains.

All children, in all cultures, know how to play. It's not something we need to teach them. But as adults, we often don't realize its value. Psychiatrist Stuart Brown argued that play not only strengthens our social skills but enables us to find balance. During the state of play, we can begin to open up to new possibilities and creative ideas. Play fosters a more resilient brain. Some scholars believe that the opposite of play is not work but depression. Mihaly Csikszentmihalyi tried an experiment where he asked his subjects not to do anything "enjoyable" for 48 hours. After just one day, participants reported increased sluggishness and difficulty sleeping. The deterioration in mood was so pronounced that the experiment was stopped.

Marian Diamond, a professor of neuroscience, performed some classic experiments on play. She divided rats into three categories, offering them either an enriched environment, a standard environment, or an impoverished one. The enriched environment offered toys and friends. The standard was a smaller box with friends but no toys. The impoverished one had neither toys nor friends.

The findings were that the animals who had toys and friends had thicker cerebral cortexes with greater neural connections. However, the rats in the impoverished environment showed decreased cortical thickness. (The cortex is the part of the brain responsible for paying attention, awareness, and cognitive functioning.) This research was a breakthrough in showing that the environment can change the brain for the better and that play may help the brain function more efficiently, developing parts of the brain that help us learn, remember, and make optimal decisions.

Think about ways that you might play with your child. It might be going to a museum, or playing catch, engaging in an art project, or roughhousing. But it can be something as simple as taking a walk together or looking at the sky. And it doesn't need to take hours—the research shows that children can thrive with even a few minutes of one-on-one time with a parent.

And it's not just children who thrive; we do as well. But many adults have forgotten how to play or don't realize its value. The recent research on neuroplasticity in the brain shows that our brains are still growing, changing, and evolving. It turns out that for adults as well, when we are having fun the brain grows and creates new connections. These in turn become the foundation for innovation. Just as meditation can change the brain for the better, increasing memory, attention, compassion, and even our lifespan, our brains need the benefits of play. It's a win–win situation. We get to relax and destress, and our brain benefits as well.

After some back and forth, Anton and Samir created this practice. They tried it right after a snowstorm, but it can be adapted for any weather or any time of year and any environment.

Adventure Walk

- Get outside; leave the phones inside. Take a few minutes to unplug. Trust that there won't be an emergency in the next few minutes.
- Breathe in; feel the fresh air as you inhale.
- Notice the temperature. Feel it on your skin.
- Look up, notice the light in the sky. What is the weather?
- Look down; feel the ground below you.
- Listen—are birds singing?
- If there is snow, could you find animal footprints? What animals have been here?
- Notice what might be growing. What plants or flowers might you notice?
- If it's warm, try resting on the grass in a park. Watch the clouds.
- If your child is interested, look at the night sky together. See if you can identify constellations.
- Meet your child where he or she is. Young children often like to watch traffic, trucks, taxis, or trains go by.
- An older child might like to stop for a cup of hot chocolate and watch as people go by.
- Talk about what you see, what you hear.
- Have a conversation.
- Listen to your child. Talk with your child. Enjoy being with your child. Allow both of you to be enriched. Repeat as often as possible.

This is compassion and self-care for you and your child. You both get to share valuable time together and to practice "being," not just doing. Not only is this good for decreasing stress and increasing brain development, but you have enjoyed the precious moments of just playing with your child.

The Piano Recital

It was a big day for Alex and her family. When I met Alex (see Chapter 2), she was wearing an "I Can't Adult Today" T-shirt. She still had her reservations, but for the most part she was enjoying parenting and watching her children grow. It seemed, though, like there was always something. Alyce, her daughter, now ten, was about to have her first piano recital. The whole family (with the exception of Alex's brother William) came to cheer Alyce on. When Alex was growing up, most of the attention and adulation in her family had gone to William, so she was making an effort to ensure that all her children felt seen and supported.

Alyce was nervous. She hasn't been playing piano for very long, but her teacher thought she was ready to perform. "It'll be a great experience," she promised. Alyce had practiced for weeks, and things were falling into place, or so it seemed . . . but when does anything go smoothly?

"It was all looking good," Alex explained. "She had been practicing and practicing, so much that I thought I would scream if I heard another mutilated version of *Chopsticks* and *Twinkle Twinkle*. She only had three short pieces to play, and they were sounding pretty good, other than the occasional wrong note.

"But the night before the recital she was so nervous she couldn't sleep. She came into my bed for comfort, which she hasn't done for years. I tried to bolster her up. 'You'll be fine, honey,' I said. 'You'll kill it. Trust me.' Ha, famous last words. Now I feel like I pushed too much, that she was doing it for me. That I wasn't really listening to her when she said she didn't want to do it. I wanted her to shine so much . . .

"Anyway, she gets up on stage, looks around at the audience, and looks absolutely terrified. She turns white. She starts to play, makes a few minor errors, but keeps it together. She then moves on to a very simple and slow Chopin *Prelude*, the most challenging piece for her, and I don't know what happened. She started the piece, made a few mistakes, then just stopped. The teacher went over to her and they talked, and she started again. And then just froze. Again. She couldn't do it. There were hushed whispers in the audience. The teacher went over to her again, they whispered, the teacher announced a brief intermission, and escorted her off-stage. There were tears streaming down her face.

"I wanted to cry, I felt so bad for her. And my mother, being her usual empathic self, puts us both down and says, 'What happened? She couldn't take the pressure? You were like that too. You always crumbled.' So then I was doubly humiliated. And furious.

"During the intermission people come over to us, fake nice and all concerned, saying things like 'Oh, I hope Alyce is all right.' Or false consolation like 'These things happen.' Or 'It's a lot to perform in front of a crowd.' I just wanted to disappear under the floor, but I had to put on a smile and a game face.

"We sat through the rest of the recital and watched all the other kids do a great job. No one else froze. She wanted to leave, but I told her it wasn't polite. She was so ashamed that she wouldn't talk to us and refused to eat when we went out to her favorite restaurant for our celebration. She was punishing herself. 'I don't deserve to celebrate.' It was awful. Just awful. I tried to comfort her, of course.

"What's hardest for me now is that I think I pushed too hard. She never really liked to play, and getting her to practice was a daily battle. It wasn't that I wanted to make her into a concert pianist, but I thought if I persisted she would come to enjoy it. Now I feel like I was asserting my will; I was trying to control her.

"So, guess what? Now I'm the one who can't sleep. I'm beating myself up. I feel like I'm tumbling down the rabbit hole yet again." She began to cry. "It feels like something is always falling apart in my life."

We all have hopes and dreams for our children. But very often, things don't happen the way we fantasize they will. In fact, rarely do things go the way we want. And usually when they don't, our response is to try harder and to control even more. I wanted my daughter to be a ballet dancer, partly because I loved ballet but never danced beyond junior high school, as my body changed at puberty and I didn't have the genetic material to be a lithe, wispy ballerina any longer. But she absolutely *hated* ballet and hated the teacher. She refused to go. After a few weeks I stopped insisting, as it was a losing battle. She was her own person, and she wasn't going to do something just because I insisted. I let go.

Of course we need to manage so many things in our kids' lives—getting them to school, making them breakfast, lunch, dinner, making sure they do their homework, getting them to lessons, sports, playdates, and so on. But often we try so hard because we are trying to heal our wounds or thwarted desires through them.

This isn't always the case, but it is good to take a calm and understanding look at what lies underneath our relentless drive to micromanage.

Reflection: A Compassionate Look at Micromanaging

- *Start by sitting comfortably, taking a few deep breaths.*
- *Let yourself settle by listening to sounds, noticing your breath, feeling the sensations in your body.*
- *Think of a situation where you felt you were micromanaging your child.*
- *Put a hand on your heart. Be kind to yourself; be gentle.*
- *What was the situation? What did you do? What did you say?*
- *What were you feeling? What were you thinking?*
- *Jot down a few notes. What is coming up for you?*
- *See if you can get underneath the urgency that you may have experienced.*
- *What was driving you? What did you need? What was the dream? The hope? The unfulfilled desire?*
- *Are you touching on any unhealed wounds?*
- *If so, what are you remembering?*
- *Let yourself rest. Be compassionate with yourself.*

Alex and I tried this practice together. This is what she reported:

"I went back to one of my fights about piano with Alyce, and now that I look back they were daily. I had this belief that kids need to learn about music and should play an instrument. There wasn't any music in my home growing up, and I think I just wanted to give my kids something I didn't have. I wanted my kids to be cultured. To have a home where sports wasn't the only topic of conversation and the TV wasn't always blaring. But I think I pushed too hard. I'd become a little dictator about it.

"And I hadn't remembered this until my mother pointed it out, but I hated being onstage in front of people. You're going to laugh, but once during a Christmas play, I think I was eight or so, I was supposed to be one of the three Wise Men. I was so scared I forgot my lines and ran offstage crying. I didn't even remember that until my mother made that nasty comment about Alyce."

To deepen her exploration, I taught Alex the following practice.

 ## You Don't Have to Control Everything

🎧 *Audio Track 6*

- Start by tuning in to your body, giving yourself a moment or two to stop.
- Notice where you might be holding stress in your body.
- How are you feeling? Exhausted? Always on? Ready for a vacation from parenting?
- Get in touch with what you think your kids should be. Reflect on the times you insist that things should be done your way.
- When have you felt that your child was not good enough? That he or she needed to be fixed? That you wanted him or her to be different?
- See what emotions you are in touch with: Fear? Anxiety? Worry? Sadness?
- What are you noticing in your body?
- What would it be like to stop fighting this fight, to put the gloves down, even for a moment? To rest? To listen to yourself? To your child?
- Just let yourself rest. Just be. Take in the stillness.
- Bring some tenderness to this struggle.
- Try to see your behavior, and your child's, with compassion, with gentleness.
- What if, even just for a minute, you let go of micromanaging your child?
- Let things be as they are.
- Take a pause from fighting with reality.
- Stop. Rest. Breathe.
- As you return to your day, see if you can continue to see yourself, and your child, through the eyes of compassion.

"This helped me get some clarity on the next step with Alyce. She's been refusing to go back to piano lessons, doesn't want to see the teacher or the kids again—she felt so ashamed—and I didn't know what to do. The more I think about it, I'll just give it a break over the summer and not force it. I think the issue wasn't the music, but that she didn't want to have to perform in front of everyone. I get that—I didn't want to perform either. But what shifted is that I don't have to make her. I can take the pressure off and let her find her own way back."

I tried this practice with Anton as well. He was surprised to realize just how "bone tired" he was. "It was a relief to let go of fighting all the time. At first I was afraid to let go of controlling my son as I thought something awful would happen. And then you gave me permission to do it just for a moment, so that made it easier. I realize that I don't have to be a slave driver all the time—just when it's necessary," he joked. "When I saw him at the museum, I realized that he has a lot of motivation when he is interested in something. He really loves those animals and remembers all this information about them. I was just insisting that he do what I thought was necessary for him to survive. Maybe I'm learning to trust him a little more rather than force a square peg into a round hole, or whatever that saying is." Anton smiled, looking more relaxed. "And we're fighting less," he added.

The Lump

When we last saw him, Tyrone was seven and Lionel and Kyra were struggling with his Little League experience. Now in middle school, he's doing well: "He has good friends, he's happy," says his dad. "Spends too much time on his phone, like most kids. We struggle about that. I can't believe that he's thirteen. But the reason we came back is that Kyra is having health problems," he said, looking worried.

"What's happening?" I asked, concerned.

"Well, a few months ago I found a lump. I didn't think it was anything, and it was a busy time of year. I put if off for a while, then finally called my doctor," Kyra said, beginning to cry.

"They said I needed a biopsy, which is scary and painful, I hear. It's in a few days. The worry and uncertainty is getting to me. Thanks for fitting us in on such short notice.

"My mom, if you remember, had breast cancer and died when Tyrone was a toddler, so I'm really worried. I have this dread, I'm worried that I'll die too young like my mom, and Tyrone is still really young. I don't want to go through this."

"I feel I'm not able to be here for Tyrone. He knows I'm going through tests, and I can tell he's worried. I'm really emotional and distracted. I look at him sometimes over dinner and burst out crying. I've never been good at keeping my emotions under wraps."

"How does he respond?" I asked.

"Mama, why are you crying?" he'll ask and then come over and give me a hug. "Everything is going to be just fine."

"But I don't think I'm going to be fine. I watched my mama die, and I don't want him to watch me die. He's too young, and I'm too young."

"I'm with you," I said, thinking of those I'd loved who had died. "But right now we don't know what is happening; we just know that things are uncertain and scary as well. What do you need right now?"

"Well, first of all I'm scared shitless, and I feel like I shouldn't be."

"Of course you are. Who wouldn't be?"

"Really? I was thinking I was a wimp. That I should just muscle through it. That's not happening. I'm melting down, and I feel so weak."

"Where does that belief come from?" I asked.

"I feel like I have to be strong, not show any weakness."

"Kyra, it's OK to be human. It's OK to have feelings, to be scared," I said.

"Yeah, but that wasn't how I was raised. I was taught to be strong. To not show my feelings—other than anger, or course," she smiled." It's hard to do it different. I'm trying not to overreact, but I don't want to die."

"I get it," I said.

"Good," she said. "I'm wondering, is there something you can do to help me chill, to be with this? I keep having images of my ma on her death-bed. Not good." She smiled. "I bet you never expected to hear that from me. I know I gave you an earful when Tyrone was a baby, but now I really need some Zen," she laughed.

"Let me teach you some practices that will help you stay as steady as possible during the procedure and to help you be with the uncertainty. I know it seems counterintuitive, as we usually try to control how we feel, but let yourself be with whatever comes up."

We can't make things look a certain way, and we can't control the out-come, much as we want to. It's hard to find balance in life, and especially hard to find some sort of balance when we're parents. It often feels like we move from one crisis to another with barely time to recover or catch our breath.

The following practice helps us find some perspective, no matter what is happening. It's useful for difficult times. When we are knocked off bal-ance, we learn to return to center. We learn not to judge ourselves for the emotions that arise but respond to them with understanding and kindness toward the pain we feel.

An image that is often useful in developing some equanimity dur-ing the trials of life is that of a mountain. No matter what the weather, the mountain remains steady and solid. While many teachers offer some variation, this practice is designed for parents, and it can help you weather whatever storm may be happening in your life right now.

Finding a Steady Center

- Start by sitting comfortably, finding your seat, or lying down if that is easier. Take a moment to be with the breath, sounds, or the loving-kindness phrases.
- Visualize a towering mountain, either one that you have visited or one that you create in your imagination. Like all things, this mountain changes, but it changes in geological time.
- Imagine that your body can become as solid as the mountain—solid, still. Let the legs be the base, the arms and shoulders the slopes, the spine the axis, and the head the peak. Let yourself be grounded, present. No matter what is happening with your family, allow yourself to be present, not to run away.
- Visualize the mountain as seasons begin to change. (You can begin in the current season and then move through the others.) See it in fall, surrounded by warm, golden light. Gradually fall gives way to winter, and the mountain is assaulted by violent storms, high winds, blizzards, ice, maybe even an avalanche. Notice how the mountain remains quiet, steady through the storms.
- Watch as the seasons flow into each other. In spring, the snow melts, the birds begin to sing again, animals return. Wildflowers bloom. The streams overflow with melting snow.
- See the mountain in summer, bathed in light, majestic. The snow is gone, except for the highest peaks. Notice that in every season clouds can obscure the mountain; sudden storms can arise and pass away.
- See the mountain through the course of the day, beginning with the first light of day. Watch the first light of morning, then the deep golden light and shadows of afternoon. Notice as the day gives way to the rich colors of sunset, and finally the dark night, filled with stars and galaxies, endless open space across the vast horizon.
- See if you can become like the mountain, still and grounded, no matter what the weather, the time, the season, the external events. Let it all come and go, accepting change, not resisting or pushing it away.

Kyra practiced Finding a Steady Center when she became worried and anxious. To this practice I added an informal mindfulness practice that helps us stay in the moment. Kyra was finding that she was having images of being on her deathbed, which of course were disturbing. I wanted to help her stay in the present moment, even with its uncertainty and worry.

💟 Grounding in the Moment

In my office I keep a bowl of natural polished stones that can be used to help people anchor and savor the present moment. This is an informal practice that can be done at any time or in any place. While we find "worry stones," rosary beads, malas, and the like in many ancient traditions, this version is inspired by the Here-and-Now Stone in the Germer and Neff's MSC course.

- I asked Kyra to choose a stone that she liked.
- On a walk or a trip to a beach or a park, a river or lake, see if you can find a stone that appeals to you.
- Start by examining your stone. Notice the color of the stone, the way the light hits the contours of the stone.
- Let yourself enjoy the stone. Rub it. Feel it on your skin. Put it on your cheek.
- Close your eyes and feel the hardness of the stone. What is the texture? Is it rough or smooth? Warm or cool?
- Let yourself "bond" with the stone. Reflect on how old it might be. Scientists tell us that the stones we find might be several million to even a billion years old.
- Let your stone help you get some perspective on what you're experiencing.
- You might notice that when you're focused on your stone, feeling it, appreciating it, there is less room for worry about the past or future.
- Let your stone help you come into present-moment awareness.

Kyra took the stone with her and held it in her hand as she was going through her biopsy. It helped her get through the procedure.

"I realized that I was making everything worse by thinking that I was dying. I was adding all this drama, and I didn't need to. As you told me a while ago, rather than thinking, 'This is it, I'm on the way out,' I've started saying to myself, in as calm a voice as I can, 'Kyra, we don't know. One step in front of the other. One moment at a time.'

"It's like, yeah, the weather on the mountain is stormy right now, but it's gonna change. In just a little while, this will pass.

"And Tyrone always helps with the humor. He's always liked Monty Python. When I'm worried or preoccupied, or want him to help a little more, or I get a little short with him he'll say, 'Mom, you're not dead yet.' So I say to myself, 'Kyra, this sucks, but you're not dead yet. Just keep going.'

"And I have to tell you a funny story. I was on the subway on my way to work, and it stops. It's common for it to stop. But I didn't want to be late, and I got worried. I get my stone out of my purse, and I start rubbing it. The subway starts up again. The woman next to me says, 'How'd you do that? Where'd you get that stone? Is it magic? I want one too.' I got a good laugh out of that."

One of the remarkable benefits of self-compassion is that it helps us develop resilience. As we become more accepting of our flaws, of the fact that we can't control our bodies, our children, our parents, or our partners, we become more able to accept uncertainty and to relax with things as they are, not as we want them to be. We learn not to hold on so tightly and to begin to let go of our agenda for how things should be.

6 "Why Can't Everyone Just Calm Down?"

HANDLING THE INEVITABLE HOT EMOTIONS

The Birthday Dinner

Stephanie had tried so hard to make Dan's 40th birthday special. Their kids, Andrew, age seven, and Michelle, age four, designed and painted their own birthday cards. With Stephanie's guidance, they worked hard to create a book of family photos and even brought Dan breakfast in bed. It was a beautiful summer day, so Stephanie planned a picnic at their favorite state park with bikes, trikes, and games. All was going perfectly.

Dan loved French food, so Stephanie made a reservation at a fancy French restaurant in the city. The kids had never been to a fine restaurant, and she realized it was a bit of a reach, but she thought they would enjoy it. She tried to do everything right—she brought toys and books to entertain them at the table if they got bored and made an early dinner reservation so they wouldn't be too hungry or tired.

Everyone dressed up in their best clothes. The kids had never seen valet parking, waiters in tuxedos, or white linen tablecloths. When they went out, it was for fast food. When the waiter arrived to take their orders, Stephanie ordered poached salmon and wilted spinach for the kids. Andrew and Michelle protested vociferously, forgetting about their "indoor" voices. "But I want a hamburger and fries and a Coke," Andrew said loudly. "Me too," Michelle added in a whine. The other diners turned to stare.

Michelle tried to quiet them down, explaining that this was a nice restaurant for Daddy's birthday. Enjoying the attention he'd attracted, Andrew saw an opportunity for even more. He picked up his spoon and banged it on the table, as he sometimes did at home. "I want a burger, I want a burger," he chanted, thinking it was funny. Michelle, thinking this was a new game, joined in.

Stephanie, humiliated, rushed them out of the restaurant, followed by death stares from the other patrons and disgusted looks from the staff. "Madame," the host scolded, "we suggest that people hire babysitters." "Yeah, a lot of fucking good that's going to do me now," she thought.

She took the kids outside, calmed them down, and gave them snacks from her purse (she had tried so hard to think of everything). She negotiated a compromise for plain noodles. And they returned to the restaurant. They somehow made it through dinner and all sang "Happy Birthday" to Dan, with the waiters joining in. Stephanie thought she had handled a difficult situation well.

However, on the drive home, Dan was quiet and cold. Once they put the kids to bed, he wanted to talk.

"At his best," said, Stephanie, "Dan is critical and always finds fault. He'll come home from work and notice if a picture is off center. He'll find a problem before he even says hello to us. I'm home all day, so I don't see that stuff.

"He hates to be embarrassed, and he was embarrassed by the kids. Maybe he was upset about turning 40 and getting some gray hairs. But we hit a familiar fault line in the relationship. I get hurt when he criticizes my parenting, which he did full force: He thought they behaved like 'barbarians.' Why did I allow Andrew to bang on the table? Why hadn't I set better limits? Why did I think I could take them to a nice restaurant? Why didn't I hire a sitter? And he went on and on and things escalated. I had poor judgment, I was too permissive, the place was too expensive. Barely a thank-you. I had tried to make it a perfect day, and I'd worked so hard to get it all right and make him happy. I got no credit for my efforts, and I ended up in tears, feeling underappreciated and devalued." She sighed. "No good deed goes unpunished. I ended up sleeping on the sofa and crying myself to sleep. Rather than this being a wonderful celebration, we ended up on opposite sides of the parenting abyss."

We've all been there. Rarely do couples agree on everything, and there are usually significant disagreements about discipline, rules, manners, money—actually many of the details of life. But often what is the hardest is that we can't see we're on the precipice of the "parenting abyss." The day starts off perfectly, then the terrain shifts and suddenly there's a major chasm. Even with the best of intentions, the special birthday party, anniversary, or vacation can go south, and what was designed as a festive celebration can turn into a full catastrophe.

Knowing where your fault lines are as a couple can help you see more clearly and help you avoid the usual "potholes" of parenting. Try this exercise:

Reflection: Navigating the Parenting Abyss

- *Take a moment and let yourself stop. Find your breath or notice the sensations of your body.*
- *Are you feeling stressed, upset, belittled? Bring loving awareness to what you are experiencing.*
- *If you just encountered a "shipwreck," give yourself some extra kindness. Put your hand on your heart and acknowledge that this a moment (or many moments) of suffering.*
- *Pause. Do a quick scan of your body. Where are you holding tension? Can you let it soften?*
- *Reflect on the following: When do you and your partner find yourself on different continents?*
- *What issues divide you?*
- *What are the areas of the greatest disagreements?*
    Eating?
    Behavior?
    Attitude?
    Academics?
    Sports?
    Chores?
    Homework?
    Money?
    Other areas of disagreement?
- *Step back a little and look at the "top hits," the charges you level at each other.*
    Too sensitive?
    Too critical?
    You never listen?
    You can't set limits?
    Too indulgent?
    Too frugal?
    Spendthrift?
    Never set a boundary?

Not organized?

Can't cook?

Add the top hits in your relationship struggles.

- *Step back again, remembering to bring kindness to yourself. Pause. This is hard.*
- *Imagine how this will look from the distance of 40 years. This is not to minimize what you are feeling but to get some perspective. Will you be laughing at the restaurant host telling you to get a babysitter? Will this be a story you repeat to the kids or grandkids, adding a pretentious French accent? Notice how its importance diminishes with the perspective of 40 years.*
- *Are you stuck replaying the inner movie of the bad birthday dinner over and over again? Are you tired of the endless reruns? Even though the story is no longer "prime time," is it still playing?*
- *Try saying to yourself, "Honey [or use your name], you tried; you really did. But you can't control everything. In fact, you can't really control anything. Not everything works out the way you want it to."*
- *Need more to break the ruminative cycle of bashing yourself? Try this: "If it's not happening now, it's not happening."*
- *Put it in perspective: "It was just a dinner. It's over."*
- *Soothe yourself; no need to let it get bigger than it needs to be. See if you can let it recede into the past.*
- *Take another few moments, breathing out, letting it go.*
- *When you are ready, return to your day.*

"This was very helpful," Stephanie said. "The problem is that we are mismatched in temperaments. He's very critical; I'm very sensitive. He's good at finding problems (not his, of course) and sees all my faults.

"Some days I wish he was nearsighted or something," she joked. "But I can feel like a failure and replay fights we had 15 years ago. And they still have the power to upset me. It's hard to forget about the harsh words. They get under my skin, and I can't forget them. When we did some couple work at the beginning of the marriage—we were fighting about everything—the couple therapist said something that was really helpful: 'Why are you going back there? Is that serving you?' Of course it wasn't. So now, when I catch myself doing endless replays of ancient fights, I just say to myself, 'Is this helping?' It makes it easier to let go. The self-compassion helps me feel it's OK to do things that are helping." She paused. "And when your partner isn't interested in working on himself, this is a necessity."

Not only is self-compassion a necessity when there is tension in a marriage; it is a life saver when our kids lash out at us (and when we lash out at them).

"You Look Like a Slut"

Amy and Sophie, Part III: When Sophie was eight (Chapter 3), Amy was concerned about Sophie's body image. Now, six years later, she's concerned about the image Sophie is projecting with what she puts *on* her body. Sophie is now in ninth grade, just starting high school. Like most kids, she wants to be popular and cool. She's trying hard to fit in and look like all the other kids. She had just been invited to her first party, and Amy and Sophie clashed over the clothes she wanted to wear.

"She comes out in a very low-cut top, much too tight around her boobs, and skintight jeans so torn they looked like something you would throw out—they were ripped that much and showed so much of her thighs it was obscene. She bought them with her babysitting money, and she never showed them to me, of course. I think she was saving them for the party. And then she added a pair of crazy high heels that were just awful. And so much makeup! She looked like a whore. I know I shouldn't say that, but she did."

When Amy saw Sophie's outfit, she "lost it."

"I couldn't help myself. I just blurted out, 'You aren't going out like that. You look like a slut. Put on something else.'" She didn't want to change, so things got heated. Of course, Tom was away, so I didn't have anyone to back me up."

"'But everyone wears clothes like this and makeup,'" she countered.

"'I don't care. You aren't everyone. Go change, now.'

"After more fighting, she put on another top and changed the shoes. She didn't want to miss the party. She was going with a friend, the mother was driving them, and they were waiting outside. On the way out the door she made a horrid face and yelled, 'Sometimes I wish you weren't my mother. I wish I had a better mother. I HATE you!'

"And I feel ashamed for what I said, but I just blew. 'Sometimes I wish I had a better daughter!' I know I shouldn't have said that. I regret that. But I was sick and tired of her shit.

"I cried a lot, I felt so angry. She had never told me she hated me before. I had some time to practice some self-compassion while I was waiting for her to come home, and I was a little less furious. But she was still pissed at me. When she got home, I said, 'I'm sorry I called you a name, that wasn't right, but you can't talk to me like that, and you can't behave like this.'

"Rather than accept my apology and take some responsibility for what she said, she lashed out. 'You are such a loser,' she yelled. 'You're just jealous because no one invited you to parties when you were in high school.' And she turned and stomped off to bed.

"We haven't spoken since, and it's coming up on three days. I didn't deserve that. I felt so disrespected. She's talking to Tom, but not to me." Amy began to cry.

"And she knows how to hurt me. I wasn't popular, and I often felt like a loser. She just went for the jugular. And the timing is terrible. Here I am, menopausal, fat and ugly, having hormonal mood swings, while her hormones are swinging in the other direction. I'm a mess. I think I need more self-compassion stuff. But she needs to be nicer to me. That really hurt. She can't treat me like a doormat. Otherwise adolescence is going to be hell."

Adolescence is challenging for almost every parent, and all of our buttons get pushed. But *if you lose it, you can use it*. That is, you can tune in to what's going on for you—see what your needs are and what is getting stirred up—and then work with your child from a less reactive place.

It's always wise to start with compassion. The following practice of sending compassion to yourself and another person is one of the core practices in the Mindful Self-Compassion (MSC) program. It is an ancient practice that dates back to an Indian teacher who taught in the 10th century. The American teacher Pema Chodron has popularized this meditation. I've adapted it for parents who need it in the heat of the moment. In fact, I can't think of a more useful practice for the storms of adolescence (theirs and ours). This practice builds on the breathing practices and the loving-kindness meditations in earlier chapters of this book.

When You Both Really Need Compassion

- Sit comfortably, close your eyes if you like, and put a hand (or two hands) over your heart or wherever you need some soothing touch. Feel the warmth and comfort of your hands as a loving reminder that you can bring awareness and compassion to yourself and this experience.
- Take a few deep breaths, letting yourself be held and rocked by the breath. Let it nourish you, hold you. Let the breath soothe you and comfort you as you inhale and exhale.

- Take a moment to find a natural rhythm of the breath. Stay with the sensation of breathing in and breathing out. If you like, imagine the breath as sustaining and nourishing you at this difficult time.
- Now focus on your inbreath, feeling the sensations of breathing in, letting your breath revitalize your body, breath after breath.
- As you breathe in, take in some nourishment for yourself—something good that you might need right now. Maybe some kindness, some compassion, some love? You can either feel this quality or use a word or an image. Take a moment and breathe it in.
- Now focus on your outbreath. Feel the sensations of breathing out, perhaps a sense of letting go, of release.
- Now call to mind your child (or whoever it is you're struggling with and needs your compassion). Visualize that person in your mind's eye.
- Begin directing your outbreath to this person, offering this sense of ease.
- If it is difficult, start with just one or two breaths.
- If you like, send some warmth and kindness—something nourishing— to this person with every exhalation.

One for Me, One for You

- Now, returning to you, just focus on the sensation of breathing compassion in and out for yourself. When you're ready, try breathing in for yourself and out for your child, saying to yourself, "In for me, out for you." "One breath for me, one breath for you."
- If you're having a really hard time, you can focus more on yourself if you need a little extra care. Of, if the other person needs more right now, it is fine to focus on his or her needs. Or, it can be an equal flow— whatever feels right in this moment.
- If there is more than one person in need, feel free to send something good to other family members or friends.
- Let your breath flow in and out, like the gentle waves of the ocean. Let the flow feel boundless, without limits, flowing in and flowing out. Let yourself be part of this vast flow. Feel this ocean of compassion.
- When you are done, gently open your eyes, feeling that you can take this compassion with you throughout the day.

This is a practice that is good to do when you experience any interpersonal conflict. Stephanie used it when she was furious with Dan, and Amy found it helped her keep a cool head in trying to repair the relationship with Sophie. After over two days of stony silence, she was able to reach out and try to talk about what happened. Sophie was defensive and insistent that Amy had acted "crazed."

"I told her how mean she was to me. We started fighting again. But then I saw how this fight could escalate and happen all over again. And again. I paused and took a breath, taking in some compassion for being the mother of an angry teen. 'I know, I got really angry. I'm sorry I blew up. But I've been thinking about what really upset me. Do you want to know?' I asked. And she did. 'I know you just want to look like the other kids, but I didn't want you to look, uh, so available. I was afraid someone would take advantage of you. I know that sounds silly, but I guess I'm an old, protective, and worried mommy.'

"For the first time in days she laughed. 'Was that it? OMG, you are so out of it! I'm not going to let anyone take advantage of me.'

Amy and Sophie were both able to laugh about it and to have a good conversation about Mom's desire to protect her daughter and Sophie's desire to be liked and accepted. Mutual apologies left them on better ground, and they even turned the incident into a private joke. Now, when Sophie needs a ride from her mother, she says "Uh, Mom, are you *available*?" and they both break out in laughter.

Amy is not alone in fighting with her daughter. And it's not just teens who have hot emotions. We all do. We all say things we regret. And knowing that you aren't alone, that most parents experience these blowups, can help when it feels like you're the most dysfunctional family on the block or the worst parent in the world. But rather than just enduring until those frontal lobes come online (and sometimes it isn't until the mid-twenties or later so it can feel like geological time), this can be an opportunity to become more mindful and compassionate.

Our children can remind us of what is missing in our lives, as well as our unresolved wounds, and this is often difficult to look at.

Roberta, for example, felt like she was in a constant battle with her son Jorge.

"It feels like we are constantly at war. We fight about everything, but it has gotten worse now that he turned 16. We fight a lot about screen time. He spends much of his time on video games, and I want him to do his homework. 'Just a few more minutes, Mom.' And the minutes turn into a half hour. He's obsessed. And when I try to set limits or insist he focus on his homework, he loses it. 'Mom, get off my back. I need a break. Stop bugging me. Just back off!' he yells, and of course I don't want to be treated that way, so I start yelling back and making threats, and it escalates. I miss my sweet little boy. But I worry that if he doesn't do his homework he won't do well in school and he won't get into a good college. Things are so competitive. And sometimes I'm so upset that I can't sleep at night."

To help Roberta get a handle on what was getting stirred up, we tried this reflection:

Reflection: Time Travel Back to Your Childhood

- *Sit comfortably; take a few breaths to let yourself settle.*
- *Think back to when you were the age your child is now. What were things like in your family? What was your experience?*
- *How did your parents treat you? Your siblings? Other family members?*
- *What were things like in school? Were there teachers who supported you?*
- *Did you have friends? What activities did you participate in? What did you do for fun?*
- *What were your dreams? Were there hopes or desires that you didn't have the words for back then?*
- *What were the wounds you experienced? The heartbreak?*
- *What were your ambitions? Who did you want to become?*
- *And what about those dreams? Did they get dismissed? Ignored? Ridiculed?*
- *Stay in touch with what you are feeling. If painful or raw feelings arise, send yourself some compassion.*

Roberta practiced this reflection at home, and what came up for her was powerful.

"I was really driven in high school. We didn't have tons of money, and I realized I had to work hard to get ahead. I tried so hard to be perfect, to never make a mistake. The way I survived was through sports. I became very disciplined. I played soccer and really applied myself. I ran every day, I lifted weights, I trained. I pushed myself so hard. I didn't take a break. I was afraid that if I slacked off I wouldn't get a scholarship to go to college, and that was my ticket out." Roberta stopped. "It's helpful, but painful, to look back.

"I think when I see Jorge slacking off and not working and playing computer games, that old anxiety and fear rises up in me. I feel it in the pit of my stomach. It's automatic, it takes me over. And if I think about it, it takes me back to being his age and all those worries about my survival.

I couldn't take a break, I couldn't relax, still can't. I think I go into a state of panic when Jorge isn't working up to his potential.

"Being able to say 'That was then, this is now' has really freed me up. It gives me a cushion from the past. I don't have to keep running."

As Roberta worked on bringing some compassion to herself, she realized that she could give herself permission to stop and do things that she loved. For example, she had been a talented artist but hadn't had the freedom to pursue art as she was so focused on achieving and being able to support herself, leave her parents, go to college, and move far, far away. She decided to enroll in a watercolor course at a local art center, which gave her enormous pleasure. As she began to nurture herself, she was able to help Jorge find a balance between the demands of school and his need to relax.

When Roberta was able to turn toward what was irritating her about Jorge's behavior, acknowledge it, and bring some awareness to her long-buried pain, the battle between them lessened. When we can take a larger and more flexible perspective and realize that we are still learning and still growing, our intense emotional response can be a trailhead that reminds us to explore our own needs, not simply react and focus on our child's achievement (or lack of it).

How Hot Emotions Impact the Body and Brain

Let's take a minute and imagine what was happening inside Amy and Roberta when they became angry with their kids. Their amygdala, the alarm center, turned on the stress response in the brain and body. Scientists call this stress response the "HPA axis" because it also involves a chain reaction between the hypothalamus, the pituitary gland, and the adrenal gland. It's like a domino effect. The amygdala sends a signal to the hypothalamus, which in turn signals the pituitary, which then signals the adrenal gland to secrete stress hormones, such as cortisol and adrenaline. The impact, however, is not a positive one. The elevated cortisol can cause a loss of essential neurons in the prefrontal cortex (our center of executive function) and the hippocampus (which controls memory). This can impede short-term memory and prevent you from exercising your best judgment. You may find that you're not making your wisest decisions when you're upset. Cortisol can also decrease serotonin and dopamine, the neurotransmitters that keep us happy. With their decrease you might be more sensitive to pain and to feeling anger. It can make you act in more aggressive ways. And the elevated cortisol may interfere with your ability to think before you speak. While the release of the stress hormones might give the body a temporary burst of energy, too much of these hormones can give us frequent headaches, decrease the function of our thyroid, slow metabolism, lower bone density, and increase our blood pressure, our heart rate, and our blood glucose level, thus increasing the likelihood of a heart attack or stroke. This has also been tied to an increase in cancers and an increase in the number of virus-infected cells.

The good news is that self-compassion can change our brain chemistry. When we tend to our painful feelings with the balm of compassion, not only do we change our emotional experience, we also change our body chemistry. The research suggests that when we criticize ourselves we trigger an increase in adrenaline, blood pressure, and cortisol. However, when we practice self-compassion we trigger an increase in the release of oxytocin, the "tend and befriend" or bonding hormone, which also increases feelings of calmness, safety, and generosity. The amygdala is soothed, and the negative chain reaction of stress begins to dissipate.

Culture Clash

I met Rachel when she enrolled in an MSC class at the hospital where I teach. She had two young children and a complicated relationship with her in-laws. They had never approved of her, and the relationship was strained, so she figured she had nothing to lose if she tried self-compassion. Maybe it would help her get through the obligatory holiday festivities without getting so upset and depressed.

Reed was from a prominent family, and she was the daughter of immigrants. They met in college. He was attracted to her intelligence, beauty, wit, and passion. She worked in public health, often traveling to war-torn countries to help refugees. Her in-laws assumed that she would quit her job when she had children and invest her energy in causes closer to home. But she loved her work, found that it gave her life meaning, and returned to travel once the children were old enough.

The in-laws did not approve, and this became a bone of contention at every family gathering. "Are you still going to Africa?" the father-in-law would ask. "Don't you think that is dangerous? And what will happen if you bring back some disease and give it to the family? Don't you think you should reconsider? I think it is irresponsible."

Rachel didn't suffer fools gladly, and if she wanted something, you didn't get in her way or tell her what to do, Reed had learned in the years they'd been together. At almost every family event there was an argument, and often tears and harsh words. Rachel would not back down, nor would Reed's parents. It got to the point where Rachel dreaded Christmas, but the kids loved seeing their grandparents and cousins. She felt she had to go but always resented it. The whole dynamic had become increasingly stressful, and Rachel started having migraines before the visits. Her internist suggested a mindfulness course.

The following practice is the one that was most effective for Rachel, and she renamed it Secret Superpower for Angst (SSA), since her son was into superheroes and often talked about superpowers—she wanted some too! (In the MSC course it is called soften–soothe–allow.)

 ### Secret Superpower for Angst (SSA)

- Find a comfortable position and take three relaxing breaths.
- Put your hands on your heart or use your favorite position of soothing touch. Remind yourself that no matter what is happening you are worthy of kindness.
- Focus on what is happening now that is causing you distress.
- See the situation. What happened? What was said? Who was there?
- Notice if any emotions arise. Can you label the emotion, give it a name? For example, you might be experiencing:
  Sadness
  Anger
  Grief
  Fear
  Despair
  Anguish
  Frustration
- You may find you are noticing a number of emotions. Pick the one that is strongest.
- Repeat the name of the emotion in a kind, warm, and understanding tone, as if you were validating for a good friend what he or she was feeling. "Yes, that is anger." "That's anguish."

Noticing Emotion in the Body

- Bring your awareness to your entire body.
- Think of the difficult situation again and bring your attention to your body, scanning to see where you feel it most strongly. In your mind's eye, sweep your body from head to toes, pausing when you feel discomfort or tension.

- Feel what you are able to feel.
- If you can, pick a location in your body where the feeling is the strongest—it may be a raw, achy feeling, a heartache, or muscle tension. If nothing stands out, zero in on where you simply notice discomfort.
- Bring some warm, kind understanding to that place.

Soften–Soothe–Allow

- Now **soften** into that place in your body. Let the muscles relax, as if they were in warm water or a whirlpool. *Soften . . . Soften . . . Soften . . .* We can't control the feeling or make it change or go away—we're holding it in a kind and tender way.
- If this is too much, try softening around the edges.
- Now **soothe** yourself because this is a difficult time.
- If you like, return to the soothing and supportive touch that works for you. Treat your body with tenderness, the way you would treat a young child. *Soothe . . . soothe . . . soothe.*
- Are there words you need to hear? Were there phrases in the loving-kindness practice that touched you? What would a dear friend say?
- See if you can offer yourself this message: "I care deeply about you." "It is hard to be going through this." "May I be kind to myself."
- If it begins to get too intense, just return to the breath.
- Finally, **allow** the discomfort to be there. Make room for it; don't resist it or try to make it go away.
- Let things be as they are, just like this. Don't insist on changing the moment or the events, even if they are difficult or painful.
- *Soften . . . Soothe . . . Allow.*
- Let go of the practice and focus on your body. Allow yourself to feel what you are feeling and be exactly as you are in this moment.
- You can remind yourself to soften, soothe, and allow whenever you need to during the day. This is a practice you can do when walking, picking up the kids, or cooking dinner. No need to close your eyes.

What Rachel realized, as she did the practice, was that she was constantly in fight mode with Reed's family. She was angry and defensive, and she was determined not to let them boss her around. The amount of tension in her body surprised her—no wonder she was getting migraines. When she worked with allowing the difficult feelings to be present, she understood something that she hadn't realized before. Just as she wanted her children to be safe and secure, they wanted their grandchildren to be healthy, safe, and secure. Things began to shift, and she could understand their perspective. She wasn't going to change her career, but she could be a little more understanding of their fears. From all they heard on the news, Rwanda was a violent and scary place—of course they didn't understand what she was doing, the beauty of the land and the people. It wasn't that Christmas became a holiday that she suddenly enjoyed, but at least every visit wasn't a major battle.

SSA is one of the core practices of MSC. Like Rachel, I think of this as a "secret superpower" you can have with you at all times. The parents I work with smile when I teach them this "superpower to go." Richard, one dad I worked with, quipped that it was his new "constant companion. I don't leave home without it." He found that he drew on it during the frustrating events of the day: the rush-hour delays, the difficult coworkers, the disappointment of a deal not coming through. He also found it helpful when the kids got upset. "The other day Kelsey was devastated. She's only 10 but has decided that her life goal is to star in a Broadway show. She tried out for the lead in the school musical. She was singing, tap-dancing, and practicing her lines for weeks. And she didn't get the part. She was devastated. And at 10 you think it's the end of the world." He made a dramatic gesture with his hand on his forehead. "And when I told her there would be many plays and many parts, she sighed and said, with a world-weary voice, 'Dad, you don't understand.' So what am I going to do? Tell her about all the disappointments that I've faced? She didn't want to hear that. So I held her while she wept and practiced with my superpower because there was nothing I could do for her at the moment that would make it better." He smiled. "And it made me feel less helpless."

It is also an effective tool for managing shame, which all parents and kids experience. And what parent, at one time or another, hasn't been ashamed of his or her child? And what child hasn't been embarrassed by his or her parents?

Shame is an intense and difficult emotion and usually very difficult to work with because it makes us feel flawed and defective. It is deeply rooted in our brains and can be experienced as early as 15 months. Shame can often cause people to isolate and withdraw, fearing rejection. It is tied to our sense of who we are. Self-compassion can help us move away from shame and self-criticism by helping us realize that we all have strengths and weaknesses, we are all vulnerable and imperfect.

"I Can't Believe He Did This!"

Chen's son, Sam, who's in middle school, took a photo of his friend Jessica with a huge smile and open mouth showing a full set of braces. He posted it on social media with the caption "For a good time, call . . . " Of course it spread like wildfire, and of course Jessica was humiliated. So was Chen when the principal called to say that Sam was being suspended for "inappropriate behavior" and to warn her that he would be expelled if it happened again.

"I'm sure he thought it was an innocent joke," she said, "but it was very poor judgment. I felt so ashamed of him. I had to leave work and go to the school to get him."

Self-Compassion: An Antidote for Shame

Shame is a universal emotion, and it is often most intense in adolescence. Fortunately, self-compassion is an antidote to this difficult emotion. Let's spend a few moments deconstructing shame. It is, in fact, an innocent emotion. It stems from the desire to love, to be loved, to be accepted, and to belong. We are all seeking approval, especially teenagers. And we need each other to survive. Shame is the deep, dark feeling that we are too flawed to be accepted and loved by others. When we feel isolated or rejected, we tend to panic and become anxious. Shame can be more intense if you grew up with critical parents, if there is a history of childhood trauma or neglect, or if you were marginalized because of race, religion, ethnicity, or gender. Shame can also be intergenerational, going back to the suffering or behavior of earlier generations. The psychologist and compassion researcher Paul Gilbert notes the multiplicity and complexity of causes but emphasizes that shame is not our fault. However, it is our responsibility to tend to it.

There is often confusion about the difference between shame and guilt. Shame is feeling bad about who we are; guilt is feeling bad about something we did. Shame goes beyond making a mistake; it is feeling that we *are* a mistake. Shame can often be at the root of other emotions such as anger, despair, and worry. We often find it when we look deeply into the roots of depression, anxiety, and interpersonal conflict.

When we or our children experience an attack of shame, feeling defective, unlovable, inadequate, or like a failure, what can we do? While mindfulness can help with difficult experiences, self-compassion moves directly to the *experiencer*—the sense that one's very self is under attack. Seeing the entire picture can help reduce the pain. We all have strengths and weaknesses, situations where we excel and others where we struggle. A saying that can help is "I'm not perfect, but some parts of me are excellent."

When we can embrace all of our complexity in warm, openhearted awareness, it helps us put challenging experiences in perspective. It can get us out of the "rabbit hole" of despair where we imagine that we are inadequate parents, we will always be defective, and our children will be defective as well.

The following variation on the Soften–Soothe–Allow component of the SSA practice helped Chen and her family take responsibility, repair the damage, and move ahead in constructive ways. (This practice is also adapted from the MSC course.)

Note: This can be a challenging exercise. If you have a history of trauma or neglect, it is wise to do this practice with a trained professional who can help you process difficult emotions if they arise. You can also try this exercise using an experience with an event that brought up mild embarrassment, such as overreacting to something, or saying something that your children (or partner) deemed stupid.

Soften–Soothe–Allow for Shame

- Start by sitting comfortably and taking a few deep breaths. If during the exercise you begin to feel upset, feel free to stop, return to the breath, or take care of yourself in another way.
- Put your hand on your heart, reminding yourself that you are here and letting some kindness flow from your hand to your body.
- Pick an event that stirs up some shame that you can feel in your body. Start with something that is about a 3 on an intensity scale from 1 to 10.
- Choose something that you don't want people to know about, or hear about, because if they knew they might think less of you.
- Start with a situation where you feel bad about yourself. Gently feel your way into the incident.

Labeling Core Beliefs

- Reflect for a moment to see if you can determine what it is that you are afraid others might realize about you. Try to give it a name. It might be "I'm flawed" or "I'm not a good parent" or "I'm a fake."

- If you find a few negative beliefs (and we often do), pick one of the strongest.
- If you are feeling isolated, know that you aren't alone in having this belief. We all experience shame; it is universal.
- Name the core belief with some warmth and kindness. For example, "Oh, you're feeling not good enough. Wow, that is painful." Or simply say, "Not good enough. Ah, I'm feeling not good enough."
- Remember that what you are feeling and thinking is a belief, not a fact. And that it rises out of the wish to be loved and accepted.
- If you need to pause, take a breath, and open your eyes, please do so.

Noticing Shame in the Body

- Now bring your awareness to your body as a whole.
- Recall the situation again and scan your body for where you feel shame. Sweep your body from head to toe, stopping where you feel discomfort.
- Now choose a location in your body where you feel the shame most strongly.
- Bring some kindness and gentle attention to that place in your body.

Soften–Soothe–Allow

- Now, in your mind's eye, incline toward that place in your body.
- **Soften** into that area. Let the muscles relax, as if in warm water. *Soften . . . Soften . . . Soften . . .* We're not trying to change anything or make the experience go away. We're just holding it in a tender and loving way.
- Now **soothe** yourself because of this challenging situation.
- If you wish, place your hand over the place in your body that holds the shame most strongly. Imagine warmth and kindness flowing from your hand into your body. *Soothing . . . soothing . . . soothing.*
- Are there some comforting words you might need to hear? Imagine that you have a friend who was struggling in the same way. What would you say, heart to heart? ("I care deeply about you. This is really difficult. I'm here for you.") What would you want your friend to know?
- Now try offering yourself the same message. Let the words and the feeling in as much as possible.
- Allow yourself to be just as you are, just like this, just for now.

Putting Compassion into Action

"The exercise helped me do things differently," Chen reported, "and be more constructive than I would have been otherwise. At first I wanted to ground him for the rest of his life, or at least disown him," she smiled. I was starting to focus on what a bad parent I was. When Jian got home, we sat down and talked. His first reaction was that this was a lot of fuss about nothing. He thought the principal had overreacted and that Sam was just being an adolescent boy. He was ready just to dismiss it as a lot of fuss about nothing. We disagreed, as I wasn't going to let him off the hook. He was clueless, he obviously wasn't thinking, and yes, it was a hard lesson, but it could have been so much harder.

"But doing the exercise got me in touch with a time when I got shamed around my sexuality in college. I had my first boyfriend, and it was the first time I was sexual. I was living in a dorm, and the walls were very thin, so you could hear things. One night when I was alone and doing my homework, I heard the guys in the room next door talking about me, making fun of me and laughing at me. I was so ashamed, and I've carried that humiliation with me for years. It made me wonder what Jessica must be feeling. So I called up her mom, we all went over, and I brought her flowers. Sam apologized, and they held him accountable. They were tough on him. It was uncomfortable, but he understood their feelings and he was genuinely sorry. He realized how much he had hurt her and embarrassed her, which he hadn't intended. I was pleased he could take responsibility and ask for forgiveness. They seem to have worked it out."

Our kids do all sorts of things that shock and embarrass us. Rod's family was going through the security line at the airport on the way to visit family when TSA found weed hidden in his jar of peanut butter. Rod thought the X-ray machine wouldn't pick it up. He was wrong. The security official pulled Ed, the father, aside and explained the situation. The police were called, and the family not only missed their flight but had a legal mess on their hands.

Sandra's daughter Katy was at the mall with a friend when a store clerk caught them shoplifting. It was their first offense, but the police were called and gave them a stern lecture. They were lucky. The store owner decided not to press charges but talked to the girls about what happened to him when people stole his merchandise. The owner suggested that the girls engage in community service as an alternative to having this misdemeanor be on file.

Both Ed and Sandra were wracked with shame and felt they had failed to impart basic values to their kids and had screwed up in their responsibility as parents. Rather than ignore it, both parents, after reflecting on their situation, became proactive. Katy was showing other worrisome behavior, and Sandra used the opportunity to get her some psychological counseling. Ed hadn't realized his son was experimenting with drugs until the incident with the TSA. They talked about it and agreed some drug education and counseling were needed. While both Ed and Sandra initially wanted to deny the problem, self-compassion helped them accept that it was an important issue and they needed to address it. Looking back, both saw it as a painful but important wake-up call.

"The House Looks Like a Pigpen"

A messy house doesn't bother some parents. Others have learned to let this battle go. Pedro couldn't stand it. Pedro came to a workshop on Mindfulness and Self-Compassion for Parents. His question was about how to get his kids to keep their rooms clean. Other parents shared similar concerns.

"I have three kids, and my house is a mess all the time. I know they say that cleaning up after kids is like shoveling before a blizzard is over, but this is too much. My daughter leaves her clothes all over her bedroom floor, my son does his homework on the living room couch, books and papers everywhere, my little one has Legos in every corner of the room, and I'm always stepping on them. It puts me in a foul mood when I come home from work. Plus, there's sports equipment everywhere—ice skates, baseball gloves, cleats, sweatpants, smelly sneakers, you name it. And it's a safety hazard! My wife says I'm a control freak and should try to ignore it, but I often end up blowing up at everyone when I reenter the chaos at the end of a hard day or hide out fuming (my wife calls it sulking). How do I let this go?"

Pedro found that practicing Soften–Soothe–Allow helped him relax and not get so agitated. "I guess I'm just a neat freak. It makes me really nervous when things aren't in order. My wife sees it as part of the territory of having a bunch of kids. The stuff makes her feel like she has a full life. It makes me feel like there's no air to breathe."

Using a sense of humor, the family worked together to create a home environment that wouldn't end up on *America's Most Embarrassing Videos*. They all made sure the house wasn't an accident waiting to happen.

I introduced the following reflection to help Pedro manage his anger and become less reactive.

Reflection: Don't Be Pulled into Their Chaos—Pull Them into Your Calm

- When you notice yourself feeling the sensations of anger in your body, give yourself a "time-in." If possible, take a break and go to a quiet spot in the house that is soothing. Sometimes the bathroom may be the only quiet place you can find.
- Set the intention to get a handle on your anger, resentment, and sense of injustice toward your child(ren).
- It may feel justified. However, if you keep replaying it, or getting behind it, feeding the hot emotions, it won't help you resolve the issue.
- This is not to say that you should silence yourself or be passive. This doesn't mean you can't set boundaries or establish reasonable limits.
- Your aim is to establish as clear a mind and as loving a heart as possible. If you aren't reacting from a place of anger, your words and behavior will be more effective.
- Start by bringing things into perspective. Look for things you admire in your child(ren). What makes you happy? What gives you pleasure? You may not feel it in the moment, but think back to what your child is doing that is positive.
- Reflect on the neurological turbulence in your child's brain. Neuropsychologists tell us the child's brain is largely chaotic and even "under construction." Allow yourself some space from the fallout. You may say to yourself, "I'm here; he's over there." Take a breath, feel the space.
- Don't take it personally. Yes, something your children did or said was nasty. But often they are just spouting off and don't mean what comes out of their mouths.
- Bring self-compassion to this moment. Yes, it wasn't right, it wasn't fair. Yes, the house is a mess and you don't like it. Put a hand on your heart. Try some soothing touch. Give yourself a hug to feel more grounded. Let yourself receive this compassion.
- See if you can meet an outburst (or argument) with kindness. Think back to when your child had tantrums. This isn't that different. Try to stay loving. See if you can stay calm and centered even if your child has dissed you.
- Speak your truth as skillfully as you can. Perhaps you are trying to protect your child from driving drunk, from predators,

from other dangers. Tell her that without getting pulled into a debate.

- Remember, this will pass. Whatever it is you are struggling with, it will change. If your child is a teenager, remember that adolescence doesn't last forever. Ninth grade (or whatever grade it is) doesn't last forever. Try to be generous with your patience.
- Think back to how you would have liked to be treated as a child, tween, or teen. The more you cultivate a foundation of compassion, of empathy, listening, kindness, and calm, the more you nourish these qualities, the more you will have a safe harbor from the storms of parenting.

"She Started It! No, He Did!": Declaring a Truce in Sibling Warfare

Janice was sick and tired of her kids' fighting. "I'm embarrassed to take my kids anywhere. One is a teen, the other a preteen, and the third is in elementary school, and they are constantly at each other, like dogs and cats! Sometimes I feel like I'm the Parenting Police."

Juan's kids were ages eight and five, and they were constantly picking on each other. He joked that the only time there was peace in the family was when the kids were asleep or eating. "And I like it quiet. I don't like constant noise. Will this go on for another decade? I'll be totally gray by then," he joked.

"My kids," says Marguerite, "try to pull me in when they fight: 'He started it. No, she did.' 'Mommy, you always take her side. You like him better.' I'm exhausted."

It Takes Only a Few Minutes

As a mindfulness teacher, I have found myself inspired by the Three-Minute Breathing Space practice from mindfulness-based cognitive therapy (MBCT), a treatment program developed by Zindel Segal, Mark Williams, and John Teasdale. They consider this practice to be the single most important practice in MBCT.

The Three-Minute Compassion Space that follows draws on the structure of the Three-Minute Breathing Space but explicitly adds warmth and compassion. We start by becoming aware of thoughts, feelings, and emotions, anchoring with an appreciation of the breath, and then expanding the field of awareness with an adaptation of the MSC practice of Giving and Receiving Compassion.

Three-Minute Compassion Space

🎧 Audio Track 7

- Start by sitting comfortably, adopting a dignified posture. If it is comfortable, close your eyes.

Noticing with Compassionate Awareness

- Ask yourself, what are you experiencing right now?
- Take a moment to notice the thoughts that are going through your mind. Greet them with kindness.
- What feelings are present? Turn toward any emotional discomfort, responding with compassionate attention.
- What body sensations do you notice? Do a quick body scan to pick up sensations of tightness, holding, bracing, pain. Greet these as well.

Anchoring

- If it is comfortable, bring your attention to the sensations of the breath. Welcome each breath with affection.
- Your breath has been with you since birth. It is your constant companion, always with you, sustaining you.
- Greet each inhalation and exhalation as you would a dear friend or a beloved child. Let yourself be breathed, held by the breath.

Opening to Compassion

- Expand your awareness so it includes your body as a whole. Notice any tension, tightness, resistance. Greet whatever arises with kind attention.
- If you become aware of harshness, criticism, confusion, disparagement, anger, sadness, or despair, notice the parts of the body where they are broadcasting from. No need to fix them or chase them away. Simply notice without judgment.
- If possible, try to breathe in compassion for any pain, discomfort, or suffering and breathe out compassion for any pain, discomfort, or suffering of any kind.
- Try this for a few breaths. Breathing compassion in, breathing compassion out.

Return to the Three-Minute Compassion Space whenever you need it during the day. Most people can find three minutes, and this easy "Compassion on the Go" practice fits into most people's day. I've found that it's helpful to parents tearing their hair out over sibling bickering, to parents providing love and care to kids who need extra help, and to the many single parents out there, who just have a lot to do on their own. What about you? When could you use this quick practice?

Learning to Listen with Compassion

It's hard to truly stop and listen to another. Often we want to jump in and fix things or just want to express our opinion about something, or we need to be right, or to let another know just how smart we are. We see these dynamics in constant interplay between parents and children and between siblings. We see these dynamics in constant play in politics. But learning to listen with kindness and understanding is an important skill to have in all relationships, and it can make a huge difference in family dynamics. It turns out that the more distrust there is, the less we listen.

I learned a deep lesson in listening many years ago when I was in training to learn internal family systems therapy. We all did a practice where for three minutes we would listen to a colleague speak without interrupting or saying anything. For a group of therapists this was a challenging and paradoxical practice as we believed that we needed to speak up and contribute our wisdom to help others. Yet the feedback we received was that simply listening and being fully present was more healing than our advice—so humbling and so important.

The following practice can be done together as a family.

 Listening with Compassion

- Start by sitting comfortably, eyes either slightly open or gently closed.
- Listen to the sounds around you. Notice the sounds of the traffic, the rain, the wind, the birds.
- Don't worry about naming the sounds, holding on to them, or pushing them away.
- Imagine that your body is a huge ear, listening to 360 degrees of sound. Listen with your heart. Listen with your entire being.
- Think for a moment—who do you know who is a good listener?

- What qualities do you sense as this person listens to you: Respect? Openness? Lack of judgment? Not interrupting you?
- What keeps you from listening to others?
- Do you feel you don't have time? Are you listening to reply, not to understand?
- As you listen to another, notice what is happening inside you. See if you can set an intention to open to another.
- Try listening from your heart, not just your head.
- What is it like not to argue? Not to interrupt?

The Zen master Thich Nhat Hanh says that compassionate listening can relieve the suffering of another. What is it like to deeply listen to those in your family?

Anisa was curious to try out this practice with her family. Diego, her husband, wasn't a great listener. When she or the kids were speaking, he would often interrupt or abruptly change the subject. She didn't like it but figured it was something she had to live with. She never realized that there was anything she could do. She would mention it from time to time, as would the kids, but he would just get defensive and feel criticized. He was not reflective and didn't want feedback on his behavior.

But because Anisa seemed happier while she was taking a class on MSC, her family was interested in what she was learning. And Anisa could be wily. "Hey guys, I learned this cool new game in class. Want to try it out? Everyone gets two minutes." They listened to each other talk and then shared their experience. What Diego had to say helped them see him in a different light. "I always feel under so much pressure, I feel there isn't time to listen or that it's wasting my time. But it felt relaxing to slow down and not feel so tense or so rushed. And I realized that I think I know what others are going to say, but I really don't," he admitted sheepishly. See what happens in your family if you slow down enough to really listen with an open heart.

Mindfulness in Daily Life

Here are some practices you can use in the midst of your routine.

 Calming the Hot Emotions of Life

The other day I was waiting in line at the grocery store. I chose the line that was the shortest because I was in a hurry to get to a meeting. But in my rush I didn't read carefully. There was a sign that said "Cashier in Training." Oops. Too late to change lines. I found my agitation building and started heaving an annoyed sigh. Yup, it was rude. And then I caught myself criticizing myself for being rude. "A lot of good that is going to do," I thought.

I tried a little breathing, felt the soles of my feet, and then gave myself a little compassion. And as I slowed down, I realized that I was making this into a big deal when it wasn't. There was nothing inherently wrong with standing in line. Nothing horrible was happening. In reality it would probably take me another five minutes or so. Not the end of the world. I didn't have to take this personally. The world was not conspiring against me to make me later for my meeting. I thought about the young cashier and how hard she was trying to learn all the codes for all the items. Turned out it was her first day. Of course she was having a hard time and was slow. My irritation wasn't helping speed things up. I found that when I made an effort I could respond to her with kindness and support rather than annoyance. There wasn't really a problem here. I was making it into a problem.

I thought of a Zen story one of my teachers likes to tell. A student asked a Zen master, "How can I avoid hot and cold?" The master says, "Why don't you go to the place where there is no heat or cold?"

"But there is no place where there is no heat or cold," the student says. The teacher laughs and laughs because in life we can't avoid either hot or cold.

He smiles and says, "Don't make hot! Don't make cold!"

Try this the next time you find yourself fuming in line at the store, getting hot under the collar in rush-hour traffic, or getting angry waiting for a kid who is running late, or the next time you're fighting with your child, your temper is rising, and you're tempted to say something really mean.

Or the next time you "ice" your partner or your child. Look at the story your mind is making up. Let yourself pause. Is this helping? There are so many ways we can make hot and cold.

 Mindfulness and Compassion Cocktail to Get through the Day

This is a nonalcoholic "cocktail" that is designed to help you stay sane through a stressful day. It is a good way to help you get through the day when things are tough—if you and your partner aren't getting along, if you and your child are fighting, if you or your kids are battling health issues, if one (or more) of your parents or in-laws is struggling with declining cognitive function, or if you need a little extra help during the storms of the terrible twos, elementary school, middle school, adolescence, college applications, or whatever is stressing you out. Come to think of it, is there any time when parenting isn't stressful?

Spend three to five minutes on each practice.

- A.M.—Before the kids wake up. Start the day with Tending to Yourself. (Chapter 1)
- Practice Drinking Coffee Meditation while making and serving breakfast. (Chapter 1)
- If you are driving the kids to school, and they begin to fight, try Self-Compassion Life Saver for Parents. (Chapter 2)
- Feeling shaky? Has it been a rough day so far? Try Ego Glue for Parents. (Chapter 3)
- During lunch break, try to get outside to get some fresh air and exercise. Try Adventure Walk (Chapter 5). Don't have time? Three-Minute Compassion Space helps in virtually no time. (Chapter 6)
- If you pick up the kids and they start to bicker, engage them in Mindfulness and Compassion in the Car. (Chapter 2)
- Homework? Playdates? Driving kids to assorted activities? Soles of the Feet is a good practice when you're driving. (Chapter 3)
- Quick run to the grocery store to pick up a needed ingredient for dinner? Uh-oh, a tantrum coming? Try Soothing Touch in the Heat of the Moment. (Chapter 3)
- Another fight during dinner? While cleaning up? Try When You Both Really Need Compassion. (Chapter 6)
- Bedtime or bath-time struggles? Try Seeing with Kind Eyes. (Chapter 1)
- Before bed, do Rewiring with Loving-Kindness Meditation for yourself. (Chapter 4)
- Can't sleep or waking up in a panic at 2:00 A.M.? You aren't alone. Try Tree of Compassionate Beings. (Chapter 8)
- Repeat as often as needed and continue when they leave for college or get a job, get married or have their own children. This is a lifelong practice. And it is never too late to start.

7 "It's All Too Much"

TAPPING THE POWER
OF COMPASSION WHEN TIMES
ARE PARTICULARLY TOUGH

The journey of parenting rarely takes place along a smooth road with magnificent scenic views. Our experience of joy and delight in our children is often tangled with obstacles and challenges. Trying to juggle kids, work, home, and family obligations is a lot for anyone, and we can feel pulled in many different directions. When we can't keep everything together and things don't go the way we want them to, we usually blame ourselves. But it doesn't mean that we're not good enough or smart enough or lucky enough or that we screwed up. Look around. Do you know any family that doesn't have challenges? That isn't struggling in some way? That hasn't experienced some hardship, death, or tragedy? The fantasy that the road should be smooth and gentle is a sure formula for suffering. There is an African saying that puts it succinctly: "Smooth seas do not create skillful sailors." And uncomplicated times do not create wise or skillful parents. It can be easier to endure difficult times and keep our suffering in perspective if we find some unexamined benefit, some silver lining within the hardship. Poet Jane Hirschfield puts it eloquently: "Suffering leads us to beauty the way thirst leads us to water."

When I think about my life, there was a period when nothing was going smoothly. It was one thing after another—my father lost his job, my grandfather developed terminal cancer, my aunt committed suicide, I had a difficult pregnancy with health scares, then an ill child, and then my father died suddenly and unexpectedly. I was reeling, and my family was stretched thin just trying to support each other and get through the day. As I look back, I realize that this difficult time helped me open my heart to how painful and tragic our lives can be and what little control we have over our circumstances. And it helped me increase my compassion and develop gratitude for the times when there is smooth sailing.

One meditation teacher encourages students to allow themselves to be a "compassionate mess" at these difficult times. But so many of us feel the need to keep it together (or at least look like we do) or have a "stiff upper lip" during trying times. Many families, including my family of origin and the family I married into, don't talk about difficult times at all (and the stiff upper lip easily turns into a stiff drink). Not everyone has an interest in processing thoughts and feelings, and some folks feel overwhelmed if they try—it can feel like opening a Pandora's box of years of accumulated pain. When things are really hard, we often don't know what to do. So we retreat or distract ourselves with our smartphones, our work, drink, food, shopping, exercise. And not wanting to impose on others, or thinking that others don't want to be burdened by our troubles, we try hard to keep up a front that everything is just fine, pretending that we have it all together. I think about Carol, one of my closest friends, who is a very private person. She suffered silently in a tortured marriage for many years, telling only her therapist. When she finally decided to divorce, most of her friends and acquaintances were shocked—on the outside things looked so good.

Talking about difficult times is no guarantee of relief either. Juanita hit a point in her life where she experienced the "full catastrophe." Her mother had a stroke, her father-in-law was struggling with cancer, and her youngest child was diagnosed with autism. It seemed that everyone needed special care. They were spread so thin no one had any reserves—either financial or emotional. "In my family we talk and talk and talk, spending hours on the phone, but it doesn't help. We end up ruminating and worrying and then no one gets any sleep. We've tried to analyze our way out of the problems, but I think they are just too big to fix with talk." She had assumed that analyzing her emotions was a good thing to do and this would help minimize their destructive impact. But after she began to practice mindfulness, she realized this wasn't the case. "I was thinking all this intellectualizing was helping, that I was being rational, and then I realized it was actually making me more upset."

It can come as a surprise to notice that trying to think our way out of problems can make them worse. Often we end up excavating past hurts or creating new worries, becoming preoccupied and living primarily in our heads, and then feeling even more helpless and discouraged. This is where compassion can play an important role.

Common humanity, one of the foundations of self-compassion, can help as well. It is a relief to realize that we all have hard times and we all suffer. During these times we often judge ourselves harshly, isolate, and suppress what we are feeling. You are not alone in having this reaction. It is universal. But withdrawing is not the answer and can increase our suffering. As mindfulness teachers say, "Pain is inevitable, but suffering is optional." The mindfulness and compassion practices in this chapter are designed to be "industrial strength" and to help you get through the trying times with kindness and perspective (and hopefully some humor), and to remember that this will pass.

Let's start by bringing mindfulness and awareness to the challenges you and your family are facing:

Reflection: What Obstacles Are You Facing?

- Give yourself a moment to sit comfortably or, even better, let yourself lie down.
- Start by putting your hand on your heart or, if you like, choose one of the forms of soothing touch (Chapter 3) that makes you feel held and safe.
- Bring some kind awareness to the "speed bumps" you are facing.
- What are you dealing with right now that is challenging, that makes you feel like you are being pulled apart?
- Are you facing health challenges?
- Issues in your relationship?
- Is your child struggling? If so, in what ways?
- Are you concerned about a family member? A friend?
- Are you having difficulty adapting to passages such as your son or daughter moving from childhood to adolescence or college or your parents starting to need your care?
- What about your own journey? Feeling as if you aren't where you expected to be and powerless to change that?
- Is the stress taking a toll on your body? Your mood? Your sense of well-being?
- What supports do you have in place that work for you?
- Take a moment of mindfulness and compassion right now. Just let yourself be; no need to do anything or fix anything.
- Maybe these speed bumps are telling us to slow down a little?
- Let yourself stop and rest, even if just for a moment.
- When you are ready, jot down the issues that feel most overwhelming.

- *Bring some compassion to yourself. Parenting can feel impossible at times.*
- *When you're ready, take a few deep breaths and find some movement in your arms and legs.*
- *Feel free to use the soothing touch whenever you might need it during the course of your day.*

There are so many ways that we feel challenged by daily life, and so many ways that things can fall apart. We don't need to be facing a terminal illness or a devastating change in circumstances. Our partner ignores us, our children don't appreciate us, our boss doesn't give us credit for our hard work, an elderly parent demands attention that we don't have time to give. "Tough times" can come from a seemingly endless list of smaller burdens that drag us down as much as from one big event.

Or they can come from the natural transitions of life. As our children get older, as part of the developmental process of separation and individuation, they often find fault with everything we say and do, frequently putting us down, often in front of friends and family. While this may all be part of the "developing brain," it still hurts and feels unfair. And sometimes adolescence continues well into the twenties (hopefully not longer). It can feel like everyone is irritable and on edge. Will it ever end? Will things ever return to "normal" (whatever that is)? Sometimes just reframing the problem can help. One piece of research I've found comforting is that tweens and teens can interpret a neutral comment as critical. No wonder we misunderstand each other so frequently.

Even happy events, such as weddings, can stir up buried feelings and resentments. And we all know what deaths and funerals can unleash. With the help of a decade or so, we can often look back at what seemed so dire and upsetting and laugh about it, but in the moment it is hard to have humor or perspective. In these times it is important to remember self-compassion and to have your own back. The wisdom of the ancient sage Rabbi Hillel still rings true: "If you are not for yourself, who will be?"

When Things Don't Work Out as Expected

No matter how much we plan, no matter how hard we work, the future we envisioned and aimed for doesn't always emerge. It's hard enough to feel like the moody, irritable teen before you barely resembles the child you've raised. Then there's helping that teen make the transition to the adult world and out of the home. It can all feel like too much.

Vanessa came to see me, devastated that Jason hadn't gotten into any school that he wanted to go to. He was waitlisted for a few colleges but was feeling dejected about not getting into his top choices. Vanessa hadn't attended college, as it was a luxury her family couldn't afford, and she and her husband had done everything they could to help Jason succeed. The counselor at the high school wasn't giving sufficient guidance, so they hired a private college adviser, spending money they didn't have and dipping into their retirement funds.

Jason loved tennis and was good at it. He made the varsity team in his sophomore year. The college adviser, however, said that he needed to take all AP courses to get into a "good" school. Math wasn't Jason's strong suit, but his parents pushed for him to get into an AP calculus class. It was hard for him to keep up, and it took so long for him to do his homework that something needed to give. Between math tutors and getting extra help from the teacher, there wasn't time for tennis. Jason was a dutiful son, and he let go of tennis. But now, after all that work and sacrifice, he felt he had nothing.

"I'm so down," Vanessa said. "I put so much time and energy into getting this to work. I'm having trouble getting out of bed in the morning. My internist suggested that I talk to someone. We placed so much hope in him. And our daughter, Rebecca, has Down syndrome and won't ever go to college. We love her, she's an angel, but Jason was our future. We spent so much money that we didn't have.

"But the worst thing is that I feel so guilty and blame myself. AP calculus was hard for him, and he would have been so much happier if we had just let him play tennis. Such a loss on so many levels," she sighed.

Our lives are all experiments. We never know how things will turn out. This is where self-compassion and resilience can make a huge difference. I tried to model some compassion for Vanessa, acknowledging that she had done everything she could and Jason had as well. She had been blaming herself for making poor decisions. Jason was dejected, feeling that he'd let the family down. "I hear him crying at night, crying himself to sleep. I tell him things will work out, but he just shakes his head. He feels ashamed that he wasted our money, that he failed, and is spending all his time alone in his room."

In adolescence, it is hard to hold a larger picture of the complexities of life, to realize that while a college rejection is hard, other opportunities will arise and other doors will open. It is common for kids to feel inadequate and to feel they have failed. Self-compassion can help us realize that we all fail and that it is part of the experience of life. Rather than fall into despair, we can learn from difficult experiences. (See Chapter 8 for more on imparting the lessons of self-compassion to your kids. The Self-Compassion for Parents Toolbox, at the back of this book, organizes all the practices to help make them accessible and family-friendly).

To help Vanessa put things in perspective, both for herself and for Jason, I asked her about what we call in MSC a "Silver Lining," something that happened to you that was devastating at the time but turned out to be useful in a way you couldn't have predicted. She thought back to when she had been passed over for a promotion. A coworker had been spreading nasty rumors about her so he would get the position. Once he got the job, he expected her to help him. "He threw me under the bus and then expected me to change the tire. The hell with that! I left that job. It was scary, as I was out of work for a while, people told me that I was stupid, I should just suck it up, but I refused to be demeaned. I landed on my feet in a better job with better pay. And an extra gift was that I met my husband in the new job, which never would have happened if I had stayed."

Try this reflection exercise when you encounter hard times. Vanessa called it "Lemonade Stand" because Jason used to make and sell lemonade in their neighborhood and she took joy in his motivation and entrepreneurial spirit. It helped her connect with his strengths. "So," she said, "when life gives you lemons, you know the saying. I'm learning you really can make something from disappointments."

Reflection: Lemonade Stand

Write down your thoughts on paper or in your phone.

- *Take a moment out of your day. Close your eyes and take a few deep breaths.*
- *Think of a time in your life that seemed hard to bear but, in retrospect, taught you an important lesson or had a positive outcome.*
- *Choose an event in the past that is now resolved and from which you feel that you have learned what you needed to learn.*

- *What was the event? Jot it down. What happened? How did you handle it?*
- *How did you turn the lemon into lemonade?*
- *What deeper lesson did the challenge teach you that you wouldn't have learned otherwise?*
- *Is there a current situation in your life where you've been handed a lemon? Jot that down.*
- *Pause. Bring some compassion to yourself in this moment.*
- *Might there be a potential lesson in this situation? Jot that down.*
- *Return to this practice during the day or weeks to come when you feel you need to change the optics.*

Vanessa used this reflection during the week. She reported she had stopped blaming herself. She also felt that she'd been able to help Jason once she reconnected with his strengths. "I told him that things don't always work out the way you want, but it builds character. That's wisdom from my grandmother as well. We explored other options—thought about a gap year, brainstormed about jobs and internships he might explore. He seems a little more upbeat about the future. He'd never seen me get that upset. I tried to keep it together, but I was really down and he knew it. It felt like a body blow. We had invested so much, with money, with emotions, for so long. But once I showed him I could bounce back, he seemed a little lighter. It's hard for all of us, but not the end of the world. He's young, and life is long. And I told him to be kind to himself. I wouldn't use the word *compassion*—he would sneer—but I just said, 'This is tough. We'll figure this out. Be kind to yourself.'"

Sometimes life gives us so many lemons that we feel that a stand is too small—we could open an entire lemonade store (or business)! For many of my students and patients, this practice has added some needed perspective. Carlos used this practice when he lost his business in a recent economic downturn and was feeling depressed and worthless. He worried that his kids would lose respect for him. Trudy, who had suffered a recent miscarriage, felt that this practice helped her develop some perspective and the grit to keep going: "I was feeling like I was defective, that something was wrong with my body, and this helped me persevere. Things don't always go your way the very first time."

What about you? When could you use this practice? This is a practice you can share with friends, older children, your partner, and family members when appropriate and when they are receptive.

When It Feels Like the Walls Are Closing In

At times, when we're feeling pulled in many directions, overwhelmed and worried, it's hard to keep going. Rob, who was concerned about his daughter's problems with "mean girls" not long ago, was now feeling "sandwiched." Rob's mother had fallen and broken her hip, and she needed nursing care at a rehab center for a few weeks to help her recover and manage the pain. After she was released, she needed his help to get to physical therapy and for her numerous doctors' appointments. These trips cut into his ability to do his job, and he was exhausted. He was also distraught about a change he had recently discovered in his daughter, Heather.

Heather had just started high school and was having a hard time adjusting socially and academically. Confronted with a whole new group of students, she hadn't made any close friends yet, and she had failed a test in American history. Stressed and irritable, she would come home from school, shut the door, and stay in her room till dinner. She complained she didn't have time to set the table or load the dishwasher. When Rob asked if she was OK, she replied that she was fine—she just had lots of homework and she hated memorizing all the dates and battles for her history class. He knew something was wrong but didn't want to push and didn't know how to approach her.

One night when he was taking out the trash, he noticed a splash of red on a tissue. Initially he thought nothing of it, but there were other tissues with dried blood. He talked to his wife, who was also concerned, and then they spoke with Heather.

"At first she denied anything," he said, "and she got angry. 'Gawd, back off, you guys. I just cut myself shaving. I'm a klutz—you know that,' she lied. We didn't believe her, but we didn't know what to do.

"'You're not hurting yourself, are you, honey?' I asked.

"Heather insisted that she was just fine. 'Don't cross-examine me,' she yelled. But at night, when I was giving her a good-night hug, I noticed a few razor cuts on her arm, partially hidden by her pajamas.

"I knew if I confronted her she would get defensive. So all I said was, 'Honey, we love you, and we're here for you. You can talk to us when you're upset.' I think she wanted me to find the tissues but couldn't say that. I think she was too embarrassed.

"The next day she asked to speak to me privately. She told me she had been cutting herself. 'Please don't be mad at me, Daddy,' she pleaded. She didn't want to worry me because I was exhausted caring for my mother. She said she was feeling worthless and ugly. She worried no one at the new school liked her or cared about her." He paused and began to cry. "What can I do to help her? It's horrible for a parent to know his child is wounding herself. And I have so much on my plate right now. What do I do? I feel like the walls are closing in on me."

When children begin to harm themselves, it is crucial to get professional help before the situation gets worse. Heather evidently did want her parents to know she was suffering. I think of the famous sentiment from the British analyst D. W. Winnicott—children find joy in hiding, "but it is a disaster not to be found."

We found a child therapist to evaluate Heather. Although she didn't want to talk at first, the therapist was warm and knew how to reach her. It took some time, but they eventually developed a rapport. She worked with Heather to develop skills to cope with the new school, the challenge of making new friends, and the increased academic load. Within a few months, Heather began to feel less depressed.

To deal with Rob's feeling of the walls closing in on him, I suggested this practice of Sky Gazing. At first he did it alone, but when Heather saw him lying on the grass looking up at the sky she wanted to join in. "That looks relaxing," she said. This is a great practice for families. (In Chapter 8, there is a variation called The Vastness of the Night Sky, which is a family-friendly practice as well.)

Held by the Earth, Open to the Sky

The following meditation is especially suited for a balmy summer day or evening but can be done in any season. If it is too cold to go out, sit by a window and look out. It can be practiced either lying down or sitting up. I have made this practice accessible for adolescents, children, and adults.

♥ Sky Gazing

- Start by lying on your back on a blanket or beach towel. While it's ideal to practice on a patch of grass or soft sand, it's fine to do this on an urban rooftop or a chaise lounge. Or any window with a view of the sky works as well.
- Start by taking a few deep breaths and let your body settle into the earth. Your eyes can either be open or closed.
- Feel yourself being held by the ground. Feel that the earth is comforting you, that it "has your back."
- Consciously relax each body part: the feet, the legs, the pelvis, the

back, the belly, the shoulders, the arms, the chest, the neck, the jaw, and the eyes.

- Let yourself rest, allowing your muscles to soften and release. See if you can let go of any tension or clenching.
- Find your natural breath, letting it come and go without controlling it or forcing it.
- Become aware of the space and openness within your body.
- When you are ready, open your eyes if they have been closed. If the sky is bright, you may want a pair of sunglasses.
- Let yourself rest while you watch the clouds pass through the sky. Become aware of the spaciousness and openness of the sky. Imagine you can bring this openness into your body.
- If thoughts, emotions, or sensations arise, allow them to pass as effortlessly as the clouds.
- No need to hold on to anything; just allow it to be held in the vastness of the open sky.
- Let yourself rest in the spaciousness within your body and outside of your body.
- See if you can carry this sense of openness with you through the day.

This is also great to do on vacation or as a respite during a stressful week. It is a meditation that helps us recharge and renew as well as develop a broader perspective on our lives and our worries.

Rob found some comfort in this practice, as did Heather. "It makes me feel like there is some space in my world when the walls start to close in," he reported. "When I start to think about all the things I have to do in caring for my mother, driving her all over town, getting her groceries, cooking for her, taking her to all her medical appointments, and my worries about Heather, I think of the sky, pause, and take a deep breath. And I've come up with a phrase that is helpful. I say, 'Yup, your mother is losing altitude, but she's still here.' And I feel grateful for that. And 'Heather is having a hard year.' And then I add, 'And the sky is blue.' It helps me remember the open sky and the sense of space, and I don't feel as trapped."

I taught this practice to Vanessa, who did it with Jason as well. She appreciated lying down during the day. Jason, who was interested in science and was intellectually curious, used The Vastness of the Night Sky (Chapter 8) as a way to learn the constellations. He liked the fact that when he looked at the vastness of the sky his worries seemed less pressing.

This is one of my favorite practices and something that I like to do on a warm summer day. It can be used in a variety of situations and doesn't need to be limited to challenging or upsetting times. It is a good practice to do when you're stressed, when you've been at your computer or work desk for too many hours, or you just need a break (better than eating, bingeing on TV, or online shopping).

Feeling overwhelmed by paperwork, Eleanor used this practice to help manage stress shortly after the death of her father. Alberto, upset by conflict within his family, used it as a way to chill out and not escalate the arguments. Jonathan, worn down by his daily commute, which seemed to take more and more time each year, used it as a way to refresh and renew when he got home. For him it was a needed pause from the stress of his work life and helped him transition to being with his family. Sometimes the entire family joined in. At times they watched for shapes in the clouds, sometimes finding dinosaurs and dragons, sometimes just listening to the songs of the birds and the crickets if it was at night. "It's stealth mindfulness for me. I get to teach the kids to relax, but not in a heavy-handed or formal way."

Working with Our Thoughts

Valerie had been through a difficult time in the past five years. She was emerging from a contentious divorce and custody battle. Matt, now ten years old, was trying to adjust to the fallout—his parents at odds and the stress of living in two households. Valerie was having trouble setting limits and boundaries with him as she didn't want to be the "bad cop," but Matt was not cooperating with her and was challenging her authority.

"It's been bad enough losing my husband and the financial and social support. The end of the marriage has been heartbreaking and very lonely, and I'm furious, of course, but what is the most difficult is that I feel like I've lost Matt as well—instead of seeing him every day, now I only get him 50% of the time. He was the center of my life, my universe. This is so unfair. Things feel so empty without him. And when I do see him, he fights with me and challenges me. On the weekends I don't have him, I feel so alone. It's not like all my friends are young and single and we can go out and have fun together. They all have family and their homes and don't want to spend their free time with me. I'm a reminder that marriages fall apart, and they don't want to think it could happen to them, that their husband could have an affair and leave.

"And I blame myself for the end of the marriage. If only I hadn't gained so much weight, I might have been more attractive; maybe he wouldn't have fallen for the perky fitness instructor at the gym. Should I have had plastic surgery?

"The worst thing is that I feel that I'm losing Matt's respect. And he's angry with me as well. This has disrupted his life big time. His dad and new girlfriend take exciting trips, they go hiking and skiing, and Matt's life with them is much more fun. I can't afford to take him to cool places. I'm in a rut where I'm constantly reliving what happened, my thoughts are spinning, and I keep replaying what happened. I feel less present for Matt. Most of the time I'm feeling inadequate and unwanted. I'm not much fun for him these days. I'm not fun for anyone."

While Valerie and I talked about how to set fair and consistent limits with Matt, we also worked on managing her depression. One of the most effective ways to work with depression is to work with our thoughts, not to believe or get behind every negative thought. When we are down, our pattern of thoughts can often settle on a theme of inadequacy and self-loathing. During the divorce Valerie felt like she was engaged in a war with her ex; now she was battling with herself. However, if we take distorted thoughts about our self-worth as absolute truth, we buttress our depression. Mindfulness can help us cultivate a new relationship with our thoughts. Rather than analyzing them or trying to get rid of them, we learn to let them be. If we can perceive a thought such as "I'm unwanted" as just a thought, we can take away its power to upset us. In mindfulness practice we are often taught to label our thoughts, such as "a thought that I am worthless" or "a thought that I am inadequate." This practice takes it a step further and weaves in compassion.

Just Because You Think It Doesn't Mean It's True

- Start by sitting comfortably and letting yourself settle. Bring your awareness to your breath or to the sensations of your body sitting.
- Come into the present moment by anchoring yourself with the practice of breathing or of listening to the sounds around you.
- When you are ready, bring your attention to your thoughts, letting them be the focus of your awareness.
- Notice how they arise, intensify, and then pass away.
- See if you can observe them but not get caught by them, just watching, not agreeing with them.
- Don't force this process, don't try to make your thoughts go away, don't try to evict them from your mind.
- Try bringing some warmth and kindness to the thoughts. If for example you notice a thought that you are worthless, or an inadequate mother, put one hand on your heart and pause. Add the other hand if you like. This is a difficult thought to be having. Yes, this hurts.

- Watch your thoughts the way you would watch the drama in a film. Or, if you like, you can imagine that you are on a train and the thoughts are part of the scenery.
- As in the previous practice of Sky Gazing, you can imagine the thoughts as clouds passing through the sky. Some are storm clouds, dark and threatening; others are cumulus clouds, light and airy. Notice them and let them dissolve.
- Connect with the spaciousness, but acknowledge that some thoughts bring storms and intense weather. Know that these will pass.
- If at any time a thought takes you away and you begin to feel scattered, or sucked into the storm of your thoughts, stop. Bring compassion to yourself. These thoughts are here. This is a difficult moment. But thoughts don't last forever.
- If you find yourself being taken hostage by a thought, pause and steady the mind. Think of every inhalation as a chance to start again and every exhalation as a chance to let go.
- When you find that you have become distracted, return to your breath or your body. Let this calm and anchor your awareness.
- When the thoughts arise during the day, you can say to yourself, "This is just a thought; this isn't the truth."

Valerie practiced during the week. At first it was hard to stay with a thought and to watch it rather than getting taken over by it. But as she practiced, she found it easier to follow her thoughts, imagining them as the view from a train. The sense of creating some distance was a relief for her. She saw herself going to her usual "end of the world" scenario and was able to interrupt that pattern. "This helped me realize that all I was feeling and believing about myself and taking so seriously were just thoughts, not really who I am."

But what was most helpful for her was that she began to see the relationship between her thoughts and her turbulent emotions. "So a thought arises about our vicious custody battle, and wow, the thought triggers this intense emotional storm. And I'm livid, I'm enraged. My fists are clenched. I'm caught in this avalanche of emotion. I hate my ex. And then I stop and I realize that there's no need for all this rage and drama; it is just a thought. He isn't in the room, the lawyers aren't here, the judge isn't here, the girlfriend isn't here. I'm just here alone in my new condo. The drama is over. I can chill!" She paused. "I realized that I was replaying this nightmare over and over and I could stop it. What a relief!"

Meditation teachers have us inquire into the nature of thought—"What is a thought?"—noting that a thought in itself is insubstantial. Still, it can have enormous power over us, and if we don't pay attention to the thoughts that have risen, we can suddenly be sucked into the drama and emotions that they evoke. However, if we can pause and realize that it is just thoughts that are stirring us up, and that they are "real but not true," often we can bypass the rage, the annoyance, the rumination, and the endless justifications.

Reflection: What Thoughts Get You Going?

Jot down what comes up during this reflection if you like.

- *Spend a moment getting curious about the thoughts that get you going.*
- *Do you have thoughts that hijack you and send you down the rabbit hole?*
- *What are they? Are you getting caught reliving the fight you had with your partner this morning?*
- *Still spinning about your mother-in-law's putdown last Christmas? Or was that a few years ago? (Don't worry, this is a judgment-free zone. We often hold on to slights for years.)*
- *Your daughter's rude comment about you still stinging weeks later?*
- *Are you obsessing about a problem your child is having in school?*
- *Or an insult from a person you consider to be a friend?*
- *Still thinking about an argument with your mother? Still harboring rage?*
- *How about that nasty comment from your boss?*
- *Not talking to a sibling or a family member? The relative who couldn't bother to come to your wedding?*
- *Come back to the moment: disengage from the thought stream. Let it pass by.*
- *Bring some compassion to yourself. Put your hand on your heart or practice soothing touch.*
- *Don't beat yourself up. You didn't invite this thought. You didn't ask it to intrude on this peaceful day.*
- *Breathe in; start again with this fresh breath. Breathe out; let it go.*

Noticing Your Critical Thoughts

There are myriad ways that can use the preceding practice in your daily life. Many of the people I work with find this one of the most helpful tools in the "Self-Compassion for Parents Toolbox" at the back of the book. Miriam found herself constantly judging her parenting, imagining that others were judging and criticizing her as well and feeling that she wasn't doing a very good job. This was an opportunity for her to notice that criticizing and judging were just another form of thinking. When she caught herself thinking, "I'm a bad parent," she managed to interrupt the thought and bring some wisdom and humor. "Well, not in every moment," she learned to say to herself. "The way I handled Jerry's meltdown when he didn't want to leave the playdate was pretty damn good." If she was feeling particularly down on herself and needed a "booster shot" to help with an especially sticky critical thought, she added the You Are Not Your Fault practice (Chapter 1) to help work with her inner critical voice.

Jake noticed a running critical commentary in his head, as if he were listening to a sports broadcast or a reality TV show: "Folks, there Jake goes; he's lost it again. Why did you say that to Sam? That was stupid. Jake is a loser of a dad. Watch him mess up again. He's failing at everything he does. How many years of therapy are his kids going to need to recover from such incompetent parenting? He is the weak link. He's fired. Get outta here!"

One technique that helped was to give these thought patterns a name. Sandy named her litany "Bad Parent." Jake called his "Loser Dad Gets Fired." Ideally, the labels help us bring some humor and perspective to our negative thought patterns. In an experiment, Jake tried singing his thoughts in different voices, as if they were a dramatic musical or an opera. As he was having fun adding trills and high notes, responding with a dramatic baritone and bass, he couldn't help laughing. And his commentary lost its power over him.

 Turn It into a Song

Try turning your critical commentary into music—whatever genre is fitting.

- Hip-hop?
- Country and western?
- Blues?
- Rock and roll?
- Folk?

- A melodramatic opera?
- A musical? Maybe add some movement.

Have fun with it. You can even create your "Top Ten Hits," things that are common themes in your inner dialogue.

When we can allow our thoughts to be seen, heard, and known and realize that they are just thoughts, our relationship to them shifts and they lose their power over us. In this way, with music, humor, or awareness, we can release ourselves from their toxic and destructive potential. In seeing and understanding what is going on, in bringing compassion to these painful inner commentaries, we can release them. This is a gift we can give to ourselves whenever things get overwhelming and we feel stretched too thin. Yes, it takes some practice and work, but the willingness to look at our "inner operas" is a gift of freedom.

Finding the "Mentor" in "Tormentor"

Teens are challenging for most parents. Even when we're not dealing with a raft of other difficult problems that are competing for our time and attention, adolescence can be a difficult period for parents. The adolescent brain is "under construction," so this is a time that is often marked by rapid shifts in moods, behavior, interests, and friends. The more we can stay calm and steady, the better off everyone is. At times it may seem like our kids or partners were put on earth to torment us, but (using a phrase from Dick Schwartz, developer of Internal Family Systems) if we can step back and see what we have to learn from the situation, they can become our "mentors." However, let's be real. When we feel dissed, demeaned, and insulted, it is hard to see anything but our rage and reactivity. How can we get peaceful enough to make this transition? Let's look at how Chrissie and Meghan kept their sanity when they felt stretched to their max.

Pink Hair and Blue Tattoos

A few years earlier, Chrissie's relationship with stepdaughter Jenny had improved since the first year of her marriage to Jenny's dad, and her main concern was their son Steven. Now Steven's ADHD has stabilized, and Chrissie is losing sleep over Jenny again.

"Dealing with this kid is one of the most challenging things in my whole life," Chrissie explained. "We seemed to find a truce, and I was managing well enough that I didn't need therapy. We learned to respect each other and get along. Sometimes we even enjoyed each other and had fun together. But now Jenny is 15, and she's hell on wheels. Everything is a fight. She challenges every boundary and limit I set. She thinks she can argue and negotiate everything. Getting her to cooperate seems harder than finding peace in the Middle East. Impossible.

"But last weekend took the cake. She goes to the mall with a friend, and she has her own money from babysitting. Plus, it was her birthday, so she had some cash from her grandmother. She comes home, get this, with pink hair and a tattoo on her ankle. It's small, but it's a real tattoo. She didn't ask my permission, or my husband's permission (he's away on a business trip, of course); she just went ahead and did it. I think she's been plotting this for weeks.

"As you can imagine, I went ballistic and hit the ceiling. I grounded her for two weeks.

"And she fights back. 'It's my body. You have no right to control my body,' she retorts. She knows I'm a huge supporter of women's rights, but she is a kid. And I'm trying to be a responsible parent. So I say, 'You live in this house and you follow the rules we set. You're too young for a tattoo.'

" 'I hate you, I hate you. I wish you weren't my mother,' she yells and storms upstairs to her bedroom. We haven't talked for days. It felt like déjà vu all over again."

For those of us who have been teens, or tried to raise teens, this may sound familiar. Almost every parent has a story to tell about piercings, tattoos, nose rings, or some other rebellion involving the body. Dr. Judith Herman, a mentor of mine and a pioneer in the study of trauma, once explained it to a group of her students in the following way: Teens may look like adults once they have developed and grown to their full height, but with tattoos, piercings, and so on, they are asserting their independence, announcing to the world that they are not adults and that they reject the norms of the adult world.

So, how is a parent to stay sane during repeated acts of defiance?

Reflection: Acts of Defiance

Start with your own history and then look at how defiance is being manifested in your family. Grab paper and pencil or your phone.

- *How did you assert your independence and autonomy when you were a teen? Sex? Drugs? Alcohol? Music? Acting out in school?*

- *In what ways did you challenge your parents? How did you deal with their limits? With the curfews they set? With rules around the family car?*
- *How is your child asserting his or her independence? Sex? Drugs? Alcohol? Music? Piercing? Tattoos?*
- *How is your teen challenging your limits or the boundaries you set?*
- *Step back and look at your behavior and look at your child's behavior. What is most upsetting for you?*
- *See if you can set aside your self-righteousness. What could you learn from your child? Is there a part of yourself, or your behavior, that you would like to address? If so, what is it?*
- *Write your answers down and then give yourself a few moments to reflect on what has come up for you.*

Chrissie tried this practice and came back humbled. "Yup, I wasn't an angel. How convenient that I forgot what an absolute terror I was! Sneaking out at night, sex with my boyfriend in the park in the middle of the night, smoking weed, as well as stronger substances. Amazing I didn't get caught. I certainly gave my parents a difficult time. But I still wished Jenny had gotten my permission for the tattoo and the pink hair."

"And what would you have said?" I asked. "My guess is that she knew the answer, which is why she defied you."

"OK, I get your point," she said and smiled. "But I'm a parent now. I don't want to condone bad behavior or let her think she can get away with it." She paused. "OK, I'm getting off my high horse. But this is the million-dollar question: How do I not lose it with her?"

The Power of Equanimity

Equanimity is frequently taught in meditation centers, but it is rarely mentioned in parenting books. Yet it has enormous value for parents. Called the "secret ingredient" in mindfulness, it helps us find balance and not get overwhelmed by life, but keep an open and responsive heart. Like mindfulness and compassion, equanimity is an ability that can be developed in the midst of life. We don't need to run away to a mountain retreat to cultivate it—the laboratory of parenting, with its chaos and frustration, is a perfect environment. It is a perfect complement to mindfulness and compassion and bolsters these practices. With equanimity we can accept things as they are, seeing clearly without getting caught in our desire for things to be different. The concept, rooted in ancient Buddhist thought, translates as "seeing with patience and understanding," qualities we need in abundance as parents. An illustration of equanimity, often used by meditation teachers, is of a wise grandparent at a playground with a toddler. As the child is happily digging in the sand, her favorite red shovel breaks and she begins to wail, inconsolable, perceiving this as a tragedy. The grandparent, who has endured true loss, doesn't diminish the upset, but comforts the child, imparting a perspective on how to manage the sorrows of daily life.

I wanted to give Chrissie an experience of equanimity and started with the following practice, which is adapted from a meditation the Dalai Lama gave to thousands at Harvard University. It uses the metaphor of a still place beneath a stormy sea to cultivate equanimity. This is a good practice for turbulent times and may become your go-to practice after a fight with your kids, partner, in-laws, coworkers, or others.

A Still Place beneath a Stormy Sea

- Start by sitting comfortably or lying down, taking a few breaths to ground and center. Feel free to use the breath, the sensations of the body, or the loving-kindness phrases to help you come into the present moment.
- Visualize a boat anchored in a deep harbor. It is a lovely, peaceful day, and the water is calm. But suddenly the wind shifts. Dark clouds roll in, and the wind and waves pick up, battering the boat.
- Notice as the storm intensifies, with high winds, hail, driving rain, and enormous waves.
- Now imagine that you can drop below the storm, perhaps in scuba gear if you like, and bring your awareness to the anchor at the bottom of the ocean.
- Let yourself rest here at the bottom of the sea, seeing the storm and wind and waves high above you.
- Even though the storm is raging, see if you can experience some calm and spaciousness at the bottom.
- Let yourself rest here, taking a break from the storms in your life and the storms and high winds of parenting.
- Give yourself a few moments for restoration and rejuvenation.

- When you are ready, take a few breaths, find some movement in your arms and legs, and open your eyes.
- As you return to the stormy surface of your life, remember that you can return to this stillness whenever you need it.

"I think I fell asleep," Chrissie said and apologized. "I've been so upset that I haven't been sleeping. It was good to get a respite from the daily struggle with Jenny. I've been taking it so personally. I know it has seemed earth-shattering this week, but I'm sure when she's in her thirties with her own kids we will look back and laugh and laugh about it. I feel much less wound up, less reactive."

Reflection: Getting Back in Balance

"Yeah, sure," you may snicker. "When did I have balance? Not since the kids were born, maybe not even then," you sigh. In addition to the Still Place practice, try asking yourself the following questions, which are designed to help you see a situation with more patience and understanding.

Grab that pen and paper again, or your phone, and jot down your thoughts.

- What situation is troubling you? What happened? What did your child (or partner) do? What was said?
- Now pause and consider. Why do they feel the way they do? What might be the reasons? With Jenny, for example, what did she want? Why the need for pink hair and a tattoo?
- Rather than getting stuck in reinforcing your position—I'm right; she is wrong—see if you can move from conflict to a deeper understanding.
- This is not hard to do, but it is hard to remember to do. Give yourself credit for making the effort.
- Ask yourself, What can I learn from this situation? Can we do this differently the next time?

Chrissie worked with these questions and the Still Place beneath a Stormy Sea practice during the week. She began to understand Jenny's perspective, and what she saw surprised her. "At first all I saw was an act of defiance, and I thought it was all about me and her need to rebel against me. As I slowed down and considered what she was feeling, I saw a little, insecure kid desperately trying to be cool and to fit in. She thought the pink hair and tattoo would suddenly make her belong. My heart opened a little more. It's so hard to be a teenage girl these days."

Good Morning, Heartache

Jessamyn felt that she'd hit bottom. She'd recently left an abusive, alcoholic marriage that had gone on for many years. While she was relieved to be out, she was feeling lonely and scared being on her own and trying to support herself and her 16-year-old daughter on her meager income as a cabaret singer. But as if that weren't enough, her 90-year-old mother, who had been her "rock" her entire life, had developed dementia. Her decline was rapid and heartbreaking. When she began to wander naked through the streets at night, Jessamyn realized that she couldn't keep her mom safe in her home any longer. All the stress and all the changes were taking their toll, and Jessamyn was waking up in the middle of the night unable to return to sleep, the Billie Holiday standard "Good Morning Heartache" running through her head.

"You'd think that was enough," she told me, "but my daughter just got suspended for plagiarism. She's a good kid and said she didn't realize she was doing anything wrong, or at least not terribly wrong." She smiled ironically. "A friend offered to share a term paper to help her out, and she's lazy and was upset with all that is going on, so she figured she could make some minor changes on the paper and turn it in. No one would notice. Didn't work, and she got caught. They suspended her for a week, and she's on academic probation. Now I have one more thing to manage. How could she have been so stupid? And so sloppy! I lost it with her, really blew up and yelled at her for being careless and lazy. For not having enough of a work ethic. I slapped her. I know I shouldn't have, but it was the last straw for me, just put me over the top. I just can't keep up. I feel like I keep getting knocked down by life. I'm just trying to keep my head above water."

Given the multiple stresses Jessamyn was experiencing, I taught her an equanimity practice to help her ride the waves of distress and keep balanced. But before doing that, I acknowledged her pain and how hard it is to parent during stressful times in our life. Sometimes it feels like we just can't handle one more stressful thing. They are, however, unavoidable, and denying them or resisting them can make it worse. There is a saying that I find useful when we are spread too thin and it is hard to manage everything: "You can't stop the waves, but you can learn to surf."

This is a useful practice for riding strong emotions, such as anger, sadness, fear, or anxiety, as well as intense desire for food or sex. This practice was inspired by the pioneering work of G. Alan Marlatt, who created a practice called *urge surfing* to help patients deal with addictions. And this is my "go-to" practice for when you are feeling knocked down by life.

Riding the Waves of Parenting

- Start by sitting comfortably, taking a moment or two to settle and anchor your awareness.
- Feel free to follow the breath, notice the sensations in the body, or use the loving-kindness phrases to help yourself come to center.
- Start by thinking of an incident with a child (or partner or parent) where you didn't behave up to your standards, acting in a way that didn't serve you or your child. (No judgment, please.) It might have been yelling, blowing your top, or becoming enraged in response to a difficult interaction.
- As you think about this incident, see if you can remember the emotion that preceded the behavior. Go back to the emotion and stay with it, labeling it if you like: "This is anger." "This is frustration." "This is sadness." "This is exasperation."
- See if you can pause before the emotion peaks or in the moment before you explode. Stay at the edge. Breathe and relax into the experience rather than resisting.
- As you reflect on the event, watch how the wave of feelings and thoughts may rise in intensity. Be with this rising and notice the sensations in your body. See if you can stay with the "rising" rather than fighting the wave or going under. Trust that the wave, no matter how big, will subside.
- Try using the breath or the loving-kindness phrases as a surfboard to help keep you steady. Don't worry if you "wobble" as you try to find your balance. Constant adjustment goes with the adventure of parenting, just as in riding a real surfboard. See if you can find a flexible, dynamic balance.
- If you "wipe out" or fall off, don't worry. We all lose our balance in parenting. We all get knocked over. Don't beat yourself up; just get back on and keep riding those waves. This is a lifelong practice. The waves really don't stop . . . and sometimes they come from all directions.
- Be kind to yourself. You're doing the best you can.
- Stay as steady as possible until the wave of emotion begins to fall and

subside. Feel free to return to your breath or loving-kindness phrases before ending the practice and returning to your day.

Jessamyn liked having something that she could do that helped. "When I'm upset I usually open the fridge to eat, pour myself a stiff drink, and feel sorry for myself. Sometimes I feel like I'm drowning in my sorrows. This helps me feel like I can get back on my feet." To add something extra on really hard days, Jessamyn tried the reflection that follows—When Do You Wipe Out?—as well. She found the reflection helped her anticipate what would push her buttons, and respond constructively, rather than losing it.

We all have things that push our buttons and situations that cause us to "wipe out." Cecilia would lose it when she opened her daughter's bedroom door and saw dirty clothes and books and sports equipment piled mile high. "It made me worry that she was going to be a hoarder. She seemed totally incapable of hanging anything up or putting anything away. It made me furious and I'd go berserk. I'd totally lose it. Now, after learning to ride the wave and keep a modicum of balance, we set a time once a week where we all pick up, my husband and me included. That way she doesn't feel targeted. And when the house is picked up, we all go out for ice cream. Much easier than it used to be."

Reflection: When Do You Wipe Out?

This is a pencil-and-paper exercise.

- *Take a moment and let yourself rest. Aaahhhh . . .*
- *Give yourself a chance to reflect on when you "lose it."*
- *Sometimes it is small things, like a kid not putting food away or not helping load the dishwasher.*
- *Other times it is the classic spilled milk. Or not cleaning up the kitty litter. Maybe not taking the dog out for a walk? Or when your kid is defiant? Talks back? Is lazy or sloppy?*
- *Sometimes it is when someone is chronically late or forgets to call or text. Or when your partner has a meeting at night and neglects to tell you and you cooked a really nice dinner, or planned a fun family outing.*
- *And it can be bigger things, like someone lying to you, deceiving you, cheating on you.*
- *Jot down what it is that sends you over the edge.*
- *Do you notice any patterns? If so, can you do anything differently?*

- *Can you discuss how to do things differently so there isn't constant fighting?*
- *See if your family can brainstorm with you to offer suggestions.*
- *Try to work out a plan to make interactions go more smoothly.*
- *Remember, while it may not seem this way, no one really wants you to wipe out.*

When You Need Industrial Strength

There are times in life when only industrial strength will do. Sometimes things are so challenging that you feel you need ten extra-strength practices instead of just one to get you through the day—or the next hour. The end of a marriage, the loss of a child, a life-threatening illness or injury, a dying parent, or an addiction can make it feel like your life is unraveling. In times like this it is hard to cope, to make sense of your suffering, or to find some larger meaning or redeeming value.

Meghan's son Johnny is now in high school, and things were going well until Johnny started smoking weed. "He had friends, was playing soccer, and then he started hanging out with this group of kids, too-cool-for-school slacker types, and they started smoking weed together. I'm not a prude, and I tried it in college and I know it is about to become legal, but I didn't want him smoking too much and losing motivation. We talked about it, and he promised that he would stop. I trusted him; I really did. And things seemed better for a while. But the last few weeks he has been acting strangely, he is keeping the window open all the time, and we noticed that he was sneaking out of the house at night. His grades are dropping, he's missing school, and I'm worried about him. The other day his eyes were looking glazed over, he was jumpy and irritable, and it seemed like something was up. He had been seeing a nice girl, and she was a good influence, but she dumped him for a football player, and since then he's been really down. It's the first time he's had his heart broken. I tried to talk to him about it, but he didn't want to talk to his mom. I get that. I never wanted to talk to my mom at that age.

"But yesterday Dan and I were folding laundry together, and he put it away in Johnny's room. Johnny was out with his friends. One of the dresser drawers was open, and something caught his eye. We try not to snoop, but Dan opened the drawer, and underneath Johnny's T-shirts were drug paraphernalia, pills, and a stash of cash. I'm worried. I hear so much about the opioid crisis that I'm scared, and I'm afraid that he'll become addicted.

"I've been a mess. I couldn't sleep last night, I'm blaming myself for this, and I was having nightmares that he overdosed. I know you'll think it's an extreme reaction, but I worry. Dan and I have plans to talk to him tonight."

"Of course you do, it's a natural reaction, and of course you are upset," I responded. "But you don't know what is happening yet, so let's take it slowly and see what is going on. Before you talk to him, let me give you an exercise that will help keep you grounded and will help you get clear."

This is a reflection that helps with clarity during difficult times and can also be done during transitions—from middle school to high school, before college, or even when your child is beginning kindergarten or elementary school. It gives you a chance to gather your thoughts, express your love, your hopes, and your fears. It isn't something that you need to give to your child unless you want to—it is a practice for you.

Reflection: Letter to My Child

Grab paper and pen.

- *Let yourself settle, turning to your breath, the sensations in your body, the sounds around you, or the phrases of loving-kindness.*
- *Take a few really deep breaths. Let yourself slow down.*
- *Begin with love and compassion. You might want to start with an image or memory that stands out for you when your child was an infant, or even during pregnancy or childbirth. What do you remember? What were the feelings?*
- *You might want to write about the connection that you felt with your child. The moments when you bonded, when you looked into each other's eyes, when he or she first smiled or laughed.*
- *Remember the sweet times together. Pushing him or her on the swings in the playground, going to the beach on vacation, traveling together, watching a sunset, smelling a flower, noticing a baby animal. Write down some of the times when you felt really close to your child.*
- *Remember the funny times as well. What did your child do or say that made you laugh out loud, that made you feel so grateful for this precious being? Write that down as well.*
- *Now think of the difficult times you've been through together—a move, a loss, a divorce, an illness, a natural disaster. How did*

you get through this hard time? What brought you together? Take note of the strengths of the relationship, how you have weathered storms and have been resilient.

- Look as well at what hasn't gone well, what you regret doing or saying, what you wish you could "do over" or "take back." Perhaps there are things you might like to change about your behavior? Challenges because your temperaments clashed? Mistakes you made? Write this down as well.
- Don't blame; don't get self-righteous. Don't assert that you are always right and virtuous and your child is misguided and stupid. Don't judge right now.
- Finally, think about how you might like to move ahead in a positive direction. How can you start again? Acknowledge that you are both fallible human beings and that you aren't a perfect parent.
- See if you can reach out, heal the wounds that exist, repair any damage, say things that you might not have said, ever, that could be healing to hear. Write that down. Accept responsibility for your failings, for the times you have misunderstood your child, the times you may have let him or her down.
- Brainstorm about a plan that would address the issues that need to be dealt with in the relationship. How can you move ahead constructively, without blaming or shaming your child?
- Take a few more minutes to write down other things that come to mind that you want to express.
- When you are ready, return to your breath, the feelings of your body, or the phrases. Put a hand or two hands on your heart. And give yourself credit for writing this letter.
- See if you can let the love and compassion expressed in this letter guide you in your interactions with your child.

Meghan wrote the letter between sessions and read it to me when we saw each other again. "Johnny is used to me yelling at him and being critical, and he was surprised that I was understanding when we talked. However, that didn't mean that we were wimps. He was pissed that we were going through his things and got all defensive about that, but as we talked it turned out that he was feeling pressured to try more drugs, and riskier drugs, and painkillers. His friends were stealing drugs from their parents' medicine chests. I think he was relieved, although angry with us.

He admitted it was hard for him to say no, and he was caving under pressure. We've reached out to the other parents so they know what is happening. And we insisted that he go to drug counseling. He doesn't want to, but he knows that he's in a dangerous situation. I think he was actually relieved, though he would never say that, that we noticed and are helping him."

Meghan asked if there was something else she could do in the middle of the night when she started to ruminate about all her failings and wish that this wasn't happening to her and her son.

For some, the following practice might require a willing suspension of disbelief. But for those who try it, it can offer a powerful shift in perspective. While it is a good practice for extreme situations, it is also helpful for everyday disappointments.

 When Things Fall Apart

- Start by sitting comfortably. Take a few breaths and a few moments to ground and settle yourself. Use whatever practice you find helpful—the breath, focus on the body, or the phrases of loving-kindness.
- Bring your attention to the difficult situation you are facing. Stay in touch with what you are feeling, what you are thinking, as well as what you fear.
- Notice where you feel this in your body. Let yourself sit in the middle of this mess.
- Imagine, and this might take that suspension of disbelief, that before you were born you decided to have this experience to help you grow.
- Imagine that you are sitting with some wise guides or elders who care about you and want the best for you. Discuss with them how these events will help you learn.
- Rather than resisting these events, can you allow them to be? Can they become lemons for you? Can you work with them?
- Sit with what arises for you and see if you see this situation with new eyes.
- What is it like to imagine that you chose this situation rather than had it imposed on you?
- Imagine that these circumstances can become an opportunity to develop new strengths and skills, not just a burden.
- As challenges continue to arise, or when you find yourself feeling like a victim, see how the bumps in the road can become a chance for growth and learning.

Meghan was skeptical but tried the practice and found it made a difference. "At first I was feeling self-pity and asking, 'Why me, why did I get a son like this?' but it helped me step back from being a victim. We ran into some former neighbors the other day that we hadn't seen for a while. Their son struggled with depression and addiction and went through rehab—a few times. It finally took, he turned his life around, and he works with addicts now. He's 30. The neighbor joked that he's really good at his work 'cause he knows recovery from the inside. But he said something that really touched and inspired me. 'I tell people my son is in the business of saving souls.' His words gave me hope."

Mindfulness in Daily Life

Do you ever find yourself wanting hope? Or at least some comfort? It's the middle of the night. You can't sleep, again. You've counted sheep, you've counted your breath, you're tried the touch points, and you have even tried labeling your emotions. There're so many you can barely count them—anger, fear, worry, betrayal, distress. Yup, parenting can be like that. Compassion helps a little, but the rumination keeps coming. It's hard to stop rumination. Your thoughts keep spinning. One meditation teacher once told me that rarely do we have useful thoughts in the middle of the night. He was right. Our thoughts, in that quiet darkness, which often seems endless, tend to be more dramatic and reactive than we might like. Sometimes it feels like morning will never come. Try something different—try getting up and doing walking meditation to interrupt the cycle of rumination. The goal isn't necessarily to get back to sleep, but to allow yourself to be a fallible, imperfect, and struggling human being, a "compassionate mess."

What we often don't realize, in the early years of parenting, as we try to get our newborn baby to sleep, is that our interrupted sleep continues for years—seems there is always something new to worry about. This practice can help when you need something more.

Mindfulness at 4:00 A.M.

🎧 *Audio Track 8*

- Just get up if you've been struggling with sleep for hours. Sometimes you just can't force it.
- Turn on a night-light so you don't trip over the furniture. Find a space to walk, even if it is small.

- Stand comfortably, eyes open, with your feet about hip distance apart.
- Let yourself feel held by the ground. If you like, imagine that the earth is supporting you, holding you, anchoring you.
- Become aware of sensation in your feet. Feel free to shift your weight from side to side.
- Start walking slowly, but let yourself remain relaxed and alert. Feel the sensations of your feet touching the ground.
- You can say to yourself, "touching, touching."
- Bring your attention to each movement of walking—the touching, the moving, and the placing of each foot.
- Notice your internal experience as you walk. (And if it's your bedroom you may be walking around in circles. Parenting feels like that as well.)
- If you like, you can expand your awareness to notice the sounds, texture, smells, the darkness and shadows around you.
- If your thoughts start spinning, or you feel overwhelmed, bring some kindness and soothing touch, placing a hand or two on your heart if you like.
- Don't try to control this, let this be easy, relaxed. You can say to yourself, "Just this moment. Nothing more."
- If this is a time when you really need industrial strength, add these phrases: "May I be safe and protected, even if there is no safety."
- "May I be peaceful, even if there is no peace."
- "May I be embraced with kindness, even if there is no kindness."
- When you feel ready to stop, return to your breath and the feeling of your feet on the ground.
- See if you can carry this awareness and compassion into your next activity.

8 Roots and Wings
THE GIFTS WE GIVE OUR CHILDREN

The journalist Hodding Carter wrote, "There are only two lasting bequests we can hope to give our children. One of them is roots, the other, wings." Once we have kids, it seems that everything is a process of learning to let them go—from the first babysitter to the toddler's first steps away from us, to playdates, nursery school, sleepovers, overnight camp, college, and varied adventures. How can we help them be grounded and trust that they will make good decisions, rather than being anxious helicopter or snowplow parents? The more we can stay compassionate and steady, the easier it will be for them to spread their wings.

In reading "Even As I Hold You," a poem by Alice Walker, I was struck by the last two lines: "Even as I hold you/I am letting go." Walker captured this constant tension poignantly. Suddenly I was transported back to taking my daughter, my youngest child, to her first day at nursery school. That morning, I thought I was looking forward to having a little more time to myself and finally having some stable childcare. However, I was taken aback by the emotion I was suddenly feeling. At the school I ran into my good friend Naomi. Our sons had bonded at nursery school a few years back, and we all had become fast friends. Naomi was an actress, playwright, and director from another country and had a deep comfort with emotions.

"How are you?" she asked.

"It's harder than I expected to send her to nursery school," I said, as my eyes filled with tears. Embarrassed, I quickly apologized.

She embraced me and said, "No apologies. This is a big step. You go and let yourself have a good cry now."

I was stunned by her warmth and compassion. If I had admitted my sadness to most of my other friends, they might have rolled their eyes, told me to get over it, or given me some indication that I was overreacting and being dramatic. Or politely let me know that they were busy right now. Naomi was older, her children were older, and she was the wise, sometimes wild, nonconforming sister I never had. And she wasn't bound by the rules of this culture.

"And go take yourself out for a nice lunch; you deserve it." She smiled as she gave me another hug.

This was something I wouldn't have done on my own; it seemed too self-indulgent. But I did. And I still remember the details of that lunch on a perfect September day over two decades later. Rather than deny it or distract myself thinking about the stable childcare I so desperately needed, I marked, mourned, and celebrated the transition. For me this self-compassionate response was radical. Although I had had years of therapy, and years of mindfulness training, I was tough on myself and tried not to complain or be a drama queen. Now, looking back, wishing I could thank Naomi (who died much too young), I realize how naturally steeped she was in the language and action of compassion.

It was a passage, the end of a stage of our lives, and I was trying to have a stiff upper lip rather than feel what I was feeling. And it was a relief to acknowledge what was happening. My concern was that I would become an emotional mess, but what happened is I didn't lose it—I actually felt that I could acknowledge the complex and bittersweet emotions.

That wise and loving advice from Naomi, plus the experience of giving myself permission to feel both the joy and the sorrow, prompted the following meditation. This practice can be helpful no matter how young (or old) your children are.

Holding On/Letting Go

- Take a few breaths. Give yourself a few moments to check in with yourself.
- Where are you now in the spectrum of either holding on or letting go?
- If your children are young, are they in daycare? With a family member, neighbor, or nanny during the day?
- Are they in school? Just beginning or full-time?
- If they are older, are they still at home? Are they living away?

- Have they returned home for economic reasons? Failure to launch? Health problems? Broken relationships?
- How are you feeling about letting go?
- Are you holding on for dear life?
- Imagine you had a friend who understood just where you are. Perhaps this friend was a little older and wiser or a more experienced parent.
- Imagine this friend could intuit what you needed before you did. What would he or she tell you? Remember, the friend won't judge you, and won't sugarcoat things.
- Stop. Listen. What would the friend say to you?
- Put a hand on your heart. No need to rush. Get in touch with what you need. Give yourself permission to respond to your needs.
- This will not make you weak, indulgent, or selfish.
- Your needs matter. It is hard to let children move on. It is hard to allow ourselves to move on.
- Set an intention to include yourself in a circle of loving and caring friends and family. Do this in your mind's eye.
- Feel yourself surrounded by warmth and wisdom.
- Return to this practice whenever you feel overwhelmed.

Talia, who came to a parenting workshop, was about to go back to work full-time after finishing a four-month maternity leave. "I was feeling rather weepy and telling myself that I shouldn't be that way. That I should just toughen up. We need the income. Knowing that as parents we're always letting go was helpful and prepared me for the transition."

John's daughter was away at a tennis camp for a few weeks. The house was unusually silent, and he missed her energy and chatter, although it was nice to be able to sleep a little later and not have to chauffeur her on weekends. His wife, Charlotte, seemed delighted to have a break and was spending time having drinks and dinner with her friends and coming home late. John was feeling lonely and began to worry about what things would be like in a few years when their daughter left home for college. "My parents weren't very emotional, so when I'm having strong feelings I wonder if there's something wrong with me. It was a relief to know that many parents feel this way. Although I do believe my mom opened up a bottle of gin when I left home," he smiled, "and never shed a tear."

Sometimes it's hard to pay attention to any needs other than your child's, even though your well-being depends on taking care of yourself too. If a child has had serious health problems or there has been a difficult pregnancy, it is often hard, for example, to leave the child with a stranger just to take a few renewing hours to go to a movie.

Jerome and Taneshya tried for many years to get pregnant, and it took longer than they expected. It was a difficult pregnancy, and the baby was premature. Although caretaking was exhausting, they didn't want to leave her with an unknown sitter. Family was far away, and there was no one they trusted to watch her. "I've never loved anyone more, and she's so vulnerable. How can I put her at risk?"

They didn't go to a movie until Kaitlin was over two years old, and that was only when a friend gave them a night with a sitter as an anniversary present. Taneshya was on edge and texted the sitter before the movie, "Everything OK?" When the movie was over, she texted again, "Is she sleeping?" While they were nervous, it felt great to get a break and do the things they loved again.

As they began to venture out into the world, leaving Kaitlin with a reliable sitter, Taneshya and Jerome created loving-kindness phrases that helped them with the separation. They came up with: "May you be safe," "May you be healthy," "May you be happy with the babysitter," "May you have fun playing while we're away," "May you sleep well and have good dreams," "May you know that we love you and we'll be home soon."

The following practice, The Warm Blanket, is enormously soothing and comforting. It can be practiced at many points during the journey of parenting. Mothers I work with have used it during pregnancy; others have used it when a child is ill or needed surgery. It is also great after a stressful day at home or work or you just need a little extra something and you're trying not to go surfing online or open up the fridge. Try it whenever you need a little more nurturance, comfort, and connection. It is best done lying down. This practice builds on the skill of visualization.

The Warm Blanket

🎧 *Audio Track 9*

- Start by lying down and taking a few deep, relaxing breaths.
- Bring some kindness to yourself by putting a hand on your heart, or two hands on your heart, or wherever you might need a soothing touch.
- Imagine that at your feet is a soothing, comforting blanket. It's made of any material you like—cotton, fleece, mohair, silk—whatever you associate with safety and security.

- Let the blanket gently cover your feet. Let the muscles soften, letting go of tension.
- Let yourself rest and take in this comfort.
- Imagine that the blanket moves up to wrap around your calves and shins. Let those muscles soften. Let this in.
- Slowly, when you're ready, let the blanket wrap around your knees, front and back. Let your knees soften and relax. Pause. Rest.
- Let the blanket move up and cover your thighs, front and back. Let the touch be just what you need. Soft, gentle, warm.
- Let yourself be held by the blanket.
- Allow it to move up to your pelvis, your buttocks. Let any tension soften.
- Let yourself rest.
- Imagine the blanket wrapping around your abdomen and your lower back. Let any worry or tension you might be holding soften.
- Feel it wrap around your belly. We often hold a lot of tension and feelings in our belly. Feel the warmth and gentle weight of the blanket. Pause. Rest.
- Feel this around your midback. Let these muscles soften.
- Imagine the blanket moves up to your chest and upper back. Again, pause, rest, take in the comfort.
- Feel it wrap around your shoulders. Arms. Fingers. Letting go of tightness, tension, allowing the muscles to soften if possible.
- Gently let the blanket move up and rest on your neck and throat. Softening, smoothing.
- Allow it to move up and rest on your jaw, your cheeks. Pause.
- If you like, feel it on the back of your head.
- Finally, let the warm blanket gently cover your forehead, and your eyes if you like, but leave plenty of room to breathe.
- Let the muscles in your face soften. Rest.
- Let your entire body be held, touched, comforted by the warm blanket.
- When you feel ready, return to your day or allow yourself to get a good night's sleep.

Parents I work with gravitate toward this practice when it's difficult to let go or be apart. Sonia used it during a difficult second pregnancy; others have used it during medical procedures (their own or their child's). Ellen, who was very worried about a major surgery for her son, commented,

"With the body scan [Bringing Kindness to the Body, Chapter 3], I think of the body as separate and discrete parts. This touches all of me and holds me together." It is also fine to add words and phrases, such as "It is difficult to let go, to simply be with an uncertain outcome. Let me be with it, let me feel it. Let me be with not knowing."

As Kaitlin got older and seemed less vulnerable, Jerome and Taneshya were able to go out for more than a movie and tried activities that involved a longer separation, such as dinner parties with friends. They found the phrases above helped them reduce their anxiety and take the next step.

Yasmina was distraught when her last child started elementary school. She no longer had anyone at home. While it was nice to have a little extra time, she missed the sweetness and hugs of the little ones. This practice was a gentle reminder that this was just the first of many leavings and many transitions, but there were other ways to stay connected.

The Warm Blanket is also a practice that you can share with your children when they want to soothe themselves. Marco, age eight, was nervous about his first sleepover with Danny. He'd slept over at his grandparents' house, but he'd known them all his life. Danny was a new friend, and they didn't know the family very well either. Marco had many worries: What if Danny teased him? What if he dared him to do something dangerous on the skateboard? What if they served him something he hated to eat, like kale? Sometimes, if he was anxious, he would sleep with his old stuffed animal, but he knew he couldn't take it with him. And what if he missed his family?

Sasha, his mom, was trying to be supportive and composed about it all, but she was apprehensive as well. Wondering how Marco was doing, she couldn't fall asleep. Although in different places, they both turned to the Warm Blanket for comfort, and it helped both of them. With this practice, as with many forms of mindfulness and compassion, no one has to know what you are doing with your attention.

Teaching Them to Survive without You

When our daughter was in middle school, she and a friend joined an exciting community service adventure in a developing nation. She'd never been without us for that long. She was thrilled, but I was a nervous wreck. Her brother had spent a semester abroad in high school and had had a great time, until he went on a school trip and became extremely ill. He was in extreme pain. His teachers got him to a doctor, but the symptoms were confusing. Maybe it was something he ate? A stomach flu? It was a mystery to the doctors, and the pain persisted. It turned out to be appendicitis, and unfortunately his appendix burst, requiring emergency surgery and hospitalization in a country where medical standards were different from what we were used to. My husband flew out immediately to be with him, and he appeared to be healing. But there was an allergic reaction to an antibiotic, and then an infection, and another hospitalization. After nearly two weeks we traded places, and I flew over to be with our ill son so my husband could return to work.

I felt alone and frightened in a foreign country, trying to navigate a different medical system, communicate in a language I barely knew in a country where women weren't treated with much respect. Now, a few years later, was I crazy to be letting my daughter travel? What if something happened to her? Were we being foolish letting her take this risk?

The week she was scheduled to leave I had my monthly consultation with a mentor, who had raised two children. I confided my worries. She said something that has stayed with me: "Your job as a parent is to teach them how to survive in the world without you." Huh? I'd never heard this before, or if I had I hadn't been willing to listen. And of course I didn't want to hear it now, and I didn't even want to think about it. All that time and effort and attention to bonding and connecting and being present and now I was supposed to contemplate not being here anymore? I didn't know what to say, and I'm rarely without words. It was hard to get my head around it. And I have to admit now, years later, it is still a terrifying thought, but I see the wisdom more clearly.

My daughter went off, there was no emergency, and it was our first taste of an empty nest. However, I wanted reassurance that the universe would be benign and that God would not be playing dice with my children. I didn't get that reassurance then, and I don't have it now. Things are uncertain, and it's not in our power to make them certain. No one can. But we still need to let our kids test their wings in the midst of our worry and fear.

The following practice is one I turn to when I need to believe that there is love and guidance, that the village we live in is not full of idiots, and there are beings in the world who care and are wise and compassionate.

This is a classic Tibetan practice, which I have adapted just for parents.

💙 Tree of Compassionate Beings

- Let yourself rest and settle for a few moments.
- Drop into your body.
- Feel the weight, the solidity of your body.
- Allow yourself to feel grounded, connected to the earth.
- Imagine that like a strong tree you have roots beneath you that go deeply into the earth.
- Notice that the roots are connected to the trunk of the tree. Visualize them connected to the core of your body.
- Feel the support of this tree.
- Let yourself be grounded, steady. Feel a sense of being anchored, dignified.
- Imagine that there are branches with leaves and blossoms above your head that reach to the sky.
- Between the leaves, in the branches of the tree, are the faces of teachers, guides, friends, benefactors, sages, saints. People who have loved you, inspired you, supported you.
- Feel your connection with each benefactor. Take in their love and guidance. Don't rush. Let it land. Feel the connection with each being; let yourself be nourished by the love and wisdom.
- Let yourself feel seen, secure, and solid.
- Feel the direct connection from each benefactor to you. Feel the support.
- Let yourself take this in. Here. Now. Absorbing this compassion and nourishment.
- You can return to this tree of compassionate connection whenever you need guidance or feel alone, adrift, or isolated in the task of parenting.

Carrie used this practice when her child went to sleep-away camp for a month. Not only was Ethan homesick, Carrie was "childsick." Initially, they both found that not being able to call had made the separation worse. Cell phones were not allowed, and there wasn't good service in the remote Maine woods. If there was an emergency, the camp would contact the parents. To assuage anxiety, the camp posted pictures of the children every few days. While it was good to see Ethan smiling and at least looking OK, Carrie had intense longings to be with her son.

To help her get through the separation, Carrie made sure she found time to be with her friends and other mothers in Ethan's class and organized a dinner at her favorite restaurant for her group. She joked that they were the "Margarita Moms," a tribute to her favorite cocktail. Her friends understood how hard it was, and she didn't feel judged or criticized—they were experiencing the same thing. When she missed Ethan, she could pause and acknowledge that it was difficult to have him be far away and not have daily contact. The other moms reassured her that she wasn't an idiot for crying during the day when she longed to talk with him or give him a hug.

Kyra's mother had died many years ago, and there were so many times when she wished she could reach out for help and guidance when things were challenging in her life. It wasn't just that she longed for her wisdom about helping Tyrone navigate adolescence or about raising a black male in a white culture. She also wanted to know how her mother had kept her own marriage strong and how she managed to keep going and positive for years while battling cancer. "My mom was my rock, my anchor. I could really use her advice. I miss her every day," Kyra said. The Tree of Compassionate Beings helped her feel more connected to her mother, and also feel the presence of the minister of her church, who had passed a number of years back. He had been a source of strength and resilience for Kyra as well. "It makes me feel that the people who loved me and helped me are looking down from that tree and cheering me on." She smiled. "I need all the help I can get."

The Importance of Reconnecting

Children often love structure and rituals, which can help them feel seen and secure. Sometimes when they return from a day at school, a sleepover, summer camp, or a longer absence, simple things can help them feel held and welcomed home. It doesn't have to be elaborate or expensive—for a younger child a visit to a favorite ice-cream shop or bakery, or a simple walk together is a way to reconnect at the end of the day. For older children, a favorite hike, playing catch, a board game, or riding bikes keeps the relationship steady and conversation flowing. As children begin to leave, there are still ways to stay connected—watching a baseball game in summer, basketball in winter, or the annual ritual of watching the Super Bowl (even from different cities) can be a way of reuniting. Talking about and expressing interest in what they are reading or watching also deepens the connection. Returning to mutual shared interests and memories can ease reentry home.

Although our son no longer lives nearby (and in fact I am writing this chapter just two weeks after he got married), one of his favorite summer activities was watching the Perseid meteor showers every August from the deck of our rented summer cottage on Cape Cod. It became a ritual to make a wish when we saw a falling star (and during the meteor shower you're likely to see a few). Even though he lives in another state and we don't always see him during the summer, he reminds me of the meteor shower when the time arrives.

See what the ritual might be for you—it might be watching a sunrise or sunset together, going fishing, or going for a favorite walk or a swim in a nearby pond, pool, lake, or ocean.

Watching the night sky can provide a vast, wide-open perspective. We can find our favorite constellations and planets—the Big Dipper, the Little Dipper, the Milky Way, Mars, and Venus. And remember that sailors used the night sky, especially the North Star, to help orient and guide them in the darkness.

The Vastness of the Night Sky

- With your child or children, or with the whole family on a clear warm night, take some blankets and find some grass, sand, or a roof.
- Look up into the night sky. Let your eyes adjust.
- See what you notice. You might name what you see.
- As you look into the vast and open space, knowing that what you see is often light years away, reflect on how insignificant our problems can seem in the light of this vastness.
- From the moon, or the starry heavens, we are barely a speck.
- See if you can find the North Star.
- Reflect on your life. What is guiding you?
- Use the moment to get a wider perspective.
- See if you can let go of hurts, slights, misunderstandings that you might be holding on to with your children or your extended family.
- In the space of this vastness, could you let go? Or perhaps not hold on so tightly?
- See if this might give you a bit more freedom, or distance from the things that are weighing on you.
- Know that these moments are fleeting. And they are precious.
- See if you could bring some of the spaciousness of the wide-open sky into your being.
- Perhaps you might want to reflect on this saying: "Body like Earth. Mind like Sky."

- Feel the love that connects you with your children, your family. And the love that connects you with this fragile planet.
- And if you like, hold hands and make a wish.
- Stay as long as you like, contemplating the vastness of the night sky.

Janelle and her son Ralph, who was in middle school, had a turbulent relationship. Her way of staying connected, when they easily could have stopped speaking many times, was continually to find a "safe zone." Even though they argued frequently, she made an effort not to dwell on the conflict and the constant putdowns or to keep their fights going, but to find things they enjoyed doing together. Janelle had recently divorced Ralph's dad, and there was tension and anger about the split. She had fallen in love with a woman, and Ralph was angry about that. But she decided that she wasn't going to get lost in endless discussion and recrimination and kept redirecting the conversation. She tried not to keep ruminating on the things Ralph said, blaming her for the end of the marriage. "I know he misses his dad; I get that. He's a kid and he lashes out. But I'm determined not to let his blame have a lasting grip on my heart. If I take it personally and get into nursing my wounds and feeling victimized by his harsh words, I can see where that would take us. There are only a few years left till he turns 18, and I don't want to lose him. I've consciously decided to give him some space to express his anger. When I'm tempted to take the low road and say mean things in return, I stop and think, 'What does my child really need from me in this moment?' Rarely is the answer 'More shit from Mom.'"

Janelle joined Ralph in activities he liked, such as gaming, in which she had no interest, and tried to find things that made him happy when his mood sank. The Vastness of the Night Sky was a practice that worked for them. She'd moved into a small, cramped apartment in the city after the divorce, but one benefit was that the building had a roof deck. After dinner they would get out the binoculars, go outside, and watch the setting sun and the night sky, finding solace in the stars and maintaining a larger perspective on their lives.

The Power of Home Base

How can we use the inevitable challenges of letting go as a way to connect more deeply? Pain and discomfort can often help us reorient our lives and find our deepest values, even discovering new meaning in our lives and value in our struggles. And how can we continue to make home a safe and secure base that will help our kids launch into their own lives, as well as a place to return for solace if things don't go as expected?

Where Do I Go from Here?

Valerie was worried about Matt going off to college. It was hard to believe that so much time had passed. In the last few years, her life had stabilized. The divorce, which had been nasty, was behind her. She had begun dating again and was seeing someone she liked. She and her ex-husband had made a concerted effort not to make Matt a pawn in their divorce negotiations, and their interactions were now cordial.

Her concern was what her life would be like when Matt left home. For almost 18 years he had been the center of her life, her reason to get up in the morning. He kept her going during the anxiety that followed the divorce. "I feel embarrassed saying this, but I think my separation anxiety is worse than his," she acknowledged. "My whole identity has been focused on being a mother. This has been the purpose of my life. I wonder what I'm going to do now. I don't want to spend the next few years gardening, getting a new puppy, playing bridge, and waiting for grandchildren like some of my friends—that sounds dismal!"

A part of the MSC program that can help Valerie, you, and other parents with difficult transitions like a child's independence and the resulting empty nest is to identify the core values that will guide you in letting go and creating a new life that has personal meaning. Our suffering depends, in part, on the values we hold. For instance, if we value providing for our family, losing a job can be devastating. If we value travel and adventure and have the financial means to take the kids along, the loss of a job can be freeing.

So much of our reaction to events depends on where we are in life and what our needs and values are at the time. Marjorie slipped on the ice and sprained her back. She needed to rest and was told not to do any heavy lifting. However, she valued being able to pick up her young children, so this was a huge inconvenience. But so much of this is relative. If your children are older and self-sufficient, a few days of rest could be a luxury that might give you a chance to binge-watch your favorite TV show.

Core values are different from goals:

- Goals can be achieved. Core values guide us before and after we have achieved our goals.
- Goals are *destinations*; core values are *directions*.

- Goals are something we do; core values are something we are, something we embody.
- Goals are set by us; core values are something we have to discover.

 Finding Our Core Values

I've adapted this practice from the MSC program to be used by parents. In the following exercise, we will discover our core values and reflect on how to live in accordance with these values. Grab some paper and a pencil.

- Ask yourself: What are the values I try to live by and that really matter to me?
- Let's look at some common core values:
    Generosity
    Compassion
    Connection
    Loyalty
    Honesty
    Fairness
    Courage
- Many of our values involve not just how we treat others, but how we treat ourselves and meet personal needs that matter to us. The following are personal core values that many people feel are important.
    Family
    Personal growth
    Exploration
    Tranquility
    Nature
    Autonomy
    Creativity
- Now let's take this a little deeper and discover the core values that have been motivating you throughout your life.
- Please close your eyes. Smile at yourself in welcome.
- Place a hand on your heart. Let yourself feel your body. This body has been with you for years, trying to live a happy and fulfilled life.

Looking Back over Your Life

- Imagine that you are near the end of your life, looking back on the years between *now* and *then*.
- Pause. What gives you deep satisfaction? Joy? Contentment? Happiness?

- What values have given your life meaning and satisfaction?
- What core values did you express in your life?
- Please write them down, including personal core values as well. (Make sure you give yourself time to reflect on your life.)

Not Living in Accord with Your Values?

- Now, please note ways that you feel you aren't living in accord with your values, ways that there is a disconnect between your life and your values—especially your personal values:

    Maybe you value time with your kids, but you spend all your time working?

    Maybe you want to spend more time with your partner, but somehow it doesn't seem to happen?

    Maybe you want to do fun things as a family, but activities and homework don't allow time to play?

- If you notice several things out of balance, choose the one that feels most important to look at during this exercise.

External Obstacles in the Way?

- There are often external obstacles that get in the way of living in accord with our values. Sometimes it's not having enough money. Other times it is not having sufficient time or having other responsibilities that take precedence.
- Reflect on the obstacles you experience and please write down what they are for you.

Internal Obstacles the Problem?

- There might also be internal obstacles that get in the way of your living in alignment with your core values.

    Are you afraid of failure?

    Do you doubt your abilities?

    Is your inner critic telling you not to take the risk?

- Please write down any internal obstacles that you notice.

How Could Self-Compassion Help?

- Explore whether self-kindness and self-compassion might help you live in accord with your core values.

    Could self-compassion help you deal with your inner critic telling you that you're not good enough or smart enough and that you're doomed to fail?

Could self-compassion help you feel confident enough to try new things, to take risks, or let go of things in your life that aren't serving you?

Insurmountable Obstacles?

- Consider if there are insurmountable obstacles to living in alignment with your core values.
- If so, can you give yourself kindness and compassion for that hardship?
- What could help you keep your values alive in spite of the difficult conditions?

Before returning to your day, spend a few moments reflecting on what you have learned.

Valerie spent some time with this exercise, looking first at her core values and then at her personal values. She had always valued loyalty and honesty, which gave her a deeper understanding of her experience of profound betrayal when she discovered that her ex-husband was cheating on her. Family had been on the top of her list of core values, as were personal growth, creativity, and social action. Devoting herself to being a full-time mom for the past few years, she had set these values aside. The external obstacles had been that she couldn't leave Matt, but that was about to change. The internal obstacle that she identified was that she always felt inadequate and timid. One of her friends, left with an empty nest after a divorce, decided to join the Peace Corps in Africa. Valerie was fluent in Spanish and had a background in nursing . . . maybe, just maybe she could try living in accord with her core values? Once she realized that people in their seventies and eighties volunteer, it seemed even more appealing.

Other parents, in classes and workshops, have been energized by this practice, feeling that it gave them permission to recover long-forgotten dreams and aspirations. And action doesn't need to be big and dramatic. Eric has just lost his job in an economic downturn, while his son Brian has just graduated from high school. What better time for a father–son cross-country road trip? And Brian could get some more driving experience as well. What have you always wanted to do but held back from, due to internal or external obstacles?

Patricia decided to try rock climbing by starting at her neighborhood climbing gym to build confidence. Hector wanted to learn how to scuba dive but wasn't a strong swimmer. He built up some endurance and then took scuba lessons.

What are your dreams? What have you wanted to do but have put off? How can your core values reflect your deepest yearning for meaning?

The importance of core values really hit home for me a few years ago when I ran into Deirdre, whose kids had gone to the same high school as mine but were a little older. Her youngest had just left for college.

"So, how are you?" I asked.

"Bereft," she responded, "absolutely bereft."

I began to dread our impending empty nest and decided to think of her story as a cautionary tale. I wanted to do all I could so that when my kids left home I would still have a rich and rewarding life while they were off exploring their interests. Leaving home is a normal and healthy developmental step, and I vowed that I wouldn't be undone just because they had launched. I remembered a line from Barbara Kingsolver's *Animal Dreams*: "It kills you to see them grow up. But I guess it would kill you quicker if they didn't."

One way to stay in alignment with your core values is to add them to your daily mindfulness and compassion practice (or your hoped-for daily practice). One thing that helped me was to think of my core values as a daily vitamin, something that took only a second to remember but would keep me healthy and strong. You can think of your core values when you wake up or at the end of the day when you're falling asleep. Or you can incorporate this into your daily meditation.

Putting It into Action

Think of your core values as a way to reconnect with yourself when you've had a rough day, when you feel that you've lost your way, or when you feel you need an anchor to ground you. These values are very much like the breath in meditation. They allow us to come back, to start again, or to set an intention. They are also a way to practice compassion when we get thrown off center—no shame, no self-recrimination. We can also realign with our values.

♥ Realignment

- Start by taking a few deep breaths and letting yourself settle.
- Start by selecting one core value that resonates most deeply right now or one that you might like to use as an anchor.

- Let it be something that helps you orient, your personal North Star.
- Write it down, spending a few minutes getting the language as clear as you want it to be.
- It can be like one of your loving-kindness phrases, but keep it personal.
- Ask yourself when you might need it the most: In the morning when you wake up? At night before you fall asleep?
- It doesn't need to be specifically about parenting, but about how you want to set an intention for how you want to live life.
- For example, you might want to say, *May I practice kindness for myself and others.* Or *May I treat my family with love and compassion.*
- Think of other ways that you might want to remind yourself of this core value on a daily basis.

Launching Can Be a Process

The transition out of the home isn't always smooth. Sometimes it is hard for both kids and parents to let go, and there is comfort in holding on to the familiar. But, at times, more growing up is needed before families are ready to separate. Thinking about letting go as a process can reduce the criticism and self-recrimination that parents often feel if the launch is in fits and starts and doesn't go smoothly the very first time. After all, if we frame it in the familiar "failure to launch" cultural meme, everyone feels like, well, they failed. Self-compassion for both parent and child can reduce suffering and stigma for everyone.

When Sana had trouble adjusting to college, and living in a dorm, she felt weak and inadequate and felt that she'd let her parents down. Her mother, Misaki, felt that she hadn't prepared her child for the transition and blamed herself.

The college wasn't Sana's first choice and was far away from her home and family, but she thought she could make it work. However, the year got off to a rocky start. She didn't get along well with her roommate, who started to bring boys to the room for "hookups" the first week. Soon Sana was "sexiled" from the room and didn't know where to go. She tried to get another room, or another roommate, but the dean of students told the girls to "work it out." The roommate told Sana to "get a life" and wasn't willing to compromise.

Sana had been a star in high school, but not so in college. She thought her teachers would be impressed by her abilities, but there were many other students who were hardworking and extremely motivated. In her first biology exam, she received only a B–, which for her felt like a failing grade. Things just weren't going well. It was hard to make friends, she didn't fit in, and it seemed like it rained almost every day. She missed her home and family. She spoke to her parents, who encouraged her to keep trying and to stick it out. But she was finding it harder and harder to get up in the morning for class, especially since her roommate frequently commandeered the room till after midnight. She fell behind in her coursework, and it was hard to catch up.

At Thanksgiving break, both Sana and her parents acknowledged that it wasn't working, and Sana took a leave. Sana and her mother both felt like they had failed. All her other friends seemed happy. Misaki felt ashamed and couldn't tell anyone what had happened. She became depressed, feeling that she had failed as a mother. Self-compassion helped her stop beating herself up and blaming herself and allowed her to put things in perspective.

In the meantime, Sana was relieved to be home, but the experience was humbling. She found a job working in a lab, took the rest of the year off, and applied and got into a school that was a better fit for her.

The practice that worked for both mother and daughter during this challenging year was the following, which got its title from Sana:

A Lotus Eats Dirt Too

- Start by sitting comfortably. Find your breath and let yourself settle.
- Feel the weight of your body. Let yourself feel grounded and anchored.
- Start with an image of a lotus floating on a pond.
- Imagine that you can follow the flower's long stem to where the plant is rooted at the bottom of the pond.
- Notice that the lotus is anchored in the mud and muck and decay.
- The beautiful bloom is not separate from the dark and murky waters but is in fact nourished by them.
- The lotus takes its nutrients from the decomposing material in the pond and in fact metabolizes them.
- Let yourself sit upright in your experience of sadness, suffering, shame, depression.
- Is there some hidden wisdom or nourishment that you can take from this experience of suffering?
- Can the lotus offer you a lesson in metabolizing the darkness and the muck of life?

- What depth, sustenance, or richness can you find in your difficult experience?
- Can you offer yourself compassion for going through this ordeal?
- Let yourself rest with the image of the lotus growing from the depths.
- You can return to this practice whenever you need to shift your perspective.

This is a practice that has many uses through the journey of parenting and of life. The meditation teacher Thich Nhat Hanh would say, "No mud, no lotus." It is one of my go-to practices for difficult times.

Rose was dealing with a recent diagnosis of cancer and wanted something that could help her get through the exhaustion of radiation and chemo and that could keep her spirits up so she could be present for her children and not fall into despair. This meditation helped her focus on the possibility that something of value could emerge from her suffering.

Letting Go Can Assume Many Forms

Letting go can be a very complex process, and it isn't always what we think it is going to be. It often involves giving up our dreams of how we wanted (or hoped) our child would be. And rarely do our children conform to our expectations. Sometimes parents lament that their child is different—a life-of-the-party extrovert may not know how to relate to a shy, withdrawn introvert, while the star college athlete may feel let down by an artistic child who has no interest in sports.

We often have to remind ourselves that it isn't all about us and that we need to love and care for the child we have, not the child we fantasized having. Derrick and Betsy came in to talk about Brett, their son who was in seventh grade. He was distracted, his grades were falling, and he was having daily headaches. It had been hard for him to transition to middle school from his small elementary school. When Betsy talked with him after they met with the pediatrician, he told her, with some hesitation and apprehension, that he was attracted to another boy on his basketball team but didn't know how to handle his feelings. He was afraid he would be ostracized if he let his feelings be known. The stress and confusion was making him sick and making it hard to concentrate. When Betsy talked to Derrick about the situation, he became furious and suggested therapy to "straighten" him out. "No son of mine is going to be a homosexual," he fumed.

But as Brett talked through his feelings, it became clear that he'd felt this way for a while; he just hadn't been able to express it. However, as Brett became more comfortable and less confused and conflicted about his sexual identity, Derrick became more enraged. "I'm from a conservative family, I grew up with three macho brothers, this isn't the way it's supposed to be. It isn't what I wanted from a son."

It took a number of months for Derrick to begin to accept Brett for who he was and to not want to fix him or change him. For him the process of letting go felt like a process of mourning. He had a complex series of feelings, at first experiencing shame and humiliation, then blaming his wife for being too soft on Brett, then me for not being an effective therapist, then the school for supporting Brett's process of discovery. When he was finally able to bring some self-compassion to his conflicting feelings, he began to settle, realizing that we are all human, we are all different and want different things, and we can't dictate who our kids will become, even though we want to.

However, Derrick truly loved his son. As the headaches began to ease, Brett made friends and continued to play basketball. He became interested in school again and joined the weather club to learn more about climate change. Derrick could see that his son was becoming his own person and a smart and articulate kid. He remembered times when he had gone against his father's expectations and how painful it was when his father withdrew his emotional support. As Derrick talked and we processed his disappointment, he realized that this wasn't about him. His task as a father was to support Brett as much as possible. He wanted Brett to feel his love, even though he still had trouble accepting his sexual orientation. Given the community they lived in, and the values of his family of origin, he knew the road would be bumpy. He realized that Brett needed him now more than ever and decided to "step up."

He found that the Self-Compassion Life Saver (Chapter 2) helped him when he became angry and upset. The Lotus practice (above) gave him hope that they would find their way through all this muck and not be "mired in this stuff for the rest of our lives." The family has rallied to be the best parents they can be for their son.

Self-Appreciation

"What? Self-appreciation? Isn't that narcissistic?" you might wonder. But isn't it interesting that appreciating ourselves as parents feels so uncomfortable and awkward, almost taboo? We work so hard at parenting; we often sacrifice, giving up our needs, our time, energy, money, and things we want so our kids can thrive. And rarely do we get appreciation from our kids (not past a certain age, at least, for most of us, and by middle school it's usually ancient history). And most of us get criticism, not praise, from our partners about our parenting. How long has it been since you heard, "Wow, you handled that tough situation really well!" When life is filled with soccer games, carpools, homework, test prep, tutors, dance classes, music lessons, the demands of aging parents, work concerns, and more, we are lucky to stay afloat.

Because of the brain's natural negativity bias, we need to work extra hard to pay attention to positive experience and to take that in. Researchers tell us that painful experiences are more memorable than pleasant ones. Neuroscientist and psychologist Rick Hanson puts it well—it's like the brain has Velcro for the negative experiences, but Teflon for the positive ones. This means that our brains lean in a negative direction. If we can notice the positive things in our life—a child's smile, our kids' good health, a beautiful sunset, as well as the positive qualities in ourselves (kindness, fairness, humor, energy, dedication)—we can begin to rewire our brain to create more happiness for ourselves and our families. What Hanson calls "taking in the good" is both rooted in science and psychologically skillful. And not only is it good for us, it will also help our kids become more resilient.

If we don't make a conscious effort, it is easy to fall into the brain's natural negativity bias and begin to ruminate on our experience. Helen Keller put it succinctly: "When one door of happiness closes, another opens, but often we look so long at the closed door that we don't see the one that has been opened for us."

We are often grateful for our children, our friends, our partners, family, home, maybe work, but rarely are we grateful for ourselves. We usually find fault with what we do and say, as do our children and often our mates. We can end up feeling invisible, unseen, and irritated that others take our good qualities and efforts for granted. Compliments are brushed off, but when we get negative feedback we fixate on it, sometimes for days, weeks, months, maybe even years.

There are many ways that we can apply self-compassion. If we look at the big picture, we realize that many of our good qualities are the result of many people and situations in our lives—our parents, our families, our teachers and mentors. So many factors have shaped who we are. Therefore, appreciating our good qualities isn't an act of narcissism; it is an act of connection and an acknowledgment of our interdependence.

When we appreciate our own goodness, competencies, and kindness, it is not that we think we are better than others or trying to put others down. It is that every parent has wonderful qualities in addition to some not so wonderful qualities. As the saying goes, "I may not be perfect, but parts of me are excellent."

Finally, self-appreciation is not selfish. It provides an optimistic foundation and resilience that we need to get through life and to impart to our families. Learning to appreciate oneself is another gift of the MSC program.

Appreciating Yourself as a Parent

🎧 *Audio Track 10*

- Close your eyes. Take a breath or two. Stop.
- Drop into your body. Let yourself rest.
- When you're ready, think of two or three things you value about yourself as a parent.
- See if you can open up to what you really, deep down, like about yourself.
- Don't be surprised if there is discomfort. This is not something we usually allow ourselves to think about.
- Allow yourself to acknowledge these good qualities. Take them in; don't push them away.
- You aren't saying that you always have these qualities or that you're better than others.
- Think about the people who helped you develop these good qualities—parents, teachers, friends, mentors, family, even your children.
- With each person, please send her or him some gratitude and appreciation.
- When we acknowledge ourselves, we also acknowledge and honor those who helped us grow and develop.
- Allow yourself to appreciate them and yourself.
- Take this in; allow yourself to feel good about yourself and your parenting, if just for a moment.
- Let it soak in; enjoy it—this may be an entirely new and novel experience.

Treniece grew up in a strict family. She was rarely praised as her parents didn't want her to get arrogant or "too big for her britches." Her parents criticized her to keep her in line. She joked that her father was the "criticizer-in-chief," finding fault with her mother and all five children. "Let's just say we weren't a 'touchy-feely' family."

The core values that emerged for her were around humility and loyalty. Her husband frequently found fault with her, telling her that she was selfish and didn't sacrifice for the family. But Treniece was doing all that she could. She was juggling work, aging parents, and three kids, one with special needs. Often it was hard to get the kids to pitch in, setting the table or helping to clean up after dinner. "Just a minute, just a minute," they would say, barely looking up from their screens.

When she tried to set limits, they would often parrot back what they heard: "You're so demanding." A friend from home visiting for the weekend told her, "Treniece, you work so hard and do so much, you don't have to take this rudeness!"

As she began to sit down and take account of all that she was doing and start appreciating herself, she was able to stand up for herself. She said that for the first time she felt like she had her own back (see Having Your Back in Chapter 4) and asked the kids to step it up. When she could own all that she was doing, she could ask for more cooperation. "I wish I could get that support and confirmation from other folks in my life, but that probably won't happen. But it was head-turning that I didn't have to wait till hell froze over. I could offer it to myself."

Gratitude

When we focus on what we don't have, or our children don't have—the awards, prizes, home runs, soccer goals they didn't make—we remain in a negative state of mind, stuck in negativity bias hell. And it's not a place we want to live. Gratitude is appreciating the good things in our lives, especially the small things that we often don't see.

This is also a relational practice that connects us with others. It is a practice that can help our children ground and establish resilient roots as they begin to spread their wings.

 Seeing the Small Things
- Start by sitting down and taking a breath.
- Yes, gratitude for being able to stop and sit down!
- Right now you don't have to do anything or take care of anyone. Ahhh . . .

- Let yourself pause.
- When you're ready, write down 5–10 small and insignificant things that you often ignore, but things that make your life easier. For example, how about:
  Buttons
  Zippers
  Velcro
  Glasses
  Sunshine
  Cool breezes
  Baby carrier
  Umbrella
  Swing
  A child's smile
- Write down what you notice.
- Drop in, see how you feel after doing this practice.

One of my meditation teachers used to say that you could change your state of mind with just three breaths. You can also change your state of mind with a quick gratitude practice. The next time you're having one of those days where nothing is going right, take a moment and pause. See what happens.

Josiah was having a frustrating day. His boss was stressed out because of a big project at work and was taking it out on him. A driver cut him off in rush-hour traffic, and he narrowly missed having an accident. When he got home, his wife yelled at him because he'd forgotten to get laundry soap because he was frazzled by the near accident. And Joey's Legos were all over the floor and he nearly broke one by stepping on it barefoot—and ended up hopping around, clutching his foot in pain. He was ready to blow up. But Joey was thrilled that his dad was home and ran over and gave him a huge hug. "Oh," he thought, "I'm grateful for that hug." And he slowed down and noticed other things in the room. "And for Legos, when I'm not stepping on them. And for Joey's Velcro sneakers so I don't have to constantly retie his shoes. And for the dog," who came over, wagging his tail in delight. Josiah realized that simply noticing a few small and insignificant things had helped him "keep my shit together." And a good dinner and a glass of wine went a long way as well.

Let this be a fun practice. No need to be serious. When Chrissie tried it, she thought of *"erasers, 'cause I always make mistakes."* They had just taken the kids on their first camping vacation, so *indoor plumbing* was added to her list. "OMG, we take it for granted!" And she included the little things that eased family interactions. "At my home, *nail polish* is the 'ego glue' for me and Jenny. When things get tough, I announce 'Mani-Pedi Emergency,' and we both laugh, do our nails, and we're laughing again. And *emojis* are crucially important; they add daily smiles to our lives and texts."

Everything Changes

Amy came in feeling sad. Sophie was going off to college in the fall. At the same time, Amy's mother was dying of cancer that had metastasized to her bones. She had been in a number of experimental clinical trials and had moved in with Amy to be closer to good medical care.

Things were better with Sophie, who had become a major support for Amy. "My mother is in pain and scared. She wants me constantly. She can't bear to be alone." All this uncertainty was challenging for her to manage, and it was hard to stay balanced through all these changes. Amy had trouble sitting quietly, but walking meditation was working for her. "I'm trying to be grateful for my mother; we've had a good relationship. Sophie has matured. She loves her grandma, and they were always close. My mom was an amazing baker and made the best cinnamon buns in the world. Sometimes Sophie will get up early on a Sunday morning to bake them just to have the wonderful comforting fragrance in the house and to make her grandmother smile. As you know, Sophie used to push all my buttons. So much of what I've learned about life has been through raising the kids." She smiled. "It's all so uncertain now, and letting go of my mother and Sophie at the same time is really hard."

Earned Compassion, Earned Equanimity

Finding balance does not come easily, for anyone. It doesn't come naturally either. It takes effort and practice. We want to hold on to pleasure and to push away pain. We want to be right and have the other person be wrong. We try to avoid shame and blame, loss and failure. We want praise, success, and more of it. It is simply how our brains are wired. For most parents, compassion and equanimity are earned, usually by being willing to look at our patterns and behaviors. A maxim in family therapy is "You can be right, or you can be in a relationship."

When Amy began to see things from Sophie's point of view, she also

began to see patterns from her childhood that were damaging and limit-
ing. In these moments, she learned that she had a choice—to continue
belittling and disparaging her daughter or to pause and try to see what
was behind her own intense reaction. When she could ask herself what
was going on and why she was reacting so strongly, she could also see the
direction where things were headed, which wasn't going to end up well for
anyone. She began to practice seeing the other choices she had. She began
to consider Sophie's needs in her thinking. Her efforts were paying off—
she was learning to respond to herself and to Sophie with more compassion and to catch herself and change course when she was about to do or
say something that was hurtful. In Sophie's senior year, their relationship
had become kinder and sweeter as Sophie felt the love, understanding, and
attention she needed from her mother.

Amy was a gardener and took delight in her vegetable patch and her
flowers. She found they kept her grounded and hopeful. When she was
feeling sad about the impending separations, she would console herself
by saying "Tough week, but the tulips are blooming." Or "I'm really sad,
and I can't imagine life without my mom, or Sophie not being around to
tease me and give me shit, but I'm grateful for the colorful dahlias and the
bumper crop of zucchini."

Since the garden helped her accept the cycle of life and the passage
of time, I designed the following practice as something she could do with
her mom (who was frail but mobile) and Sophie or alone. This is a practice
that can be done outside, in a real garden or park, or as a visualization.

Moving On/Letting Go

- Start by sitting comfortably, either in a real garden or in an imagined
  one.
- Feel your essential dignity. Spend a few moments grounding and centering with the breath or the sounds around you, letting in the sounds
  of the birds and insects in the garden.
- Let this garden be filled with flowers and plants that you enjoy—all
  colors and shapes and sizes.
- Let yourself walk through the garden in life or in your mind's eye,
  noticing the colors, the fragrance, the sunshine, or the rain.
- Notice that all the flowers and plants are in different stages of life.
  Some are just sprouting, some are about to bloom, some are in full
  bloom, some are fading, others are dying.
- Bring equal attention to all—the full fragrant blooms as well as the

ones that have wilted or died back. Notice the ones that have been eaten by insects, seeing the holes and even the skeletal forms.

- Notice that even in this garden, all life has a beginning, a middle, and an end.
- Stay with this: all relationships, all endeavors, all activities arise and pass away.
- If you like, stop and focus on just one flower, spending some time with it, really looking, noticing, bringing your full attention to it.
- Try doing this for five to ten minutes. See what happens.
- Watch as bees and butterflies come to gather the nectar. Watch as the wind rustles the leaves.
- Know that tomorrow, or the next day, this flower will fade, wilt, and die.
- Let yourself rest in the garden, taking in and appreciating the beauty, fragility, and transience of it all.
- Know that this is the nature of life and of all things.
- You might want to reflect on the words of Frida Kahlo: "Nothing is absolute. Everything changes, everything moves, everything revolves, everything flies and goes away."
- Take a few breaths, stretch, and return to your day when you are ready.
- See if you can carry the awareness of the impermanence of all things into the day and into your next activity.

"There's Hope for Me."

"So yesterday there was a huge fight between Alyce and Maddy, her younger sister," Alex told me. "Maddy teased her and Alyce responded by punching her in the belly, hard. I sent Alyce to her room for a time-out. And then I start to get all upset that they're fighting, and I worry about their future relationship. But then I hear this noise in the living room and I go to investigate. Maddy is acting it all out: she's singing, dancing, punching her fists, turning it into high drama. She's saying things like 'I'll never talk to Alyce again for the rest of my life. I hope she gets eaten by a wild monster one bite at a time.' The intensity is like something out of a Grimm's fairy tale."

"But then Alyce's time-out is over, she apologizes to Maddy, who then apologizes for provoking her. 'Let's ride bikes,' Alyce says. 'Sure,' Maddy agrees, and off they go, laughing and smiling and giggling like best friends."

"It really got me thinking. So this is living in the present moment. So this is what mindfulness and compassion can look like. I could just relax and trust the kids. That was a first! And I started remembering how my brother William and I would fight when we were kids. But I didn't ruminate. I didn't hold a grudge. I didn't lose sleep. We'd tussle, it would be over, and we would be friends again. I realize that I'm ostensibly an adult, but I hold on to things. I'm still angry about stuff he said 15 years ago. I'm angry about what my husband said last week. I'm not in the moment, I'm in the basement dusting off all the old baggage and acting like my anger is some precious heirloom. I learned a lot just paying attention to how the girls fight and then move on. Now I'm having compassion for how I've lost the ability to just laugh and let it go."

"I'm beginning to see how this could be more fun for all of us. Alyce isn't taking piano anymore—so glad that struggle is over—and wanted to try art. I took her to a parent–child art class at the museum. We were looking at a Picasso, and the teacher said that when Picasso was in midlife he wanted to see the world with the freshness of a child. He tried to regain that spontaneity, exuberance, and vitality. The kids loved that story; they felt validated."

"But I realized that I'd been so overwhelmed and focused on control that I didn't appreciate my children—I didn't delight in them. I barely saw them. The mindfulness and compassion helped me hold a larger perspective. I marvel at the fact that their fight became a chance for me to see their strengths rather than just worry about their aggressive behavior. And for me to let go." She paused and smiled. "You know, I think there is hope for me."

Self-Compassion for Parents Toolbox

This overview suggests ways that the practices and reflections presented in this book might be used in stressful times. The practices can be used individually or practiced in combination. Of course, each person is unique. These are merely suggestions based on my experience of what has worked for other parents. Many practices can help in many different situations, so you will find them in a number of categories. Please feel free to find the ones, either alone or in combination, that suit your needs. And feel free to share with your children if you think they will be helpful. A number of the practices also have an audio guide (see the end of the table of contents for information).

Achievement Worries

- Putting It in Perspective (Chapter 4, page 90)
- Achievement Isn't Everything (Chapter 4, page 91)

Addictions

- Riding the Waves of Parenting (Chapter 7, page 189)
- When Do You Wipe Out? (Chapter 7, page 190)
- Letter to My Child (Chapter 7, page 192)

Anger

- What Pushes Your Buttons? (Chapter 1, page 19)
- Seeing with Kind Eyes (Chapter 1, page 20)
- Self-Compassion Life Saver for Parents (Chapter 2, page 39)
- Ego Glue for Parents (Chapter 2, page 44)

- What the Hell Is This? (Chapter 2, page 51)
- Soles of the Feet (Chapter 3, page 74)
- The Wounds We Carry (Chapter 3, pages 74–75)
- The Rain/Hurricane of Self-Compassion (Chapter 5, pages 121–122)
- Secret Superpower for Angst (SSA) (Chapter 6, pages 153–154)
- A Still Place beneath a Stormy Sea (Chapter 7, pages 186–187)
- Letter to My Child (Chapter 7, page 192)
- The Vastness of the Night Sky (Chapter 8, pages 206–207)

Body Issues

- The Baggage We Inherit (Chapter 3, pages 64–65)
- Bringing Kindness to the Body (Chapter 3, pages 66–68)
- Resetting the Image of the Body (Chapter 3, page 69)

Bullies/Mean Girls

- Self-Compassion Life Saver for Parents (Chapter 2, page 39)
- Soles of the Feet (Chapter 3, page 74)
- Wounds We Carry (Chapter 3, pages 74–75)
- Fierce Compassion (Chapter 3, page 77)
- Oxygen Mask for Turbulent Flights (Chapter 4, pages 106–108)

Colic/Fussy Baby

- Bouncing the Baby Meditation (Chapter 1, page 18)
- Self-Compassion Life Saver for Parents (Chapter 2, page 39)

Conflict

- The Parenting Pause (Chapter 1, page 13)
- Navigating the Parenting Abyss (Chapter 6, pages 144–145)
- When You Both Really Need Compassion (Chapter 6, page 148)
- Time Travel Back to Your Childhood (Chapter 6, page 150)
- Secret Superpower for Angst (SSA) (Chapter 6, pages 153–154)
- Acts of Defiance (Chapter 7, pages 184–185)
- A Still Place beneath a Stormy Sea (Chapter 7, pages 186–187)
- Getting Back in Balance (Chapter 7, page 187)

Control/ Micromanaging

- Letting Your Child Emerge (Chapter 5, pages 125–126)
- Seeing Your Child Clearly (Chapter 5, page 130)
- A Compassionate Look at Micromanaging (Chapter 5, page 135)
- You Don't Have to Control Everything (Chapter 5, page 136)

Daily Life

- Bath/bedtime struggles: Seeing with Kind Eyes (Chapter 1, page 20)
- Dirty Diapers (Chapter 1, pages 28–29)
- Drinking Coffee Meditation (Chapter 1, pages 29–30)
- Dirty dishes? Laundry?: Mindfulness of Hands (Chapter 1, page 31)
- Exploring together: Adventure Walk (Chapter 5, pages 132–133)
- Grocery store (and other endless) lines: Calming the Hot Emotions of Life (Chapter 6, pages 165–166)
- Don't Be Pulled into Their Chaos—Pull Them into Your Calm (Chapter 6, pages 161–162)

- Mindfulness and Compassion in the Car (Chapter 2, pages 59–60)
- Playground: Loving-Kindness at the Playground (Chapter 4, pages 115–116)
- Potluck dinners: The Zapped Potluck Gathering (Chapter 4, pages 112–113)
- Rainy days: Silly Walks (Chapter 3, pages 84–85); Finding Beauty, (Chapter 3, pages 85–86)
- Tantrums: Soothing Touch in the Heat of the Moment (Chapter 3, pages 82–83)
- Traffic jams: Calming the Hot Emotions of Life (Chapter 6, pages 165–166)

Depressed Feelings

- What Would Your Best Friend Say? (Chapter 1, page 26)
- You Are Not Your Fault (Chapter 1, page 27)
- Self-Compassion Life Saver for Parents (Chapter 2, page 39)
- The Rain/Hurricane of Self-Compassion (Chapter 5, pages 121–122)

- Grounding in the Moment (Chapter 5, page 140)
- Just Because You Think It Doesn't Mean It's True (Chapter 7, pages 179–180)
- What Thoughts Get You Going? (Chapter 7, page 181)
- When Things Fall Apart (Chapter 7, page 194)

Difficult Emotions

- What Is Your Default Position? (Chapter 2, page 43)
- Ego Glue for Parents (Chapter 2, pages 44–45)
- When You're Struggling (Chapter 2, page 47)
- Soften–Soothe–Allow for Shame (Chapter 6, pages 157–158)

- Turn It into a Song (Chapter 7, pages 82–83)
- When Things Fall Apart (Chapter 7, page 194)
- Mindfulness at 4:00 A.M. (Chapter 7, page 195)

Disappointment

- What Is Your Fantasy? (Chapter 3, pages 72–73)

Fears

- Self-Compassion Life Saver for Parents (Chapter 2, page 39)
- Fierce Compassion (Chapter 3, page 77)
- In This Moment (Chapter 3, page 80)
- Having Your Back (Chapter 4, page 97)

Feeling Overwhelmed

- Finding *Yourself* (Chapter 1, page 8)
- Tending to Yourself (Chapter 1, page 9)
- What Do I Need? (Chapter 1, page 10)
- What is Overwhelming for You? (Chapter 2, pages 53–54)
- Winds of Parenting (Chapter 2, pages 55–56)
- Ego Glue for Parents (Chapter 2, pages 44–45)
- Hitting the Snooze Button (Chapter 2, pages 57–58)

Gratitude

- Finding Beauty (Chapter 3, pages 85–86)
- Adventure Walk (Chapter 5, pages 132–133)
- Seeing the Small Things (Chapter 8, pages 219–220)

Holiday Stress

- What about Your Family? (Chapter 4, page 100)
- Rewiring with Loving-Kindness Meditation (LKM) (Chapter 4, pages 102–103)

Illness

- The Sounds of Life (Chapter 1, pages 22–23)
- Bringing Kindness to the Body (Chapter 3, pages 66–68)
- Finding a Steady Center (Chapter 5, page 139)
- Grounding in the Moment (Chapter 5, page 140)

Letting Go

- Holding On/Letting Go (Chapter 8, page 198)
- The Warm Blanket (Chapter 8, pages 200–201)
- Moving On/Letting Go (Chapter 8, pages 222–223)

Meltdown

- When Have You Needed a *Life Raft?* (Chapter 2, pages 35–36)
- When Have You Shown Kindness to Others? (Chapter 2, pages 36–37)
- Self-Compassion Life Saver for Parents (Chapter 2, page 39)
- Putting Self-Compassion to Work in Your Life (Chapter 2, page 40)

Resilience

- Having Your Back (Chapter 4, page 97)

- Appreciating Yourself as a Parent (Chapter 8, page 218)

Separation

- Tree of Compassionate Beings (Chapter 8, page 204)
- The Vastness of the Night Sky (Chapter 8, pages 206–207)

- Finding Our Core Values (Chapter 8, pages 209–211)

Sibling Battles

- Three-Minute Compassion Space (Chapter 6, page 163)

- Listening with Compassion (Chapter 6, pages 164–165)

Stress

- Touch Points for Stressed-Out Parents (Chapter 2, page 49)

- Rewiring with Loving-Kindness Meditation (LKM) (Chapter 4, pages 102–103)

Tough Times

- How Has It Been for You? (Chapter 4, page 96)
- Having Your Back (Chapter 4, page 97)
- What Obstacles Are You Facing? (Chapter 7, pages 170–171)
- Lemonade Stand (Chapter 7, pages 173–174)

- Sky Gazing (Chapter 7, pages 176–177)
- Realignment (Chapter 8, pages 212–213)
- A Lotus Eats Dirt Too (Chapter 8, pages 214–215)

Uncertainty

- Working with the Uncertainties of Parenting (Chapter 5, pages 219–220)

- The Rain/Hurricane of Self-Compassion (Chapter 5, pages 121–122)

Worries

- What Are Your Worries? (Chapter 4, pages 119–120)
- Mindfulness at 4:00 A.M. (Chapter 7, pages 195–196)

- Tree of Compassionate Beings (Chapter 8, page 204)

Resources

Books

Ariès, P. (1962). *Centuries of childhood: A social history of family life.* New York: Vintage.

Baratz, J., & Alexander, S. (2012). *Awakening joy.* Berkeley, CA: Parallax Press.

Bluth, K. (2017). *The self-compassion workbook for teens.* Oakland, CA: New Harbinger.

Brach, T. (2003). *Radical acceptance: Embracing your life with the heart of a Buddha.* New York: Bantam.

Brach, T. (2013). *True refuge.* New York: Bantam.

Chodron, P. (1997). *When things fall apart: Heart advice for difficult times.* Boston: Shambhala.

Chodron, P. (2002). *Comfortable with uncertainty.* Boulder, CO: Shambhala.

Coleman, M. (2016). *Make peace with your mind.* Novato, CA: New World Library.

Dalai Lama. (1995). *The power of compassion.* New York: HarperCollins.

Druckerman, P. (2014). *Bringing up bébé.* New York: Penguin.

Germer, C. K. (2009). *The mindful path to self-compassion.* New York: Guilford Press.

Gilbert, P. (2009). *The compassionate mind.* Oakland, CA: New Harbinger.

Goldstein, E. (2015). *Uncovering happiness: Overcoming depression with mindfulness and self-compassion.* New York: Atria.

Goleman, D., & Davidson, R. (2017). *Altered traits.* New York: Penguin.

Gopnik, A. (2016). *The gardener and the carpenter.* New York: Farrar, Straus and Giroux.

Hanh, T. N. (1998). *Teaching on love.* Berkeley, CA: Parallax Press.

Hanson, R. (2009). *The Buddha's brain.* Oakland, CA: New Harbinger.

Hanson, R. (2014). *Hardwiring happiness.* New York: Harmony/Crown.

Hanson, R. (2018). *Resilient.* New York: Harmony.

Harris, D. (2014). *10% happier.* New York: HarperCollins.

Hayes, S. C., Strosahl, K. D., & Wilson, K. G. (2011). *Acceptance and commitment therapy: The process and practice of mindful change* (2nd ed.). New York: Guilford Press.

Hoffman, K., Cooper, G., & Powell, B. (2017). *Raising a secure child*. New York: Guilford Press.

Hulbert, A. (2004). *Raising America*. New York: Vintage.

Kabat-Zinn, J. (1990). *Full catastrophe living*. New York: Dell.

Kabat-Zinn, M., & Kabat-Zinn, J. (1997). *Everyday blessings: The inner work of mindful parenting*. New York: Hyperion.

Kornfield, J. (1993). *A path with heart*. New York: Bantam Books.

Kornfield, J. (2008). *The wise heart*. New York: Bantam Books.

Kornfield, J. (2017). *No time like the present*. New York: Atria.

LeVine, R., & LeVine, S. (2016). *Do parents matter?* New York: Public Affairs.

Lythcott-Haims, J. (2015). *How to raise an adult*. New York: St. Martin's Press.

Naumburg, C. (2014). *Parenting in the present moment*. Berkeley, CA: Parallax Press.

Neff, K. (2011). *Self-compassion: The proven power of being kind to yourself*. New York: William Morrow.

Neff, K., & Germer, C. (2018). *The mindful self-compassion workbook*. New York: Guilford Press.

Peterson, C. (2015). *The mindful parent*. New York: Skyhorse.

Pollak, S. M., Pedulla, T., & Siegel, R. D. (2014). *Sitting together*. New York: Guilford Press.

Salzberg, S. (1997). *Lovingkindness: The revolutionary art of happiness*. Boston: Shambhala.

Salzberg, S. (2011). *Real happiness: The power of meditation*. New York: Workman.

Salzberg, S. (2017). *Real love: The art of mindful connection*. New York: Flatiron Books.

Siegel, D. J. (2013). *Brainstorm*. New York: Tarcher/Penguin.

Siegel, D. J., & Bryson, T. P. (2012). *The whole-brain child*. New York: Bantam.

Siegel, D. J., & Hartzell, M. (2003). *Parenting from the inside out*. New York: Tarcher/Perigee.

Tsabary, S. (2017). *The awakened family*. New York: Penguin.

Willard, C. (2017). *Raising resilience*. Boulder, CO: Sounds True.

Williams, M., Teasdale, J., Segal, Z., & Kabat-Zinn, J. (2007). *The mindful way through depression*. New York: Guilford Press.

Helpful Websites

Center for Mindful Self-Compassion
www.centerformsc.org

Center for Compassion and Altruism Research and Education, Stanford University
http://ccare.stanford.edu

Center for Mindfulness and
Compassion, Cambridge Health
Alliance, Harvard Medical School
Teaching Hospital
www.chacmc.org

Cognitively-Based Compassion
Training, Emory University
www.tibet.emory.edu/cognitively-based-compassion-training

Greater Good Magazine, Greater
Good Science Center, UC Berkeley
www.greatergood.berkeley.edu

Institute for Meditation
and Psychotherapy
www.meditationandpsychotherapy.org

Internal Family Systems,
Center for Self Leadership
www.selfleadership.org

Mindfulness-Based
Cognitive Therapy (MBCT)
www.mbct.com

International Sites

Australia
www.adelaidemindfulness.com

Canada
www.mindfulnessstudies.com (Toronto)
https://ottawamindfulnessclinic.com
(Ottawa)

New Zealand
www.annafriis.com

United Kingdom
Compassionate Mind Foundation
https://compassionatemind.co.uk

Notes

Introduction

PAGE 1: "To be a mother": Olsen, T. (1965). *Silences.* New York: The Feminist Press, p. 18.

PAGE 2: "In no other country": Lerner, M. (1957). *America as a civilization: Life and thought in the United States today.* New York: Simon & Schuster, p. 562.

PAGE 3: Mindful Self-Compassion (MSC) Course: Neff, K., & Germer, C. (2018). *The mindful self-compassion workbook.* New York: Guilford Press. To find a course, either online or in person, go to *www.centerformsc.org.*

Chapter 1

PAGE 7: Motivating ourselves with kindness: For an extensive summary of self-compassion research, go to Kristin's Neff's website, *www.self-compassion.org.*

PAGE 8: "I have yet to find the man": Schwab, cited in Coleman, M. (2017). *Make peace with your mind.* Novato, CA: New World Library, p. 53.

PAGE 11: Brach teaches that a simple pause: Brach, T. (2003). *Radical acceptance.* New York: Bantam, p. 71.

PAGE 14: "When we pause": Brach, T. (2003). *Radical acceptance.* New York: Bantam, p. 52.

PAGE 27: "You are not your fault": Meditation teacher Wes Nisker, cited in Coleman, M. (2017). *Make peace with your mind.* Novato, CA: New World Library, pp. 33–37.

PAGE 28: "our emotions can be trained": Goleman, D., & Davidson, R. (2017). *Altered traits.* New York: Avery.

PAGE 32: "the one that is most pleasant": Murphy, S. (2002). *One bird, one stone.* New York: Renaissance Books, p. 85.

Chapter 2

PAGE 35: "And speaking of fairy tales": Jamison, L. (2017, April 9). In the shadow of a fairy tale. *New York Times Magazine*, p. 51.

PAGE 48: our brains are wired: McGonigal, K. (May 16, 2016). *Changing the default with mindfulness*. Sounds True Neuroscience Summit.

PAGE 54: "awake attention to what is happening": Boorstein, S., cited in Salzberg, S. (2011). *Real happiness: The power of meditation*, p. 106. New York: Workman.

PAGE 57: Labeling feelings: Creswell, J. D., Way, B. M., Eisenberger, N. I., & Lieberman, M. D. (2007). Neural correlates of dispositional mindfulness during affect labeling. *Psychosomatic Medicine, 69*, 560–565.

PAGE 57: "hitting the snooze button on an alarm clock": *www.nytimes.com/ roomfordebate/2012/11/25/will-diaries-be-published-in-2050/diaries-a-healthy-choice*.

Chapter 3

PAGE 66: "variation introduces compassion": See Chapter 12 in Neff, K., & Germer, C. (2018). *The mindful self-compassion workbook*. New York: Guilford Press.

PAGE 69: "I read an essay": Bhikkhu, T. (Winter, 2014). Under your skin. *Tricycle Magazine*.

PAGE 69: Jill Soloway: Hess, A. (May 7, 2017). Being seen stops us from being. *New York Times*, AR28.

PAGE 74: "It's one thing to know that we have": Mark Coleman, in *Make peace with your mind* (2017; Novato, CA: New World Library, p. 158), asks what it would be like to welcome all your painful emotions, which is the basis of this practice.

PAGE 80: "One thing that can help": Hanson, R. (2018). *Resilient*. New York: Harmony. This book offers a profound understanding of the negativity bias and many ways to work with it.

Chapter 4

PAGE 90: self-compassion researcher Kristin Neff: Neff, K. (2011). *Self-compassion*. New York: William Morrow, pp. 22–23.

PAGE 92: ability to see themselves objectively: Research reported by Neff, K. (2011). *Self-compassion*. New York: William Morrow, p. 20.

PAGE 102: "dose dependent": Pace, T. W. W., Negi, L. T., Adame, D. D., Cole, S. P., Sivilli, T. I., Brown, T. D., et al. (2009). Effect of compassion meditation on neuroendocrine, innate immune and behavioral responses to psychosocial stress. *Psychoneuroendocrinology, 43*(1), 87–98.

PAGE 107: "finding your own phrases": See Chapter 10 in Neff, K., & Germer, C. (2018). *The mindful self-compassion workbook.* New York: Guilford Press.

PAGE 109: default mode network: Raichle, M. E., MacLeod, A. M., Snyder, A. Z., Powers, W. J., Gusnard, D. A., & Shulman, G. L. (2001). A default mode of brain function. *Proceedings of the National Academy of Sciences of the USA, 98*(2), 676–682.

PAGE 111: our lives are connected: The story about Robert Thurman that inspired this practice is found in Salzberg, S. (2011). *Real happiness.* New York: Workman, p. 148.

Chapter 5

PAGE 119: As Maya Angelou wrote: Angelou, M. (2008). *Letter to my daughter.* New York: Random House, p. xii.

PAGE 129: "the American question": This story is recounted in Druckerman, P. (2012). *Bringing up bébé.* New York: Penguin, p. 82.

PAGE 130: try this reflection: This practice was inspired by the idea of seeing the gifts in our children as well as our own gifts. See Kornfield, J. (2017). *No time like the present.* New York: Atria, pp. 201–217.

PAGE 131: Playing can help our children: For an excellent discussion of the research on play, see Goldstein, E. (2015). *Uncovering happiness.* New York: Atria, p. 154ff.

PAGE 140: "While we find 'worry stones,' rosary beads": Neff, K., & Germer, C. (2018). *The mindful self-compassion workbook.* New York: Guilford Press, p. 195.

Chapter 6

PAGE 147: "It is an ancient practice": Germer, C. K. (2009). *The mindful path to self-compassion.* New York: Guilford Press, p. 255. For the current MSC version of this practice, which inspired this practice: Neff, K., & Germer, C. (2018). *The mindful self-compassion workbook.* New York: Guilford Press, p. 112.

PAGE 152: Hot Emotions: For a philosophical understanding of anger from the perspective of Buddhist psychology, go to Kornfield, J. (2008). *The wise heart.* New York: Bantam. For a neuroscientist's perspective on "cooling the fires" of anger, see Hanson, R. (2009). *Buddha's brain.* Oakland CA: New Harbinger.

PAGE 153: "soften–soothe–allow": See Chapter 16 in Neff, K., & Germer, C. (2018). *The mindful self-compassion workbook.* New York: Guilford Press.

PAGE 157: "This can be a challenging exercise": For an excellent discussion of shame, see Chapter 17 in Neff, K., & Germer, C. (2018). *The mindful self-compassion workbook.* New York: Guilford Press.

Chapter 7

PAGE 168: "Suffering leads us to beauty": Matousek, M. (2015, April 10). Felt in its fullness. *Tricycle Magazine*. Retrieved from *https://tricycle.org/trikedaily/felt-its-fullness*.

PAGE 171: neutral comment as critical: When teens are shown a neutral face in brain scans, it can activate the amygdala, whereas this is not the case with adults. This can help us understand their often intense and confusing reactions. In Siegel, D. J. (2015). *Brainstorm*. New York: Tarcher/Penguin, p. 107.

PAGE 176: Sky Gazing: I learned this practice from Lama Willa Miller. It can be found at *www.naturaldharma.org*.

PAGE 189: pioneering work of G. Alan Marlatt: Marlatt, G. A., & Gordon, J. R. (2007). *Relapse prevention: Maintenance strategies in the treatment of addictive behavior*. New York: Guilford Press.

Chapter 8

PAGE 197: "Even as I Hold You": Walker, A. (1979). Even as I hold you. *Good night, Willie Lee, I'll see you in the morning*. New York: Doubleday.

PAGE 204: classic Tibetan practice: I learned this practice from Lama Willa Miller, who calls it "Refuge Tree Meditation." It can be found at *www.naturaldharma. org*.

PAGE 209: "to be used by parents": This practice was first developed by Hayes, S. C., Strosahl, K. D., & Wilson, K. G. (2011). *Acceptance and commitment therapy: The process and practice of mindful change* (2nd ed.). New York: Guilford Press. It was further adapted by Neff, K., & Germer, C. (2018). *The mindful self-compassion workbook*. New York: Guilford Press, Ch. 14.

PAGE 217: "When one door of happiness closes": Keller, H. (2000). *To love this life: Quotations by Helen Keller*. New York: AFB Press.

PAGE 218: "Another gift of the MSC program": See Chapter 23 in Neff, K., & Germer, C. (2018). *The mindful self-compassion workbook*. New York: Guilford Press.

PAGE 219: "the small things we often don't see." Adapted for parents from Neff, K., & Germer, C. (2018). *The mindful self-compassion workbook*. New York: Guilford Press, Ch 22.

Index

About the Author

Susan M. Pollak, MTS, EdD, is a psychologist in private practice in Cambridge, Massachusetts, and the mother of two grown children. She is a longtime student of meditation and yoga who has been integrating the practices of meditation into psychotherapy since the 1980s. Dr. Pollak is cofounder and senior teacher at the Center for Mindfulness and Compassion at Harvard Medical School/Cambridge Health Alliance and president of the Institute for Meditation and Psychotherapy. She is the coauthor of *Sitting Together: Essential Skills for Mindfulness-Based Psychotherapy* (for mental health professionals).

List of Audio Tracks

Track	Title	Run Time
1	Tending to Yourself	3:01
2	Self-Compassion Life Saver for Parents	2:25
3	The Baggage We Inherit	11:18
4	Soles of the Feet	4:27
5	Having Your Back	9:14
6	You Don't Have to Control Everything	8:50
7	Three-Minute Compassion Space	3:43
8	Mindfulness at 4:00 A.M.	4:30
9	The Warm Blanket	8:22
10	Appreciating Yourself as a Parent	5:29